MORE

A MEMOIR

MICHAEL MASSEY

LITTLE CREEK PRESS®
AND BOOK DESIGN
MINERAL POINT, WISCONSIN

Copyright © 2023 Michael Massey

All rights reserved. No part of this publication may be reproduced, distributed, or transmitted in any form or by any means, including photocopying, recording, digital scanning, or other electronic or mechanical methods, without the prior written permission of the publisher, except in the case of brief quotations embodied in critical reviews and certain other noncommercial uses permitted by copyright law. For permission requests or other information, please send correspondence to the following address:

Little Creek Press
5341 Sunny Ridge Road
Mineral Point, WI 53565

To contact Michael directly: www.mikemasseymusic.com

ORDERING INFORMATION
Quantity sales. Special discounts are available on quantity purchases by corporations, associations, and others. For details, contact info@littlecreekpress.com

Orders by US trade bookstores and wholesalers.
Please contact Little Creek Press or Ingram for details.

Printed in the United States of America

Cataloging-in-Publication Data
Names: Massey, Michael, author
Title: More. A Memoir
Description: Mineral Point, WI Little Creek Press, 2023
Identifiers: LCCN: 2022921672 | ISBN: 978-1-955656-43-6
Classification: Biography / Personal Memoirs

Book design by Mimi Bark and Little Creek Press

For Joni Sue

TABLE OF CONTENTS

PROLOGUE 1
1. FIX YOU 3
2. CAT'S IN THE CRADLE 6
3. WHAT'S MY AGE AGAIN 8
4. FIFTEEN 10
5. TWO OF US 12
6. AGE OF AQUARIUS 14
7. CHANGES 18
8. WE'VE ONLY JUST BEGUN 21
9. TOMORROW NEVER KNOWS 24
10. WOND'RING ALOUD 27
11. MAGIC CARPET RIDE 30
12. EVERY DAY IS A WINDING ROAD 32
13. THE FOOL ON THE HILL 34
14. COMFORTABLY NUMB 37
15. 1979 40
16. ON THE ROAD TO FIND OUT 45
17. WILL YOU STILL LOVE ME TOMORROW 48
18. THRILLER 50
19. WALK ON THE WILD SIDE 54
20. I'M WAITING FOR THE MAN 57
21. HOTEL CALIFORNIA 59
22. YOU CAN'T ALWAYS GET WHAT YOU WANT 61
23. (I'VE HAD) THE TIME OF MY LIFE 64
24. GO YOUR OWN WAY 67
25. MY KIND OF TOWN 69
26. STARMAN 72

27.	SPINNING WHEEL	75
28.	DON'T GIVE UP	78
29.	FALLING APART	81
30.	REWRITE	83
31.	THE IMPOSTER	86
32.	NICE TO SEE YOU AGAIN	89
33.	BAD REPUTATION	91
34.	(JUST LIKE) STARTING OVER	94
35.	WORKIN' FOR A LIVIN'	97
36.	ON THE ROAD AGAIN	100
37.	MARRY YOU	102
38.	BORDER SONG	104
39.	SMOKE! SMOKE! SMOKE! (THAT CIGARETTE)	107
40.	THE PIANO HAS BEEN DRINKING	110
41.	VIDEO KILLED THE RADIO STAR	112
42.	GET ME TO THE CHURCH ON TIME	114
43.	THE BOYS ARE BACK IN TOWN	116
44.	I AM THE WALRUS	118
45.	LIVING IN MY MOM'S BASEMENT	121
46.	THIS IS AMERICA	123
47.	A HAZY SHADE OF WINTER	125
48.	MASTER OF PUPPETS	127
49.	LAWYERS, GUNS, AND MONEY	129
50.	HANG ON SLOOPY	131
51.	HEAD	133
52.	MERCY, MERCY ME	135
53.	ALL MEN ARE LIARS	137
54.	CHASING PAVEMENTS	139
55.	HELP	142
56.	WALKING ON A WIRE	145

57.	PAINT IT BLACK	147
58.	THE SOUND OF SILENCE	150
59.	HERE COMES THE SUN	153
60.	OSCAR MAYER WEINER SONG	157
61.	THE TIMES THEY ARE-A-CHANGIN'	159
62.	TAKIN' CARE OF BUSINESS	178
63.	WISH YOU WERE HERE	180
64.	DOCTOR MY EYES	183
65.	TAKE ME TO THE RIVER	185
66.	I HOPE YOU DANCE	188
67.	OUR HOUSE	190
68.	GO! YOU PACKERS GO!	193
69.	WHAT A WONDERFUL WORLD	195
70.	THE MUSIC MAN	198
71.	1999	201
72.	MONEY	204
73.	ALL THE SMALL THINGS	206
74.	THUNDERSTRUCK	209
75.	BUTTERFLIES	213
76.	CABARET	215
77.	I WAS LOST	219
78.	ATTACK OF THE DELICIOUS	221
79.	AIN'T TOO PROUD TO BEG	224
80.	DO YOU HEAR WHAT I HEAR?	227
81.	COME AWAY WITH ME	229
82.	FATHER AND SON	231
83.	REFLECTIONS	233
84.	ON BROADWAY	237
85.	THE ENTERTAINER	239
86.	VAMPIRES WILL NEVER HURT YOU	242

87.	NOSFERATU	245
88.	GOOD RIDDANCE (TIME OF YOUR LIFE)	248
89.	DON'T STOP BELIEVIN'	250
90.	THE SOUND OF MUSIC	252
91.	DO IT AGAIN	256
92.	TOTALLY NUDE	258
93.	SOMEONE LIKE YOU	261
94.	SMALL TOWN	264
95.	I WON'T BACK DOWN	266
96.	BEHIND BLUE EYES	269
97.	BLACK FRIDAY	271
98.	DADDY LESSONS	273
99.	EVERYBODY HURTS	275
100.	SPIRIT IN THE SKY	278
101.	INCA ROADS	281
102.	BAD MOON RISING	285
103.	IT'S THE END OF THE WORLD AS WE KNOW IT (AND I FEEL FINE)	290
104.	VIRUS	293
105.	I WANT TO THANK YOU	296
106.	BIRTHDAY	299
107.	UNWRITTEN	301
108.	START ME UP	305
109.	ANGEL OF MORNING	308
110.	LOOKIN' OUT MY BACK DOOR	312
111.	LIFE'S BEEN GOOD	314
CAST OF CHARACTERS IN ORDER OF APPEARANCE		318
ABOUT THE AUTHOR		322
ACKNOWLEDGMENTS		323

PROLOGUE

THE FIRST HALLUCINATION was the belief that my teeth were melting. The second was being certain I was missing a gig in Lake Geneva. Third, though it was nearly midnight, my friend Billy was sitting on my dresser in the bright sunlight, laughing at me.

And then came the trolls.

Let me back up just a bit. You see, I had quit drinking alcohol five days prior. After two decades of drinking almost daily, I was consuming at least a fifth of hard liquor and a twelve-pack of beer daily and writing bad checks to get it. I was maintenance drinking 24/7. I was reaching under my bed for the brandy bottle whenever I woke out of an uneasy, passed-out slumber, determined to keep enough down to stop the shakes before throwing it up.

I have no business being an author. It is yet one more thing I don't know I can't do. My intent is to entertain and shock you, to make you laugh and cover your mouth in shame. To make you feel. To take you down a rabbit hole so deep, there seems little hope in finding your way out.

But find my way out, I did. This is my story. We'll wind through the early years, setting me up for this path. We'll negotiate the incredible highs and the crushing lows of the music business from Los Angeles to New York City, Canada to Texas, shamelessly dropping a few famous names along the way. Ultimately, we'll end up in the present where I am twenty-nine years sober, raised two daughters, enjoy a loving, amazing, supportive marriage of thirty-two years, have a fulfilling career as a performer, songwriter, composer, now author, and I can't wait to see what the future holds.

To set the mood, I have adopted song titles for chapter titles, giving the songwriters full credit. And due to the preponderance of names I insisted upon using in my story, my editor suggested I include a Cast of Characters. It can be found at the end of the book.

Join me on the telling of this journey, a timeline of my life using flashbacks to a downward spiral and treatment for alcoholism interspersed with coming of age and the joys and pitfalls of a life in music. When I emerge from the fog of substance abuse and rehab, chastened and humbled, the story becomes chronological, negotiating a sober, boundless world.

If I can help encourage just one of those among you who are struggling or someone you love to see that it's possible to make the change, to find your way out of that rabbit hole and feel how beautiful life can be above ground, it will all have been worth it.

1. FIX YOU

(Chris Martin, Jonny Buckland,
Will Champion, and Guy Berryman)

IN SEPTEMBER 1993, Robin, my wife of only three and a half years, unable to live with my deception and brandy-soaked delusions, finally threw me out. She had tried so hard to be patient, tolerant, and kind, and I had tried so hard to quit for her, to be the man she knew I could be—that I thought I was.

I had just returned from a gig in Baudette, Minnesota, with Jim Ripp. We returned to the scene where our duo, Circle Park, played raucous, successful shows to tourists in the resort fishing community on the Canadian border for the prior year and a half. It was a bad week. I morosely stayed in my room most of the time, lost my voice early in the week, and struggled at shows. I would take clandestine trips into town to get bottles of Windsor Canadian whiskey, my drink of choice up there, to stay stocked but not appear to be drinking too much publicly. Jim was monitoring my consumption at Robin's behest. The joy was gone from performing, and my skills had deteriorated.

And I was lying to everyone and to myself. I was hiding pints all over, in coat pockets and sofa cushions, in shoes in the closet, in bushes, and under the driver's seat. I could pretend well and thought I had most of them fooled. Turns out I was the fool. You can't hide alcoholism in broad daylight if that sour, pungent smell of alcohol seeps out of your pores. The glassy yellow-red eyes with dark circles beneath. The flush of red in a hopeless face. I tried to quit. I awoke every morning for the previous three years, determined to quit drinking that day.

Then the tremors would start, with an uneasy, disoriented queasiness rattling around in my stomach. I would hit the liquor store when it opened at nine and get a pint, slamming a few swallows before I left the parking lot. If I could keep it down, I would feel that warmth course through my veins, comforting and calming. I must have hit every liquor store in Dane and the surrounding counties at least once. I couldn't have any of those clerks thinking I had a problem. Then, just as my heart rate returned to normal and my brain cleared from the influx of the fix, the guilt would crash in. I had failed ... again, which would cause me to drink more to ease the pain of my moral decay. I would start to look to the promise of tomorrow and repeat the same folly for endless days, weeks, and years. Hope, failure, guilt, and despair—an insidious, despicable disease. It rips your heart out, numbs your conscience, and most heinous of all, it destroys the ones you love as they watch you slowly die.

At this point, I wasn't drinking for the high, for the euphoria that normal people get with a couple of drinks. I was drinking to feel normal.

I was rationing the amount to stop the involuntary trembling of my extremities. I was drinking to clear my head from the fog of temporary withdrawal caused by going more than a couple of hours at a time without a booster shot. Long gone was the concept of having a drink socially. I needed it to function as a human being. With all of its sugar content, brandy would taste like caramel to me. I was like a starving vampire sated with fresh, warm blood, and like a creature of the night, I lived between the shadows. Reality was fleeting and soft around the edges. I had often fallen from the perch of respectability but always found a cushion when I landed. I was extremely lucky.

But I couldn't say all of this. Who would understand? And I wasn't hurting anyone, or so I justified to myself. I wasn't a mean drunk, but I didn't care about anything. Consequences be damned. When I could slip into the cocoon, all was right with the world. There were a few instances through the years when after a fender bender or a speeding ticket, if the police had decided to breathalyze me, they would've called in backup because they would've thought the apparatus was malfunctioning. Surely, he couldn't be lucid at that level.

    So, I left.

    Defiantly.

2. CAT'S IN THE CRADLE
(Harry Chapin)

I GREW UP IN A LOVING, middle-class family where my mom cared for the house and my dad went to work every day. I was the oldest of five Massey kids. Me, Scott, twins Kevin and Keith, and our "Angel of the Morning," Joni. We were the nuclear family of the 1960s. The American dream beckoned, and because my father fancied himself upwardly mobile, we moved around quite a bit. By third grade, I had lived in five different places, with the sixth coming just a couple of years later. This was not terribly troubling as I made friends relatively easily and was up for the adventure.

Let me be clear that anything I say here is not to disparage the memory of my late parents. It was a different time. A plethora of sitcoms on network television and magazine articles portrayed a dutiful wife having a drink prepared for her weary, working hubby when he arrived home after a hard day's work. It was the cocktail generation. It was normal. I fully believed that every house in America had a five o'clock beer time. Why wouldn't I? It was not until much later that I realized not everyone's parents had a beer every day at five, then switched to brandy after dinner, and that Bloody Marys weren't weekend morning rituals followed by day drinking.

My parents were great, though they were thrust into it painfully young. My mom was seventeen, and my dad was nineteen when I was born. A hasty marriage. Such was the protocol when teenage hormones won in the late 1950s. And there are no manuals for being parents when you're barely out of your cap and gown.

For the most part, alcohol wasn't detrimental to our lives, but it was always present. It was pervasive and accepted. It was social, a time when neighbors would sit together on front porches and share cocktails all the time—every day.

One memory does stand out. I would have been four and my younger brother, Scott, two. My mom packed us up and took us to the bus stop. She was so happy and excited. When I asked where we were going, she said it was a surprise. We got on the bus heading uptown, reached the Capitol Square, and hopped off in front of the theater that was playing the newly re-issued *Lady and the Tramp*. As we stood at the box office, my mother's excitement quickly turned to panic. My father had taken money out of her wallet that morning and forgot to tell her he was going to "stop with the boys" after work. My mom broke down in tears, and I vividly remember comforting her. "It will be okay, Mommy." We got back on the bus toward home, and my mom was oddly quiet, but due to her strength and resolve, she recovered quickly, and by the time we hit the near eastside, we were laughing.

Suffice it to say that never again was there any covert pilfering of my mother's purse.

3. WHAT'S MY AGE AGAIN?
(Mark Hoppus and Tom Delonge)

IT WAS AN INTENSE TIME to be a child in America. Space exploration was new and dangerous. Martin Luther King Jr. and Bobby Kennedy were assassinated in 1968. I was nine. My generation witnessed the first war to be beamed into our living rooms on the nightly news, drug culture was in full bloom, and anti-war protests rocked our hometown. I had just turned twelve when Sterling Hall was bombed on the UW–Madison campus, tragically killing Robert Fassnacht, a physics researcher. The explosion woke me up. I remember finding syringes in the gutter on Williamson Street when we left Marquette Junior High at lunch. Seventh and eighth graders were talking about fucking like they knew what they were talking about, and some did. We grew up fast and didn't know we shouldn't.

The day before Easter in 1971, our entire family went out of town to visit relatives for the weekend. That night my friends found the door open on a train car sitting on the tracks next to a restaurant supply warehouse on the east side. They stole a case of liquor, proceeded to drink it, then stumbled and shouted their way around the streets of the drowsy city. The police finally caught up with them as they sat on a front porch, unable to talk coherently or walk. One of the cops wanted to book and take them to jail to teach them a lesson. The other was a little more compassionate. After a lengthy discussion, the law gave them rides home for their parents to administer the punishment.

After hearing the news through the grapevine, my mom sat me down. She asked if we had been home, would I have gone with my friends on the excursion. The answer was written on my face, and at this point in my life, telling a lie was worse than anything, so I said, "Yes, I would have." She looked at me differently after that. Her baby wasn't a baby anymore.

The first time I got drunk was on the campus of Texas Lutheran University on a church choir trip to Houston, Texas, in August 1973. On the cusp of fifteen, I had been strongly involved in the culture of Trinity Lutheran Church for most of my life. I taught Sunday school, participated in the youth group, and sang in the choir for years. The trip to Texas was a big deal. We feverishly rehearsed a high-energy show and booked performances in churches and community events in cities down and back, mostly staying in the homes of families from the churches. At a naval base in Tennessee, one of our senior girls was scheduled to give a youth sermon before our show. Due to nerves, she referred to Christ's "erection" instead of resurrection, and a room full of sailors busted a gut trying to stifle laughter. The All Lutheran Youth Gathering was billed as the largest Lutheran youth convention in history. We filled the Astrodome.

I was an incoming sophomore, and a senior had smuggled some vodka in his luggage. Growing up in a family where alcohol was pervasive, I was eager to hop on that train and appear cool to the older guys, much to the chagrin of my more reserved group of friends. I vividly remember feeling it in my eyes first, a subtle blurring of vision and a warmth that traveled from my throat to my extremities. Getting tipsy and wobbling on my feet drew howls of laughter, and soon, I was enthusiastically laughing along. In a dorm at TLU, just outside San Antonio, a very impressive drinking career found its genesis.

My dad started letting me have a beer once in a while, and the slight buzz that ensued was glorious. Increasingly, I snuck one on him when he hadn't offered it. I started snaring a couple to drink on the way to dances at East High. He never missed them, and I found they gave me courage. As a freshman, I was a model student with a perfect GPA (except for algebra, sorry Mr. Richter). I played football for East White had started teaching myself piano, writing my first song, "Midnight Sky." I don't remember it. Probably a good thing.

But the straight and narrow was beginning to veer.

4. FIFTEEN
(Taylor Swift)

FIFTEEN IS CRUEL. You're smarter than everyone, and you can't drive legally. Then my good friend Mark Davini's mother went to Europe and left her VW Beetle sitting forlornly in the driveway.

Mike Ripp was a kid I was starting to hang out with who lived down the street. I was fooling around with a plastic toy ukulele that belonged to my younger brothers and had learned Henry McCullough's exquisite guitar solo from McCartney's "My Love." I was playing it when he came over, and suitably impressed, he asked, "Do you wanna be in a band?" A lifelong friendship and musical collaboration was born on the strength of that performance played on a toy.

The world glowed in technicolor, and we rearranged our priorities. We discovered weed and cheap beer and worshipped at the altar of Deep Purple and Jethro Tull, Black Sabbath and The Beatles, Yes and Pink Floyd, The Rolling Stones, Bowie, and J. Geils. It was all endless and exhilarating.

School became an afterthought. We'd make it to first period, hang around until homeroom, then sneak out, hit a restaurant for breakfast, head to Mark's to listen to music, and smoke and plan our destiny—to be rock stars.

The school would mail letters to our houses telling our parents what classes we missed, so it became a cycle, a game, to skip more school and intercept those missives before we got caught.

We found a drummer. Ron Hoffman went to a different high school but lived in the neighborhood. He had a beautiful black Ludwig drum kit and a basement to rehearse in. His parents, part owners of a restaurant chain, encouraged our endeavors.

The band became our focus. Mark Davini was on keys, Michael John Ripp on guitar, Ron on drums, and yours truly was on lead vocal. We decided we needed a second guitarist to flesh out the sound and put up a flyer in a local music store. Rick Paulson, a guitar-wielding hockey player from yet another high school who owned a fabulous red Fender Mustang and an amp, answered the ad.

I knew then, without question, my passion and direction. I wanted to make a life in music, and though our abilities didn't meet our aspirations, the endless idealism of youth made us confident we'd get there. Rehearsals whet our appetite to learn more and perform. Our goal was to have a set to play for the upcoming summer. There were gigs to be had and mountains to be conquered. We were worldly and golden. We were going to be famous. We scraped together $2.99 and sent Charlie Ferguson, who was fifteen but six-foot three-inches with a mustache, to the store for a case of Huber returnable bottles again and again.

5. TWO OF US
(John Lennon and Paul McCartney)

ROBIN SAID I COULD COME HOME when I quit drinking for good. No cutting down. We'd tried that ad nauseum. I had to be done. Finité. I left and moved into an apartment with Mick Whitman, my ex-musical partner who was a kindred spirit. His shithole apartment wasn't so bad. His wife had thrown him out as well. We had a lot in common. We rarely had food in the refrigerator, but it was never devoid of beer. Once in a while, he'd score some coke, and we'd spend that transitory evening feeling like rock stars. We decided to get some gigs. We tried writing songs, but there was no energy, no purpose, no spark.

We played a gig at a club down the street. What was once second nature to me was Sisyphus personified. I couldn't sing, and my hands had lost all intuition. I chalked it up to having one too many. We tried again and it was worse. These days I was reaching for the bottle under the bed the second I regained consciousness from a restless, tormented sleep. Forget pints. I was buying fifths now, with checks that bounced sky-high. After a week or so of not really eating, I remember thinking that I should go grocery shopping. I had to go to a supermarket across town, one in which I didn't have a rubber check hanging on the bulletin board of shame. I drove drunk. I filled the freezer with microwaveable entrees and never prepared one.

I was working for Murphy Music, a recording studio specializing in jingles for advertising. I had been there a year, selling their services to a dismal record of success due more to the quality of the product I was selling than to my substantial efforts. The side benefit was that I could use the equipment and spent many evenings until dawn writing and recording. So I had little income for a year, but I had an office, a place I spent numerous evenings passed out in my chair, waking when people were reporting for work in the morning. The saving grace of the situation was that the folks at the larger studio complex that housed Murphy were wonderful people who became lifelong friends. The Concept Productions crew will figure prominently later. Also in the win column was meeting Harvey Briggs and Bruce Geiger, guys using Concept for some recording projects that would loom large in my early recovery.

BUT NOW. It's Wednesday, October 13, 1993, and I'm looking out the second-floor apartment window, watching a car burn in the parking lot below. I called the fire department, and though the station was just a couple blocks away, they took twenty minutes to respond. It was only Simpson Street. People were standing around with beers in their hands like it was a Fourth of July picnic, watching it burn as if it were entertainment. At that moment, the horror of my path began to dawn on me. What was I doing here? What had I done? How far had I really fallen? Wasn't it yesterday I was in New York recording for Atlantic Records? Despair like I've never known washed over me. I saw my surroundings clearly for the first time. The threadbare furniture, the filthy, unkempt apartment in a severely depressed neighborhood. I began to cry. I called Robin and told her I was done. I was never drinking again and asked if I could come home. She said, "I've heard that before. Let's see how you do the next couple days." She came over for a little while on Thursday night and didn't even really want to sit on the tawdry sofa, but she did and comforted me and said I could come home tomorrow if I could remain successful. I came home the next day, a depleted man.

As I walked into our modest, stylish apartment, seeing the life we were building together gave me hope for the future. But I was feeling adrift. I had no balance. My thoughts were incomplete and disjointed. I knew I had to get through withdrawal and that it would be the worst I'd ever experienced. Little did I know what was coming.

6. AGE OF AQUARIUS
(James Rado, Gerome Ragni, and Galt Macdermot)

LAURA—I first met her in fourth grade at Lowell Elementary School. She was the new kid who had moved in with her grandmother just a block away, from some exotic faraway place called California. She was smart and reserved, and we became the best of friends. But it was only a little over a year before she rejoined her mother on the west coast.

In the spring of 1974, Laura was back, fifteen now, tall and lean, whip-smart, and curious about the world.

We challenged each other intellectually, traded poetry readings from the vast library in the old house, and engaged in spirited political, social, and historical discourse. We supported each other unconditionally as only young lovers can and explored our bodies in ways new and dangerous, always accompanied by open, honest, and sparkling communication. But there had been changes on the West Coast in early July, and her mother needed her. She was to fly out on the fifth. We were devastated. We'd been living every moment, consciously not addressing an uncertain future. I pleaded for her to stay. The evening of the fourth, we went to the fireworks and ended up back at her house for one last night.

When it came time for me to go home, her uncle sat in the living room with us. He asked if I'd like to spend the night. I said I'd sleep on the sofa, but Laura said, "No. He's sleeping with me."

Uncle Vince offered his room on the third floor of the grand old house. Soft lighting, fresh linens, lovemaking so tender, so delicate, both of us for the very first time.

Early the next morning, after a painful, tear-filled goodbye, I watched the jet lift into the sky and get ever smaller. I never saw her again.

SUMMER IN THE CITY—John Sebastian, Mark Sebastian, and Steve Boone

Boone's Farm Strawberry Hill, America's bottom shelf wine of choice though Laura preferred Annie Green Springs Peach Creek. We added these delights to the menu of Huber and weed in the summer of 1974, when the legal drinking age was eighteen, and it remained the sixties in so many ways. Charlie still made his pilgrimages to the grocery store for the returnable bottles, but if he wasn't around, we hit the Quonset hut liquor store on Cottage Grove Road for the wine, asking ingoing patrons if they'd grab us a bottle or two. An amazingly high percentage did, with a smile.

We enjoyed warm summer evenings on trails along the north shore of Lake Monona (where legend has it, Chief Blackhawk led his band of Sauk through our city). Under the wooded canopy with waves at our feet, we expertly solved the world's problems, always with wine.

Side note: Mark Davini and I were the last holdouts to start smoking cigarettes. Everyone else had for some time. Finally, the peer pressure became too great, and we caved. We smoked a carton of Kent in one day. Instant karma.

WE DECIDED TO PROMOTE a concert in Ron's garage. (Yes, really. Where do you think the cliché came from?) We had chosen the name Lucifer for the band, an appropriate homage from nice Catholic and Lutheran boys. There was another band on the east side called Satan. We cornered the market. Someone who was on the entertainment committee for St. Bernard's

Catholic Church saw us in the garage and hired us to do our first official show! Lucifer at St. Bernard's. Beelzebub, Dracula, Matthew, Mark, Luke, and John were all on the guest list.

High off our triumphant debut on the stage in the gym in front of a respectable crowd of family and friends, we confidently booked more gigs for the summer. After a forgettable second show, we heard about a friend organizing a benefit at an enormous airplane hangar for the Civil Air Patrol. (It's all who you know.) We set up in anticipation of the throngs of people who would imminently walk through the door.

Three showed up. My parents didn't even come.

We decided to promote a show in my basement. We made flyers and put them on every telephone pole in the neighborhood. We got a light show which was three colored floodlights in a wooden box spray painted black. The tension built all week until the day of the show.

No one showed. No one.

I've got a Polaroid of that show. I'm wearing an argyle sweater vest.

The crowning achievement of the summer was getting a gig at the east YMCA. It was a respectable gig in a series for teens. We were set for July 3. The show went beautifully. We played well, and there was an estimable audience, including Laura. We had arrived. We were a band. It had taken about nine months from the first note played.

We shared in a musical awakening, getting a taste of the hard work behind making it look easy. After hours of rehearsal, there were the knowing glances when a groove kicked in and sounded like something. In our idealistic, romantic minds, we sounded just like our idols, but in reality, it was a victory just to make it through a song without noticeable mistakes. As the summer progressed, we were slowly becoming more of a unit, achieving a synergy that only came from time spent together.

Lucifer's only paid gig was at Queen of Apostles High School that fall. After we paid for the U-Haul, we had enough left for a pizza.

The bonds of friendship forged that year are enduring and strong. Mark is a dear friend, and Michael John and I still play and record together decades later.

MICHAEL MASSEY

That summer gave me a place in the world. I had experienced love, and ingrained in my mind was the certainty that I would make my life in music or die trying. It also introduced me to the most powerful addiction—adrenaline. Heart racing, lights in your eyes, feeling the volume viscerally. Lace it with applause, and it makes heroin look like Skittles.

7. CHANGES
(David Bowie)

I WAS PLAYING MORE PIANO and writing songs on the 1898 Edmund Gram upright manufactured in Milwaukee, a piano that forever cursed me. To make it sound halfway decent, you had to slam the keys. I mean, pound them. As a result, I've broken numerous less-hardy instruments and given myself arthritis in my wrists through the years.

As a junior, I attempted high school again and met and started dating Linda, a gregarious, smart, athletic sophomore. I credit her with saving me both socially and scholastically. She introduced me to a new circle of people actively working toward a better academic future. By association, a new world of parties, sporting events, and friendships appeared. Without her in my life, I almost certainly would have dropped out or attended an alternative high school where my path would have been far different. Our relationship would continue on and off, mostly off and long distance for five years, with a couple of fractured reunions a few years later. In taking an honest look at our arc, alcohol and the stupidity of youth irreparably damaged any possibility of an actual future. Because of the spectral, fleeting nature of Laura's presence in my life, Linda shares the distinction of being my first love. She also holds the title for the number of songs inspired in my career, an honor she's not entirely enamored with, as evidenced by a letter I recently found. In it, she's emphatically angry with me for a reason that isn't clear but I'm sure warranted. She ends the letter by snarling, "At least you'll get a song out of it."

Lucifer was either fizzling or on hiatus for any number of reasons. Michael John had found a new love that was taking much of his concentration, Rick was a varsity hockey player and justifiably attended to it, and I had rediscovered high school. I was delighted when I got a call from the manager of a rival band that had all the pieces in place to achieve the next level of success. He invited me to dinner downtown and recruited me. Legend would go on to extensively play high schools and community concerts for the next two years, but more importantly, I was introduced to people who would dramatically affect my life for years to come.

Senior year, Linda's family moved to New Jersey, but her influence and the social climate to which she had introduced me remained. I gravitated toward a growing friendship with Legends' rhythm guitarist Rob Fish. Rob lived in a beautiful English Tudor on the shore of Lake Mendota with his parents and three sisters. Their home was sophisticated, stately, and elegantly appointed. I became aware of a different world that existed, one of culture, affluence, and refinement. It ignited an inner goal to make that my future reality.

Second semester I enrolled in an experimental program called Walkabout that was proof of the remaining existence of 1960s hippiedom. I jest, but it was one of the best things I've ever done. The concept was to take subject requirements and transfer them to real-world applications. I was a student music teacher at my elementary school. I wrote songs for credit and studied music theory with the help of the illustrious Fred Carr. Mr. Carr was a soft-spoken soul who had played jazz in New York City in his younger days. He was loved by all who entered his classroom. Knowing I was doing a semester of self-study, he prepared a packet of college-level music theory, and his door was always open when I needed clarification. For the physical education requirement, I went on an extensive hike, packing along the Appalachian Trail for eight days with four women. What, at first glance, seemed like paradise to a seventeen-year-old guy turned out to be a lesson in shared humanity. Eight days of ten-mile hikes with a thirty-pound pack, sparse personal hygiene, and dehydrated camp meals tend to minimize the romantic.

Walkabout gave me autonomy. It gave me direction and, most importantly, cultivated self-motivation that I am proud of and still utilize. When I walked across the stage to "Pomp and Circumstance," I had dragged myself through two years of barely passing, bookended with two nearly perfect years resulting in a 2.5 cumulative GPA. Hardly admirable, but I graduated. Thank you, Linda. Though you never really acknowledged the transformation you instilled in me, I will forever be grateful.

But the most surprising thing about senior year is that until the graduation parties, I drank much less. It was the only time period from age fifteen to thirty-five when alcohol wasn't pervasive in social activities. To this day, I'm not sure why.

8. WE'VE ONLY JUST BEGUN
(Roger Nichols and Paul Williams)

THE SUMMER AFTER high school graduation, Legend fell apart. It seems some people decided that college was a legitimate avenue to creating a future. That left the rest of us with the insatiable rock star dream to pick up the pieces. Michael John Ripp re-entered the picture to join Rob on guitar. Mike is a relatively quiet guy with a wicked sense of humor and impeccably dry comic timing. We were the best of friends, had shared our coming of age in Lucifer, and this was an exciting new step. Tony Cerniglia, Legend's fine drummer, stayed the course. Tony has a drive, energy, and focus that is enviable. A superb musician, he became the band's undisputed leader and handled any business dealings. All we needed was a bass player. An ad was put in the music store, and a six-foot two-inch Adonis named Butch Christianson answered. Butch was an affable jokester and competent musician, and having fun seemed to be all that mattered to him. We spent many summer afternoons planning the future while lounging in the opulence of his mansion in the Highlands. We later found out that the beautiful stone-for-stone recreation of a French chateau with a pool overlooking the lake wasn't a home his alleged father was renting. The actual owners of the house were in Europe for the summer and returned one day to our mutual shock and disbelief. Butch had been squatting, and he simply disappeared! Butch? You out there, Butch? Is that even your real name?

MORE

Another ad, another bass player. A slight, bespectacled dude with long, frizzy black hair came down to audition. Very quickly, it was apparent he could play circles around us. His technique, knowledge, and dexterity were light years more complex than the self-taught band he was auditioning for. I'm happy to say Pat Hynes accepted the gig. He's an amazing musician, a hilarious guy, and still a friend. Pat would come a long way for rehearsals and usually arrived with Budweiser after a hard day's work. There is some speculation that he was abducted by aliens a couple of times on the way home to Beaver Dam, but that is a story for another time.

Over the next year, we changed our name to Chaser and became an adequate cover band with a distinct Midwestern flavor playing clubs around Madison. The examples of locally successful bands that we tried to emulate played covers of glam rock from the mid-seventies and current AOR radio staples from the likes of Nugent, Foghat, Cheap Trick, Steve Miller, etc. Our first big gig was on a Monday night at the Stone Hearth, and for years I kept the poster: Chaser and Falcon, 25-cent admission, 25-cent taps.

Side note: The Stone Hearth was a club off the University of Wisconsin campus. I had the good fortune to see Cheap Trick, Journey, AC/DC, and many more in its intimate confines before record sales and celebrity rocketed them to worldwide fame.

While working on the band, I also enrolled at Madison College, taking a music-heavy course load. At my mother's prompting, I auditioned for The New College Singers (NCS), the resident show choir, a brand-new experience for me. The class met after school every day. Also new to me was the concept that you hung out with and dated people in the group—a cult of personality.

A couple of weeks later, I had the "Singers" over for a party when my parents were out of town. After an evening of drinking, I fell asleep, fully clothed, on top of the bedding with a woman in the group. As I pried my bloodshot eyes open the next morning, my eleven-year-old twin brothers pointed at me and laughed. When my parents returned the next day, they couldn't wait to exclaim, "Mike was sleeping with a girl!" No amount of reasoning could convince my mother of the innocence of the situation. She threw me out of the house, and I hadn't even gotten laid. I was lucky enough to be rescued and moved into a wonderful apartment on the lake with longtime friend and Legend crew member Scott Duckwitz. It was a fabulous time living there, partying hard and working hard. I was doing double duty with the band, learning the choreography and vocal parts for an NCS show, taking thirteen credits, and working part-time for my father, detailing cars to pay the rent.

9. TOMORROW NEVER KNOWS
(John Lennon and Paul McCartney)

ON SATURDAY, October 16, 1993, three days after I took my last drink, I started feeling jittery. Not the shakes that were common when I needed a hit of booze, but deeper. These tremors were internal, like they were coming from inside my head and radiating through the rest of me. I would have sudden spasmodic jerks of my hands and arms like electrical charges were misfiring. I tried to hide it from Robin. I had diarrhea like hot water rushing through me. I just needed to get through it and get to the other side.

On Sunday, four days abstinent, I felt eerily calm when I awoke. The day gave me hope that I was through the worst of it. Under the calm, however, was a building feeling of dread. As nightfall approached, the dread became more pronounced. I had the sensation of losing control of myself. I looked in the mirror and was convinced my teeth were melting, that they were disintegrating before my very eyes. It didn't make any sense, but I could see it happening. I called Robin to the bathroom in alarm. She couldn't see anything wrong, but I was having a panic attack saying, "Look. Can't you see it?" We called my dentist and friend, Chris Kammer. He said that couldn't be the case, and privately he expressed deep concern to Robin about my well-being. I thought that maybe I was legitimately losing it and blamed withdrawal. *All I have to do is make it through the night, and all will be well. Tomorrow would be a new day.* We went to bed, and

I believed with all my heart that I just needed a good night's sleep, and we'd be in the clear.

I was drifting off to sleep when I rocketed up in bed with the sudden incoherent realization that I was missing a gig I had contracted in Lake Geneva with two very accomplished musicians I had never played with before. I was convinced. I felt horrible and sick that I had let them down. I had never done that in my career. It took Robin a bit to calm my confusion, saying it must have been a dream, but it wasn't a dream. It was a concrete reality to me.

Trying again for sleep, though it was approaching midnight, my bedroom filled with sunlight, and there, sitting on my dresser, was my friend Billy Erickson laughing like we were holding a shared secret, a joke only he and I knew, and he was having a grand old time. I couldn't tell if he was laughing at me or with me. I turned over, blocking him out, determined to get to sleep and heal despite the growing fear I was hallucinating and that my withdrawal had reached a stage I might not be able to negotiate until, once again, it was daylight.

Then came the trolls.

They were ancient and grizzled and stood three feet high, with razor-sharp teeth filed down to needles. They wore coarse, dirty burlap clothes and stunted boots with long, grimy hats only semi-erect. Not engaging me with more than a few sideways glances, they proceeded to waddle menacingly around the room, climbing on my dresser and emitting guttural, grumbling sounds. I can still see them. I keep them close in memory. They have been a significant force in my continuing sobriety.

With the last vestiges of my rational self, I got out of bed and told Robin that I was going to shower and that when I was done, she should take me to the hospital. I was lost. I was done. I was over. My beautiful wife had to help me shower. I was shaking uncontrollably. I was terrified and couldn't stand on my own. Robin helped me dress, assisted me downstairs to the car, and gingerly poured me into the passenger seat.

I don't remember much of the drive to the hospital except that I looked out the window, lost in empty thought most of the way there. When we arrived at the hospital, whatever internal force governs the body's reaction to trauma vanished. The ER docs had to hold me down, frenzied and hysterical, on the examining table. The rest of the night was a blank until I awoke in intermediate care the next day. I don't remember singing "Hey Jude" at the top of my lungs. I don't remember them inserting a catheter. (But I remember it coming out three days later!) I don't remember the anti-psychotic drug Haldol being administered. The amount of Valium given to me that night to calm me down and slow my heart was obscene. An ER doc commented that he wished this was being videoed so it could be shown as an instructional tool and deterrent from alcohol use for kids.

I don't remember being taken to an eighth-floor hospital room. I have no memory of being so violently reactive that they needed to restrain me in the ER and then to my bed in the intermediate care wing. I was mostly unconscious for the first full day. On the second day, I would revive for brief periods and bizarrely mime the actions of lighting and smoking a cigarette and having a drink. Massive amounts of Valium, the Haldol, combined with the trauma of acute alcohol withdrawal, had reduced me to a shell. You could not get any lower on this side of the grass.

The simple fact is that I would have died had I not made it to the hospital. I would have been a statistic. My daughters' lives wouldn't exist. Robin would have buried me and moved on, traumatized by the death of her first husband. I would be dead from alcohol withdrawal—at thirty-five.

10. WOND'RING ALOUD
(Ian Anderson)

TONY CERNIGLIA'S DAD, Joe, was head of Tri-State Security, responsible for the safety of the performers and keeping order at the Dane County Coliseum, the 10,000-seat concert venue in Madison. He occasionally hired us to monitor backstage, exposing us to the workings of shows of that magnitude. All 5'11" and 155 pounds of me, guarding the stage. On November 16, 1977, Jethro Tull came to play. I was assigned stage right. There was a handsome, young, articulate guy dancing around to Tull in an expensive, tailored sport coat with a Chrysalis Records lapel pin. After a few minutes of eyeing each other up, I introduced myself to Rick Ambrose. I asked if the pin meant he was a working part of Chrysalis, Tull's record label. Indeed, it did. He was the director of national publicity. We talked about Tull's music for a bit as Ian Anderson flew around the stage, and then he said, gesturing to the house, "You know, if all of these people decided to come back here, there is nothing we could do."

After a laugh, I said, "I've got this band ... ."

He asked when my next gig was. I said, "Tomorrow night."

As luck would have it, Jethro Tull had the next night off, so he said, "Maybe I'll stay and watch and catch up with the tour the next day." We exchanged small talk and laughter for the rest of the show, and when it was time to call it a night, he asked where the gig was and was serious about attending. I picked him up at the Edgewater Hotel at five o'clock the next day and drove to the gig at a hotel in Mount Horeb, a small town twenty miles west of Madison. We gave it all at that show, still not believing our good fortune to have a record label present. Our performance of all covers was adequate but being our own worst critics, not at a level I was hoping we could achieve. After the gig, Rick came into the dressing room (which was a kitchen) and said, "If you guys can write songs and perform them with that kind of energy, I'd like to get involved."

Not long after, Rob took a fall on stage that profoundly affected him. He lost his balance during a choreographed bit, fell into his speakers, and hit the deck, lying flat on his back while his amp teetered precariously over his head, threatening to plunge earthward. He felt pressured to go to college and give up this silly dream anyway, so he succumbed to a more conventional life and left the band. Rather than add another guitarist, we decided Michael John Ripp could handle the six-string duties on his own and became a four-piece.

We started a dialogue with Rick on the West Coast, sending inspiration and ideas via the U.S. Postal Service, hoping to knock some of the Midwestern out of us. He would send cassettes of new bands on the coasts and implored us to emulate the Stones, Aerosmith, Queen, and Bowie instead of REO Speedwagon, Styx, and Ted Nugent. He would send handwritten lyrics in his flowing penmanship, and we would attempt to put them to music. He flew numerous times to Wisconsin to work with us and write. We recorded every rehearsal and jam and went back and found licks and passages that eventually became songs. We had about a dozen of our own songs to supplement a substantial repertoire of covers when we started a house gig at a club called Harlow's and played as much as we could.

Our covers changed from playing the top forty hits to our rock versions of classic songs like Donovan's "Hurdy-Gurdy Man" or the newer and interesting Talking Heads and The Cars. (In fact, Rick had a version of The Cars demo that ignited a bidding war in the record industry. Before their stunning debut album dropped, we had been playing "Just What I Needed" and "Let the Good Times Roll" for months. Locals thought they stole OUR songs when they both took the radio by storm. Rick landed us a booking agency out of Minneapolis, The Good Music Agency (sometimes not so affectionately known as the Good Mileage Agency), with national reach. Plans were being made to hit the road and sign an official management contract with him. Nightflight Management was born.

I went to the New College Singers and said I was out. I had rehearsed with them for months and never got to do a show. They assigned my John Travolta solo to someone else. I finished my one semester at Madison College with a 3.6 GPA, erasing my high school mediocrity.

Then Pat faced a terribly difficult decision. He was recently promoted to foreman at his factory job and made excellent money. He loved playing with us, and we loved the guy whose virtuosity gave us a solid foundation and instant credibility. He had started dating Linda, who eventually became his wife. She preferred he stay and get serious about life rather than hit the road for no money and the unknown. Good money and love won the day. Pat reluctantly resigned from the band.

Now what? Investigating through channels, we heard about a great bass player-singer who had recently left a longtime project. Stevie Johnson came down and auditioned and had us from the start with his tastefully manic style. His unique, energetic stage presence, excellent vocals, and serious skills on the bass were the final pieces to the puzzle. Almost instantly, there was a feeling playing music that I had never experienced before. The sum was greater than the individual parts. You could feel it in your chest. Stevie also owned a van and trailer, PA system, and lights. He wasn't totally keen on abandoning reality and hitting the road on a fantasy, but Tony and Rick convinced him that the band would make the payments on his equipment and vehicle and the possibilities were enormous. Stevie was on board, and we were on our way!

11. MAGIC CARPET RIDE
(John Kay and Rushton Moreve)

WE WERE SCHEDULED to embark upon our first tour in March 1978. In February, Ambrose flew me to L.A. to generate some buzz and introduce me to a few music-industry people. The Mississippi River was the farthest I had traveled besides the church trip to Houston. This was uncharted territory, and I loved every second like the wide-eyed kid I was. He picked me up at LAX in his black Mercedes, and I marveled at southern California's sunshine and palm trees. Beverly Hills! Sunset Boulevard! Places I had only seen on TV or in movies. We went to his Whitsett Avenue Studio City apartment to get cleaned up for dinner. We were meeting a writer by the name of Cameron Crowe.

I don't remember much of our dinner because I drank too much. I also know that I tried to be someone I'm not. We went to the magnificent Yamashiro Restaurant in Hollywood, and I didn't have the first clue as to Japanese protocol or tradition. I was trying, and I'm sure failing miserably, to come off as a worldly rock star. My misguided arrogance and unwarranted false confidence, fueled by alcohol, were a huge disappointment. I cringe to think about it even now. At the time, Cameron was an active writer for Rolling Stone and had been covering the industry's giants since he was very young. Undoubtedly my disingenuousness was telegraphed a mile away. I'm not saying we would've become the best of friends, but years later, after seeing his semi-autobiographical film Almost Famous, I literally cried to think I could have just been my wide-eyed self and maybe actually gotten to know him instead of relegating myself to a forgotten asterisk.

A few months later, I asked Rick if he had seen Cameron around. He said, "No. No one's seen him. It's like he disappeared off the face of the earth." It was then he had enrolled undercover as a twenty-two-year-old senior at Clairemont High School in San Diego to write Fast Times at Ridgemont High.

THE NEXT NIGHT I found myself above the Starwood Club on Santa Monica Boulevard in the chrome and glass office of Kiss manager Bill Aucoin. I could not believe this was happening. I did better during that visit, wasn't too wasted, and held what I thought was a good conversation, trying not to be starstruck by the priceless Kiss memorabilia surrounding me.

I walked out of the office onto the club's balcony and saw two others, one of which was Jackie Fox, bass player of the Runaways. I ordered a Heineken and returned to my seat, and soon they came over to join me. We had a great time just talking and went to breakfast afterward. Jackie was a sweet woman, and we exchanged a couple of letters and phone calls because that's what you did in 1978. I was never able to reconnect with her on our subsequent trips to L.A. My loss.

Rick also introduced me to Pamela Turbov on that trip. Pam would become a great friend, opening doors and my eyes to the wonders of Hollywood. The next couple of years in her company would bring a whirlwind of introductions, clubs, movie premieres, and joy. Pam is an incredibly accomplished person in many facets of the music business, signing acts to record labels, artist management, music supervisor for film, and more. (I'm happy to say we've recently reconnected.)

So, I got my feet wet on the West Coast. Now it was back to frigid Wisconsin and hitting the road with my mates for Chaser's first tour!

12. EVERY DAY IS A WINDING ROAD
(Sheryl Crow, Jeff Trott, and Brian Macleod)

WHEN YOU'RE NINETEEN, every day on the road is something brand new. Our crew was Mike, Tony, Stevie, and me. Tim "Cheesie" Ringgenberg was on sound production, and Mike Murray on lights and spotlight. When we got to a city, we'd set up and then find a room in a motel, flipping a coin to see who got the bed, who got the mattress on the floor, and who got the box spring, although I think Tony and Stevie got the bed more often than were the odds.

We averaged four shows a week and toured at least ten months a year from 1978 to 1981. We slowed our pace in '82 and '83. When we weren't traveling, we were writing and rehearsing. We took it very seriously, except I quickly realized a dangerous perk of this vocation—free booze. Every club had free tap beer, and most clubs provided everything free for the band. I would start drinking when we got to a club and stop when we left, doing a show somewhere in between. In many cities, if we had a layover or if it was a multi-night gig, we'd go to the club in the afternoon and rehearse, starting the cycle just a bit earlier in the day.

We were increasingly sprinkling in Chaser songs among the covers and not telling the audience until after we got applause. Time and repetition were changing them, molding them into something new. There is no substitute for playing live and experimenting with your own creation. You keep what works and discard what doesn't, and before you know it, the tightness of rhythm and arrangements click into place.

The ending of the first tour is somewhat legendary. Exhausted after a run through Minnesota and South Dakota, we ended up in Iowa. In Council Bluffs, just across the river from Omaha, we were scheduled to do five sets per night for five nights. It was brutal. On Thursday night, we hatched a scheme to get out of our contract a couple of days early. I was going to collapse on stage. We talked it through on break, and sure enough, I made it to mid-set and hit the deck. Murray came running from the lights, Tony came around from behind the kit, and they were attending to my lifeless body. They picked me up and carried me back to the dressing room, where I remained "unconscious" for a minute or so. I slowly came to and didn't know where I was. I acted like I wanted to go back onstage. The show must go on, and all that, and the owner said, "No. Why don't you guys call it a night? In fact, maybe you should just pack it up, head home, and get him to a doctor." Mission accomplished.

13. THE FOOL ON THE HILL
(John Lennon and Paul McCartney)

WE HAD A HOLE in our schedule in June, and Ambrose flew Michael John Ripp and me to L.A. for a few days to meet more people who could help our cause. On the flight out of Chicago, our American Airlines DC-10 dropped precipitously a few minutes after takeoff from O'Hare. The flight attendants hit the floor, and the fainter of heart screamed. The pilot came on and apologized for the rough air and said, "To make it up to you, we're going to be serving free champagne all the way to L.A.!" They were passing out bottles to everyone—not glasses, bottles. A doctor and a lawyer got so drunk they came to blows over a political argument. There was blood everywhere! LAPD had to escort them off on arrival. Mike and I consumed our share and asked for a second bottle. Does anyone remember when you could smoke on planes? That flight was a cloud!

Ambrose picked us up in a white Lincoln stretch limo. When we asked him why, he said, "I want you to see what you're working for."

The first night Rick had a previous engagement, so Mike and I were left to fend for ourselves. We wandered down the street, found a dance club, The Sugar Shack, and hung out until bar time. The next night, we were to have dinner at Le Dome on Sunset with Russ Shaw, president of Chrysalis Records, and Tony Toon, Rod Stewart's publicist. We proceeded to do a Viking amount of substances to ready ourselves for the evening: Quaaludes, coke, champagne, cognac, weed, and beer. Once we were seated at the classic French restaurant, introductions were made. I felt like Mike and I were holding our own in the company of luminaries. The drugs probably helped temper the panic at being so far out of our league. We ordered steak tartare for an appetizer. Neither Mike nor I had the slightest idea what it was, but it had "steak" in the name, so it must be okay, right? When the raw ground beef showed up, slathered in raw onion slices, Michael John valiantly attempted a few bites. He was braver than me. I must have looked silly trying to read the French menu because Tony came to my rescue and said in his British accent, "Why don't you do as I do? I have them find me a nice piece of meat and cook it medium rare." Now you're talkin' my language!

After our orders were taken, a familiar gentleman stopped by the table to say hello to our dinner companions. When I realized it was Bernie Taupin (Elton John's lyricist), I leaped out of my seat, introduced myself, said I was a big fan, and shook his hand, probably scaring the shit out of him.

After dinner, Tony proclaimed, "Let's all go to Rod's house. He's in Hawaii!" It was a tightrope act to walk between acting like we'd been there before and being starstruck kids. The gates swung open on Rod Stewart's opulent Holmby Hills mansion. After a tour of the house, all white furniture, white Steinway, white spiral staircase, tropical birds, and a waterfall in the backyard, we retired to the pool house for cocktails and swimming. By then, we'd supplemented the buzz, which was in full swing. I tried to play a new song I was writing on the piano in the pool house, but my hands felt like canned hams on the keys. I couldn't play or sing. It was awful. Ambrose gently pulled me away from the keys. I'd classify this as a missed opportunity, but everyone was so fucked up they wouldn't have remembered even if I'd put Freddie Mercury to shame.

I was really getting high now, and Mike and I, not wanting to go all out, opted to swim in the Olympic-sized pool in our tighty-whities. There were a couple of bikini-clad women at the pool, and I found out later that they were paid escorts designed to make the young, green imports from the Midwest more comfortable in this all-male environment. I wandered into the enormous in-ground Jacuzzi in the pool house alone, wanting to get away for a little while. I settled in the corner and put my head back to relax. The next thing I knew, there was a hand on my crotch. My eyes flew open to a naked Tony Toon sitting next to me. I removed his hand and said, "I'm sorry if I've misled you, but no. Not into it." He skulked out. We limped home to Rick's and passed out.

The next afternoon, Tony called Rick and, in that clipped British accent, asked, "Is my friend still going to Hawaii with me then?" Apparently, somewhere along the roller-coaster ride of the previous evening, I'd said I'd love to go. That answer was no.

We were so hungover and sick the next day that we passed on a dinner reservation with John Waite, singer extraordinaire of The Babys, and his then-girlfriend, movie star and Bond girl, Britt Ekland, at Pip's in Beverly Hills.

On our last day in California, we went to Laguna Beach. The sun and the ocean were magnificent. I burned my lips until they blistered and suffered all the way home.

Side note: In April, Chrysalis recording artists, The Babys, were on a leg of a tour opening for REO Speedwagon in Madison. Rick was traveling with the band for a few days, and I went to the Edgewater Hotel to pick him up and drive to the show. We were standing in the lobby when a breathless John Waite, clad in a leopard skin jacket, bright red hair, and full makeup, including blue eye shadow, burst from the elevator and strode across the lobby like a peacock exclaiming, "Has the limo gone?"

It had indeed departed without him, and Rick took him by the arm, looked at me, and said, "We need to go now!" So, I drove my mother's 1972 Oldsmobile Delta 88 with John Waite in the back seat to the Dane County Coliseum.

As we crested the hill on Wisconsin Avenue and had a view of our magnificent capitol building, he leaned over the front seat and declared, "My God, what an impressive building!" I gave him a geography lesson and explained that Madison was the capital of the state of Wisconsin. He sat back, satisfied.

14. COMFORTABLY NUMB
(David Gilmour and Roger Waters)

MY WRISTS WERE TIED to the bedrails, not because I was formulating a getaway but because I was so ruined and filled with Valium that I didn't know what I was doing. I wasn't to be trusted. The lighting was kept dim, and I floated between worlds. Those five days in the hospital in intermediate care, one small step down from ICU, are like an unfocused lens in my memory. On Wednesday, three days after admission, they removed my restraints and the catheter. I was so disoriented that at one point, I got out of bed, found my street clothes in the cupboard, and put them on over my hospital gown and IV. I was going to go outside and have a cigarette! They caught me waiting at the elevators with the down arrow illuminated, leaning on the IV pole, complete with hanging bags of fluid, I had navigated through the hallway. That little excursion earned me a bed alarm for the duration of my stay.

Robin came to visit regularly, bringing her love and encouragement. I made a call to Tony C. and didn't recall much of what I said, just that I needed to call him. As the milligram count slowly declined in my force-fed Valium cocktail, I gradually became aware of reality but had no plan or concept of my situation. I just was. I lay listless and quiet, trying to formulate coherent thoughts.

Doctors said that if I had continued my alcohol consumption at the same level, I likely would have died from liver failure within a month.

MORE

My brother Keith came to visit. Until this point, I had no recollection of the many people, including Robin, who had lightly approached how to proceed beyond my purgatory until he said, "Mike, you know you're going to need treatment, right?" Perhaps it was because it was Keith. Or maybe it was because I had regained a sliver of perception, but this time it got my attention. Treatment? I tasted the word on my tongue, and the thought of it brought relief. My brother, in that softly lit hospital room with night pushing at the window, by his seemingly innocuous question, had given me what I so desperately needed at that exact moment—hope.

Robin had gifted me a journal to write thoughts, poems, and lyrics the previous Christmas. She had brought it to the hospital, and at five thirty in the morning on Friday, October 22, the day I was to move to the residential treatment center from the hospital, I picked it up and put pen to paper, still under the waning influence of Valium:

> *Hello to the real Mike Massey. Still a long way to go, but there is light at the end of the tunnel. It will be beautiful to relate to life and loved ones as myself.*
>
> *Whether it be the bloom of roses, or the thorn in my side, it will be as me and not induced by chemicals.*

Later that morning, I wrote the most important page of prose in my life. It was my "switch," and I had flipped it. I truly believe that at the moment I finished writing, I was solidly on my way to recovery:

> *In a time of great need, it is comforting to know that many people care about you as a person and not what we can become when influenced by illicit outside stimuli. The euphoria of chemicals is far outweighed by the peace and solace of sobriety.*
>
> *Life isn't easy or simple, but the trials and tribulations one faces do not seem as insurmountable when the mind and body are clear to tackle them head-on.*

I apologize to anyone I may have slighted or hurt along the way, and I will do my damnedest to rectify any wrongdoings I have incurred in my past.

God snatched me back from the brink of death. I will find a way, or ways, to justify His decision.

So, on this day, I look forward with trepidation and excitement to embark upon this Boot Camp for Life.

I WAS EMBRACING the idea of confronting and breaking the endless cycle of Hell I'd been caught in for years, and as I started getting flashes of lucidity creaking through the fog, it was becoming clearer that I owed my life to the woman I loved. Her unconditional love and support through these times that would have found a weaker person running, not walking, in the opposite direction was nothing short of amazing. *Amazing* is an overused word in the English language, but it's most appropriate here. She has had a line she's used in our darkest hours, which never fails to inspire. "We'll get through this" is a simple thought. But coming from Robin Valley-Massey, you know she means and believes it every time.

I was scheduled to go to a residential facility for a fifteen-day inpatient treatment program. NewStart was the Meriter Hospital option that was available to our health insurance. I took a taxi to my home for the next two weeks, a path that I both anticipated and feared. As we came up the long drive and I saw the facility for the first time, nestled on a prairie surrounded by woods just outside the city, I felt a sense of detachment. I was standing outside myself, looking at an uncertain future. Waiting for admission, I spotted a basketball lying in the corner. I asked if I could shoot a few, and they thought a little exercise might be good. I took the ball out to the asphalt parking lot and found I had forgotten how to dribble. Even though I hadn't been given any Valium that day, the residual half-life of a week's worth of the drug was still battling my blood for supremacy. I could hardly stand. I couldn't jump. Once, I hit the deck hard. I tore a hole in my thick corduroy pants and my knee, a deep wound that would outlast my rehab stay. I shot hoops by myself for ten minutes. None went in. Not one.

15. 1979

(Billy Corgan)

ROCKY MOUNTAIN HIGH—John Denver and Michael Taylor

On October 23, 1978, Jethro Tull was performing at Chicago Stadium, and Rick pulled another rabbit out of a hat and decided to get us a photo opportunity. We were impersonating radio contest winners from Minneapolis and got after-show backstage passes to meet and greet the members of Tull. Ian Anderson, not being a stupid man, knew something was up, but he was delightful and went with it, at one point saying, "You're not contest winners. Who are you?" We came clean and, as Ian knew Rick well, had a good laugh. Rock history has never had a more dynamic and cerebral performer than Ian Anderson. It was a memorable and inspiring event, not only watching the masterful performance but actually having a conversation with the man himself. We left Chicago with our heads in the clouds.

As '78 gave way to '79, we toured incessantly, not realizing how much better we were becoming as performers and writers. We were perfecting new songs under fire and building stamina that only the early twenties allow. Our usual circuit was Wisconsin, Minnesota, the Dakotas, Iowa, and Illinois. It's incredible how many rock clubs and ballrooms there were at the time.

Plans were made to go to L.A. in August for a month. We would stay at Rick's new apartment in Beverly Hills: 145 Canon Drive. We were also going to record. On the way out, we spent a glorious week playing at a club in the shadow of Rocky Mountain National Park in Estes Park, Colorado. We stayed in a cabin a stone's throw from the Big Thompson River. I befriended a woman who worked at the club, and she was a lovely tour guide, showing me the expansive, majestic beauty of Colorado. We toured the shops and restaurants of the beautiful small resort town. We went into the park in the dead of night and saw mysterious lights near the summit at 14,259 feet, Longs Peak. There was no way anyone was up there. She was on the roster at Colorado State and kicked my ass in tennis. It lives in my mind as an example of the beautiful, transient friendships that surprise us if we're open to it. Those pieces of time help define what you eventually become.

Thank you, Jeane, for that life memory.

Those familiar with the horror film Alice, Sweet Alice know the mask involved. If not, look it up. We found one in a thrift store and planned a prank for our beloved crew member Mike Murray, who was a slasher movie buff. We waited until late in the evening, and Murray and Ripp retreated to their room to watch TV. Ripp was in on the gag. We were in a cabin in the Rocky Mountains. I went out into the pitch-black night with a flashlight, butcher knife from the kitchen, and the mask. I scratched on the screen with the knife once, twice, until Murr started saying, "Did you hear that? There it is again!" I scratched once more and flicked the flashlight on the mask outside the window. Mike Murray screamed. I ran around the cabin, came back in the front door, and was serenely lying on the floor watching TV when he came flying out of the bedroom. He may still be traumatized by the experience. (I recently saw Michael, and we laughed about the story, but he said half seriously, "You guys are lucky I lived through that experience.")

I don't think Ambrose thought through what it would be like to have six guys descend upon his quiet Beverly Hills neighborhood. At night there was very little floor or sofa space unoccupied by a slumbering would-be rock star. But there we were. We had a singular goal, and nothing was going to stop us. There is something powerful about the selfless determination of a team striving for greatness, and we were a team.

I LOVE L.A. —Randy Newman

It was a heady time. There was zero doubt in our minds that this was the logical progression to the success we believed we would achieve. We would sit around throwing out song ideas, work on marketing the upcoming gigs, and enjoy being in each other's company. We rented rehearsal space at Uncles, a warehouse in Van Nuys owned by Jack Lee, songwriter of "Hanging on the Telephone" for Blondie. We were scheduled and played Madame Wong's Chinatown as a springboard to the more prestigious Wong's West. We played a club in suburban Glendora where Van Halen cut their teeth. We played the University of California, Davis. We opened for the family band that inspired the Partridge Family, The Cowsills, at the Starwood. All of this was a warmup for going into the studio and in preparation for the Holy Grail: Whiskey a Go Go.

We went into Sound Lab Studios in Hollywood and, because we'd done hundreds of shows in the past eighteen months, could record thirteen songs in thirteen hours, perform, and mix. Now Ambrose had something to shop to these record labels we were playing for.

Jet Records was among the first to be interested. Sharon Arden (later Osbourne) was the A&R rep for the label, had heard our demos, and was in communication with Rick. She came out to a show and really liked the band. I'm not sure why those negotiations broke down, but rumor has it she had carnal designs on a band member, and the casting couch was spurned. (Later in the eighties, I would call her backstage at the Coliseum in Madison on an Ozzy tour, and she left all-access passes for me at the stage door.)

Pam Turbov was hosting a gathering at her beautiful Coldwater Canyon home. We all went and had a grand time meeting new people and acquainting ourselves with Hollywood. Among the attendees was Playboy Playmate, model, singer, and rock star muse, Bebe Buell. Pam appeared with authentic fencing foils, and Bebe and I, in true Hollywood rock and roll silliness, proceeded to sword fight across the living room and up and down the stairs. Errol Flynn would've been envious. We're lucky somebody didn't poke an eye out.

Another night at Pam's, I wandered down to the basement and found a bloke playing around on a keyboard. We traded licks for a while and got on smashingly. Quite a few laughs later, he said he had to go, and we said our goodbyes. I felt pretty sheepish when I found out it had been Ian McLagen, the keyboardist for Faces, Small Faces and The Rolling Stones.

Pam's Coldwater Canyon home was a magical place. You never knew who would show up and hang out on any given night. Pam and her good friend Orly decided to make me up on one occasion. The result was a combination of Ziggy Stardust, Marilyn Manson, and a regal vampire. Another night, I was dressed only in a beautiful silk kimono, worn a couple of weeks earlier by Roger Taylor of Queen. It was Hollywood. I was living a life beyond my wildest dreams.

I can't remember why I didn't or couldn't attend, but Pam invited me to accompany her to the wedding of Nick Lowe and Carlene Carter. These are the things I think about all these years later and wonder, what if?

We ate an inordinate amount of meals at the Beverly Hills Café just a block away from Rick's on Wilshire Boulevard. So many that two of the servers, Nicole and Anne, became good friends. One night six of us borrowed and squeezed into Nicole's Datsun 240z and drove up to Mulholland Drive. The views were fantastic. I can't help but wonder how much has changed in that vista since. Another warm memory is sharing a six-pack of Henry Weinhard's on the beach with Anne. The insistent ocean breeze turned decidedly cooler after a blazing sun sank in the ocean, and I comfortably draped my arm around her shoulders. Do you ever wonder where the people who briefly touched your life in your youth are now? I hope they're doing well.

The Whiskey a Go Go was legendary even to a bunch of kids from Madison, Wisconsin. The roster of performers that graced that stage is epic and historic. Everyone from The Doors to Led Zeppelin, Janis Joplin to

MORE

Jimi Hendrix, The Police, AC/DC, Motley Crue, Kiss, and countless others who went on to do great things. You could feel the ghosts of all those who had gone before us with grand aspirations and purpose when you walked in the door. We were ready. We shared the bill with the L.A. band, Smile, represented ourselves well, and played an energetic show. It was a feather in our cap. We were doing it.

In taking stock of the first tour to L.A., we were pleased. We'd played ten shows, recorded a thirteen-song demo, and raised our profile. It was up to Rick now to circulate the demo and lead us into the next phase.

On the way home, we were scheduled to play a club in Denver for five nights. After two nights, the club owner fired us, saying we didn't play enough cover material. Our contract explicitly said we needed to play at least fifty percent cover material. It didn't specify top forty material, which is what he wanted. We were holding up the provisions of the contract, although many of our songs were our versions of more obscure music or deeper album cuts. We had just enough money to make it home, but we weren't going to take it lying down. Ambrose sued the club owner for lost wages. When the court date rolled around, Tony and Rick met in Denver. The judge ruled in our favor. It seems he was a trumpeter in Tommy Dorsey's band before occupying the bench.

WE RETURNED TO the Midwest and had a growing following in every city we played. We were now close to selling out at home. One night in Des Moines, a telethon was on television when we returned from the club. Jeff Conaway of *Grease* and *Taxi* fame was hosting it. Eva and Wendy, two local friends who had come back to our hotel after the show, drove me to the TV station. Jeff was delightful, and I played two songs at three in the morning on Des Moines television, not quite three sheets to the wind and hoarse as hell. But I did my part. When we returned to the hotel, all the lights were out, and it was quiet. I was extremely disappointed my mates hadn't watched. As I entered the room, they jumped up, yelled, and turned the lights on, celebrating my star turn on Iowa TV.

16. ON THE ROAD TO FIND OUT
(Yusuf/Cat Stevens)

WE CONTINUED TO write and tour for the rest of '79 into '80. We were really proud of the new songs. There were distinctly different flavors to things but still sounded like Chaser. Our musical influences were wide-ranging. We all grew up to our parents' pop and country records of the fifties and sixties, and The Beatles cut a large swath through pop culture and our psyches. As we came of age, glam metal, prog rock, jazz, punk, and new wave all made inroads into our lives. Chaser's music encompassed elements of it all, blending into a growing, powerful, unique sound that was our own. It had the crunch of metal with accessible melodies over the top. We layered keyboards and piano to make it different but familiar. And it was our lives.

We booked an intensive two-week tour in L.A. in May. We would be playing shows just about every night we were there. Rick had moved into yet another apartment in Beverly Hills, and there was no way he would allow us to defile this one. Peter Leeds, Blondie's manager, invested in and financed the tour. We took up residence at the Tropicana Hotel on Santa Monica Boulevard in a lovely private bungalow. When I say Peter financed the tour, I mean he financed our traveling expenses and hotel, not our personal expenses or food. When you're on a three-band bill every night, the take at the door only goes so far. To say we were living frugally is a significant understatement. We'd make the trek down Santa Monica to Ralph's supermarket and eke out bread, deli meat, Campbell's soup, and in my case, beer. Though we were stretching to make ends meet, we were in L.A. We were working for our future.

Rick hosted a party at his new Almont Drive digs, partly housewarming and partly for us, and invited press and industry people. I succeeded in doing my best impersonation of a wanton rock star, and it wasn't good. Jan Golab did a mini interview with me, and I got a quote in *Oui* magazine, an offshoot of *Playboy*. I ended up getting shit-faced, threw a drink in Rick's face after an argument, and seduced a Dutch model named Annettka, who had graced the cover of *Vogue France*. She left a hundred messages for me at the front desk of the Tropicana, and I never returned them. Looking back, I can't find any motivation for such behavior except perhaps a creeping, unearned sense of entitlement augmented by alcohol and lifestyle. It saddens me now.

At Wong's West, Bill Murray showed up, fresh off wrapping up *Caddyshack*. He'd heard there was a band from Madison and came down to check it out. Bill went to college at UW–Madison, and his family vacationed in northern Wisconsin when he was a kid. Bill walked up to Mike Murray at the lighting board and chatted for a while. After the show, Mike brought him back to the dressing room and introduced us. Bill and Tony had a particular connection and gravitated toward a lengthy conversation. He wanted to know if The Plaza Tavern was still there. It was and still is. We gave him a square Chaser button and later watched *Saturday Night Live*, anticipating him wearing it on air. Alas, that never materialized.

Pam and I attended the premiere of the original movie *Fame*. An honest-to-goodness Hollywood premiere with the cast in attendance and a word from the director beforehand. I was constantly struggling between not believing these things were happening and allowing myself the hope that this would be my new normal. For Pam, it was just another day. She owned it.

The reason for our May tour was so record labels could come to see the band after hearing the demo we recorded the previous August. A smattering of people came to various shows and gave us mostly good reviews, although they wanted to hear more music. We had it; we just needed to get it recorded.

However, as the chips fell, eight major record labels had RSVP'd to our show at Flipper's Roller Boogie Palace on the corner of Santa Monica and La Cienega. Eight! Also among the attendees was Geoff Workman, engineer/producer for Journey, The Cars, Foreigner, Motley Crue, and Queen, among others. Stevie and Geoff ended up partying into the night.

We were usually on top of our game on any given night in any given city. On this night, I drank too much to try and steady my nerves and ease the pressure, and I had one of my poorest shows in recent memory. I was off balance, didn't sing very well, felt forced in my movement on stage, and seemed tongue-tied in my rapport with the audience. You only get one chance to make a first impression, and I felt like I had let everybody down. Usually an energetic, poised performer, I couldn't hear the monitors and felt awkward throughout. It was as though all the shows and all the rehearsals were for naught. I promised to do better next time. If there was a next time. Surely, they wouldn't hold one mediocre night against me.

ANOTHER DIFFICULT SHOW was on the campus of USC for a noon concert in the bright sun after drinking heavily the night before. I was soaking wet two songs in and powered through. We came off remarkably well considering the circumstances.

Elvis Costello had left behind a white dinner jacket at Pam's house. She asked me if I wanted it. I loved it! I incorporated it into my stage wardrobe and wore it for months, hoping a little of Elvis's magic might wear off.

It was time to head home. We had a new batch of songs to record and a full schedule of gigs. It was hard to leave L.A. behind this time. I felt like I could have represented so much better. Can I have a do-over?

17. WILL YOU STILL LOVE ME TOMORROW
(Gerry Goffin and Carole King)

THERE WERE PARTIES where a significant percentage of attendees were naked. There were three-ways and four-ways. Nothing was out of bounds, and that was before Chaser went on the road.

Attitudes surrounding sex in the seventies were different. It was the philosophical tail end of sixties free love, and the worst STDs could be cured with a shot of penicillin or some shampoo. Add to it the mystique of musicianship and the perception of celebrity, and you have a cornucopia of flesh searching for fulfillment.

I lived in a fantasy world. I operated under the misconception that all of our destinations were separate from reality. Although I had sexual liaisons in many of the cities we visited, I kept in touch with the people involved, returning to them when our schedule brought us back and many times exchanging letters in the interim. But in my head, they were make-believe. They weren't real. This was compounded by talking with other touring musicians who also knew my assorted friends biblically. My real relationship was back home, and there was a serious disconnect that I was doing something terribly wrong. On one weekend, my girlfriend, Ronda, from Madison, and a few of the road romances decided to converge on the same city. I was a wreck. I discreetly walked around to each table and said that I wouldn't be able to see them because of the unexpected arrival of my girlfriend, and they were all fine with it, or so they said, and subsequent trips to their towns found no negative residual effects.

It is a major regret, the self-absorption and single-mindedness I lived for many of those years. My ignorant selfishness hurt many people I genuinely cared about, good people who didn't deserve my brand of undependable love. And there was love. I valued my relationships highly but was incapable of commitment, to my detriment. Ronda and I would be on and off for five years, engaged, then not engaged, until my capricious nature finally became too much to bear in the relationship. My infidelities were immature and thoughtless, an extension of the rest of my life and how I perceived it would unfold. The primary contributing factor was alcohol abuse, the disintegration of morals, and the abandonment of logic that accompanies it. The other reason was that I was convinced I was on the precipice of rock stardom and would be above reproach. It was a time when being outrageous was a prerequisite to the position, and I was fully invested.

18. THRILLER
(Rod Temperton)

IN THE SUMMER OF 1980, we rented some mobile equipment and got set up to record a new demo in Stevie Johnson's barn. The sound was fabulous, reverberating off the thick, rough wood in the expansive building. Rick flew in to oversee. We knocked out a great-sounding collection of new music to arm our fearless leader with more ammunition in the record-label wars. He deployed to the front, and we fell back into touring constantly and writing more. Because Rick couldn't physically be with us all the time, we added Mike Ripp's younger brother Paul as assistant manager and official photographer. He was under orders to document as much as he could of our daily activities and was fantastic. Paul and I were the best of friends, and he was a great addition to the team.

We landed an opening spot for Off Broadway, an Atlantic Records artist, at Headliners in Madison. Rick had been talking with Atlantic, and it was getting more serious. Atlantic/Geffen A&R guru John Kalodner and West Coast Operations Manager Les Garland flew in to do double duty, checking on their existing artist and getting introduced to a prospective new one. The backstage photo we took that night made it on the cover of *Radio and Records* the following Monday morning. *Radio and Records* was a radio station bible, highlighting trends, new artists, and record label signings, and delivered weekly to most radio stations in America. Rick's phone rang off the hook. Kalodner had worked with Aerosmith, Journey, Heart, and Foreigner, among others. Les Garland went on to have a legendary career in the music business, including co-founding MTV. We didn't realize our luminary company at the time, but the industry took notice.

When we weren't traveling, we were rehearsing. Tony's parents, Joe and Kay Cerniglia, created a space in their home that fed and nurtured our creativity and growth. You take things for granted when you are a young, arrogant prick of a rock singer, and I hope they knew how valuable it was and how much we appreciated it.

That year we had a burst of inspiration and wrote our best batch of songs yet. We were experimenting with structure and tone. A depth of lyric was produced, leaving behind sophomoric lust stories. Melody was being married to accompaniment better than ever. We tested and perfected them on the road and then did rough demos so Rick could add them to the arsenal.

Side note: We were booked to play Hibbing Community College in Hibbing, Minnesota, the birthplace of Bob Dylan. The student promoters assured our agent that it was to be a giant event in the school's gymnasium, but they forgot one small detail—acquiring a permit to serve alcohol. On any college campus in America, and especially in northern Minnesota, alcohol is a necessary element of any event. We played to a sparse, teetotaling crowd but performed an inspired show for those who were there. After our usual extended improv of "Take Me to the River," Stevie Johnson didn't end and kept playing a bass groove. After a few seconds, Tony joined in on drums, followed by Mike Ripp and me, and we created a new song spontaneously on stage. As it was taking shape, the room disappeared for me, and it was just us, giving life to something completely new and different, feeling as one. "Someone Like You" would become one of Chaser's most beloved songs, and that shared, instinctive, impromptu magic remains an indelible, cherished memory.

Halloween on State Street in Madison was a world-class event in the late seventies and early eighties. Other Big Ten universities would bus people in to add to the statewide crusade. It was a colder, bigger Mardi Gras. We landed a slot on the gigantic stage at the bottom of Bascom Hill facing east six blocks to the state capitol building. Standing fifteen feet above the crowd, I saw nothing but bodies as far as I could see. Estimates were that 100,000 attended Halloween 1980. I flew through the performance, fueled by the energy of the massive crowd. We played an inspired show, poised and dynamic, proving we could command a big stage.

Afterward, Rick had flown in unannounced. Perhaps thinking that he'd put less pressure on us, he hadn't divulged that staff producer Genghis and A&R person, Roger Probert from Atlantic Records New York, were meeting him in Madison for the show. They loved it. We met the next morning for breakfast, and they wanted to sign us to a demo deal. The plan was for them to fly in and work in pre-production and then we would go to New York and record a demo at Atlantic Studios, 60th and Broadway, with Genghis producing. Happy Halloween! It was just a couple weeks shy of three years since I had walked up and introduced myself to that dapper gentleman stage right at Jethro Tull.

We would hit the road again and work on perfecting our craft. All of Rick's resources and attention now turned to Atlantic. He worked feverishly for new promotional ideas and swag. We were getting our ducks in a row. Genghis and Roger flew in that spring, and we had a wonderful, amiable pre-production session. They were part of the team. We were booked for the first week in June in the studio in New York!

All of this was glitz and glam on the surface, but there were signs of strain beneath the veneer. I was constantly drinking, and while the performances were good, for the most part, there were times when I was far from my best due to alcohol. Forgotten lyrics, subpar voice, erratic behavior, and fatigue could be chalked up to the rigors of the road, but if I had been taking care of myself, the effects wouldn't have been so pronounced. I started disappearing after the show and not helping as much as I should have for the teardown. After a show in Dubuque, Iowa, and a few too many, I found a booth in the deserted club and fell asleep while the boys struck the stage and packed up. Leaving for Des Moines the next day, I realized with a panic that I had left all of my stage clothes in the dressing room the night before. We would be going just a few blocks from the club on the way out of town, and I pleaded with Stevie to make that detour so I could retrieve some pretty valuable and stylish outfits. He didn't respond, looked straight ahead, and climbed the hill toward the west and our next destination. I was sullen and perturbed. I was so self-absorbed I didn't realize that they were trying to teach me a lesson.

On April 10, we were booked to open for Survivor at Haymakers in Schaumburg, Illinois, a suburb of Chicago. Survivor was a huge draw in their hometown of Chicago due in part to lead man Jim Peterik's legendary turn in the Ides of March. This was one year prior to their meteoric success with "Eye of the Tiger." Survivor sound-checked and left us the stage to set up. But they left us nothing. They weren't going to strike any gear, and the drums were center stage with about two feet of room to the front. What now? Emboldened by our upcoming trip to New York, we weren't going to take any shit. We hung our 10-foot-square banner center stage in front of their drum kit. We set up Tony's drums stage left and the keyboards stage right with Mike Ripp and Stevie just inside of them. We came on and kicked ass. It was new and different, and we used the energy to our advantage. When I wasn't on the keys, I claimed that two feet in the front of the stage as my territory and rocked and strutted like my life depended on it with our blazing logo as a backdrop. Survivor had to work much harder than they had anticipated to follow us.

Necessity is the mother of invention, and we used that stage setup once in a while going forward. It opened a huge center area on the stage that was visually unique and fun to use.

Ambrose had facilitated a meeting at that Chicago show for Tony with Elizabeth, in charge of Ludwig Drums endorsements. Rick had brokered similar deals for Tony Brock of The Babys and Barriemore Barlow of Jethro Tull, so he was well acquainted with her and the process. Tony would go on to enjoy many years of this prestigious arrangement of deep discounts, promotional items, and access to the newest products. He was a member of an elite club.

19. WALK ON THE WILD SIDE
(Lou Reed)

WEDNESDAY, JUNE 3, 1981, we drove out of the Lincoln Tunnel into Manhattan, which was like the *Wizard of Oz*, from black and white into color. New York City! We settled in at Hotel Empire, 63rd and Broadway, across from Lincoln Center and three blocks from the studio. Even the air was electric! We dropped our luggage at the hotel and went directly to the studio.

The legendary Atlantic Studios has been home to sessions for everyone from Led Zeppelin to The Stones. John Coltrane, Charlie Mingus, and Keith Jarrett. The Allman Brothers, Cream, and the Bee Gees. Roberta Flack recorded "Killing Me Softly" here, and the Queen of Soul, Aretha Franklin held court. More ghosts, we hoped for a séance.

A genial production manager greeted us. He was an older man from Trinidad with an infectious smile, booming, accented voice, and a resonant laugh. He told me some juicy stories about Mick and Keith from their days recording in Studio B. What happens at Atlantic Studios stays at Atlantic Studios. (My editor implored me for more details here. Though the statute of limitations has long passed, and existing stories in the public knowledge are legendary surrounding The Stones, I reserve the right to remain mum on the subject.)

We were prepared. We had spent the past few months doing shows all over the Midwest and then worked with Genghis and Roger in the C's basement on fine-tuning. It was just a matter of getting the performances. We had also brought cases of low-alcohol beer, which we promptly loaded into the fridge. It wasn't said, but I believe the L.A. beer was due mainly to the fear the singer might overindulge and ruin everything.

We were booked into the smaller of the two rooms, Studio B, which The Stones had preferred over the larger Studio A. Foreigner had just vacated the larger room during the recording of *Foreigner Four* because they thought they heard the air ducts in the tracks. It had been good enough for any number of historic recordings but not for them.

We spent the rest of the first day getting acclimated, warming up, and dialing in the sound. When we were satisfied with the logistics so we could come in the next day and get to work, we knocked off and convened at a pub at 56th and Broadway. It would become our hangout when we weren't working. And when we weren't working, the alcohol level in the beer returned to full strength. It was a raucous, happy night filled with anticipation for the days to come. It was also a different New York City in 1980 than the seemingly Disneyesque version of midtown today. It was dark. There was a grit in the air. Times Square sported the sex trade and people playing percussion on trash can lids, with fires burning in the cans. At Columbus Circle, lone shadowy people lurked in the doorways of broken buildings where luxury towers stand today. Walking back to the Empire at bar time required some self-awareness.

We spent the next day getting basic tracks. Because of the frequency of our live shows, it was second nature. I sang scratch-track vocals and was going to overdub later to give them the attention they needed and deserved. It was a productive day, and Genghis was happy with the tracks. We had decided upon six songs for the demo, enough for substance but not too many to dilute the time to make them the best they could be. We reconvened at the pub, and after dinner and a few drinks, I was tired and wanted to get a good night's sleep for my voice the next day, so I ventured out on a solo walk back to the hotel. There were a couple of dicey moments when I felt I was being followed, but I had always prided myself on street sense and trusting my intuition. In fact, after the exhilaration of that walk,

I have done the same thing in every city in North America and Europe I've visited since. I will go out for a solo walk, usually after midnight. It makes me feel alive.

Our third day found me working hard to get the best vocal takes possible. I'll never forget standing on the opposite end of the room from the mic with headphones on, waiting to get started. I put my hand in my pocket, and skin scraping fabric sounded like an earthquake. I had never in my life experienced that level of audio technology. I felt pretty good, and after multiple tries on each song, it was declared a wrap. I always feel like I can do better, and that day was no different, but I deferred to opinions and time. Background vocals, keyboard overdubs, and guitar solos were next.

Everyone's mood was upbeat. Our preparation had resulted in tight, energetic performances, and Genghis was ready for tomorrow's mix. We retired for the last time to the pub and celebrated. Rick was ready to unveil a surprise guest who would sit in on tomorrow's mix. One of the songs we had recorded was titled "Andy" and was loosely based on the exploits of a certain New York-based pop artist and enigmatic social giant. Rick's brother was going to bring none other than Andy Warhol by to peruse his song!

20. I'M WAITING FOR THE MAN
(Lou Reed, produced by Andy Warhol)

MY FIFTEEN MINUTES with Andy Warhol was actually about an hour. I was doing a piano overdub on the six-foot Baldwin grand in Studio B when Rick's brother arrived, and Andy gingerly walked into the mix room. Everyone watched through the angled, double-paned window while I got a good take. I pulled open the sound-insulated studio doors and joined the conversation. There was a reverent joy in the room. It was Andy Warhol! He was wearing a tailored sport coat draped elegantly on his slight frame over a subdued checked shirt embellished by a crooked, plaid bowtie for good measure. His famously unkempt "hair" was in full disobedience. After pleasantries and introductions, we played the rough mix of our song "Andy" and pretended not to side-eye him looking for a reaction. As the song faded out, Warhol smiled, turned, and said he liked it. We tried not to telegraph our sigh of relief. We piled into Studio B for a group photo, with Rick and Roger joining us for the opportunity. The slatted wood on the walls, designed for audio, provided a fitting backdrop. Andy grabbed a pair of headphones and put them on.

Everyone started filing out of the studio into the control room, and I went to the piano to gather some of my things. Andy lingered behind, walked over, and engaged me with a meek smile. We talked a little about keyboards and pianos, and I showed him some things on my synthesizer and played a little of a new song I was developing on the piano. Warhol proceeded to take a tiny camera out of his pocket and started snapping pictures of me. He must have taken at least 10. He excitedly told me about his camera. It was a state-of-the-art Japanese prototype that took high-resolution photos despite its small scale. (It was rumored that an image from this session made it to the back page of *Interview* magazine, though I never saw it.) Standing in this moment, I regretted not knowing more about Andy Warhol, his work, and his groundbreaking, remarkable life. I knew I was in the company of a twentieth-century icon with an opportunity few outside of the glitterati ever get to experience, and I didn't know what to say. We exchanged some more small talk, and Andy joined the rest of the crew in the mix room. He worked the room for a bit and then was gone as quickly as he had appeared.

It's an hour I've wished I had back a thousand times. I could have asked him about specific pieces or series. I could have asked about his processes from inception, application, to finish. I should have asked him what it was like before the fame—just an artist with a vision. But all I could manage was polite small talk. This Midwestern boy had fifteen minutes of fame alone with the person who coined the phrase and misspent it. It continues to be a gnawing disappointment that I wasn't knowledgeable enough to have a substantive conversation or ask questions that mattered.

"You can easily judge the character of a man by how he treats those who can do nothing for him."—Johann Wolfgang von Goethe. That one of the most famous people in the world took the time to come over and hang with a young, up-and-coming rock band says a lot about the man. He would die at a tragically young fifty-eight, five and a half years later. Rest gently, Andy. Thank you for your kindness.

With the demo mixed, we packed up for home. We left the promotion department at Atlantic with merchandise ranging from t-shirts and jackets to square buttons and clocks with our distinct logo. By all indications, everybody was on board at the label, and we believed we would return to New York to do a proper album after the demo had made its way to the top for approval. We drove straight through from New York to Madison, negotiating construction and torrential thunderstorms in Ohio, but with Stevie Johnson at the wheel, he aimed us toward the heart of the deluge, and the storm didn't stand a chance.

21. HOTEL CALIFORNIA
(Don Felder, Don Henley, and Glenn Frey)

ADMISSION TO NEWSTART was hazy after a steady diet of Valium and my brain reeling from being deprived of alcohol for the first time in years. Feeling small and lethargic, I was led to my cinder block room, painted institutional green, with a locked window and no removable objects or sharp surfaces. The bathroom door was padded vinyl with a Velcro fastener. The first night, my roommate and I didn't speak, and he disappeared the next day, leaving me with my own room for the duration. The staff rifled through my luggage.

I shuffled down to a buffet-style dinner held in a large community room. We would say the serenity prayer, which I had absently learned, and exercise. I had worked out regularly in hotel rooms on the road while doing at least four sets a night, five days a week, so I was shocked and dismayed when I couldn't do a sit-up. Not one. Ditto a pushup. Was I really in such pathetic condition? I lay on the floor looking at the ceiling, hyperventilating from my efforts, and vowed I would work out every day for the rest of my life.

I had no appetite. Zero. But I choked down a tasteless chocolate parfait that first night. I was assured my appetite would return. I weighed 135 pounds, twenty pounds less than when I was healthy, and my body had morphed into a small protruding pot belly surrounded by atrophied muscles straining to complete simple tasks.

The first few days, I didn't say a word to anyone, didn't participate in group therapy, didn't socialize, was completely disengaged, was underwater, my movements in slow motion, and my thoughts jumbled and incomplete. I would go to meals, try to eat, and after a time, managed one sit-up and one pushup. I didn't view it as a triumph.

I would retire to my room after dinner, hearing laughter coming from the sitting room and kitchen. My mind and body were healing, but it was taking everything I had.

Later the counselors and staff told me there was significant concern surrounding my catatonic state. They weren't quite sure what they would do if I didn't improve.

Boot camp had started, and I had a long way to go.

22. YOU CAN'T ALWAYS GET WHAT YOU WANT
(Mick Jagger and Keith Richards)

THE REST OF THE SUMMER of 1981 was a whirlwind. Our stature had risen because of the New York trip and subsequent press. Photos of us with Warhol circulated widely. Jonathan Little, program director of Madison's top CHR radio station Z-104, added our recording of "Camp It Up" from the New York session to maximum rotation. It blew up, becoming a top request for the rest of the year. Jonathan had been a priceless mentor, and we had played him countless new songs over the years to get his feedback and advice. He had heard "Camp It Up" not long after we wrote it, thought it could be a hit, and with the Atlantic recording, he had a production value he could put on the radio.

We played numerous high-profile gigs at outdoor festivals and opened for Gary Numan, Billy Squier, and NRBQ, among others, in theaters and clubs around Madison. In a microcosm of how the music business keeps you humble, we went to Chicago to play the WLS Rockfest at the 9,000-capacity International Ampitheatre. We were on the bill with Loverboy, The Go-Go's, Quarterflash, The Knack, and Survivor. Later that night, we were booked in Rockford on the way home at a tiny club where the stage was just big enough to fit Tony's drums. The rest of the band had to set up on the dance floor. No wonder I drank.

MORE

Word from New York was slow in coming, but we had been assured by A&R, the Promotion Department, and others that it was just a formality to get the approval from the powers that be at Atlantic. We were shoring up arrangements while continuing to play as many gigs as possible. We went about our business as though that was the next logical step in our career.

Then came the news. Atlantic had passed.

It didn't compute at first. Doug Morris, president of Atlantic Records, had passed on the project. It didn't make any sense. They had sunk a substantial sum into pre-production, our trip, and all of the studio time. It was estimated that their investment in New York alone was around $35,000 (adjusted for inflation it would be more than $114,000 today). It was a drop in the bucket and a tax deduction for the powerhouse label.

We were devastated.

We had gotten ahead of ourselves and become overconfident. As it turned out, there was a competition of sorts, and they had awarded demos to two bands with the understanding that one of them would ultimately get the album deal. Kix was signed to Atlantic, and we were left hanging.

I had never known disappointment like this before. It was a done deal, or so we thought. We were adrift. Rick said to keep writing and we'd try again. He was somewhat of a magician to help us pick up the pieces after being shattered. I believe we produced some very good material after Atlantic, but we found most of the doors to labels had closed after putting all of our eggs in the East Coast basket. Our writing had become more emotional and satisfying, but as our profile waned, we scaled back our travel and got day jobs to pay the bills.

In retrospect, I've spent the rest of my life trying to recreate the magic feeling that Chaser gave me. We were a team. We sacrificed everything to achieve the end goal. We played so many shows that we could intuitively improvise and come back together seamlessly. It was both a product of the times and our youth. The idealism that was pervasive in our every day was never to be a part of my life again.

We played shows, but they were increasingly becoming more work than pleasure. Plus, we had actual day jobs that took time and energy away from that concerted effort to succeed.

In one last burst of brilliance, we were tapped to open for Cheap Trick on February 26, 1982, at the sold-out 8,000-capacity Chick Evans Field House in Dekalb, Illinois, the Northern Illinois University track stadium. Rick worked feverishly to get A&R people that had shown interest to the show. Nobody made it. It was the single finest show Chaser ever played. All the coaching to be a swaggering front person Rick had given me through the years was in full view. He taught me to command the stage. I had to be on my toes at all times, literally. I had to play up and out, ignoring the first few rows. "Never look into a camera. Move independently of the music and the beat; it's more interesting." All of our efforts and time spent honing the craft of arena rock culminated in this moment. The band was nearly flawless musically, and we played with majesty and power, fully belonging and owning the big stage. If A&R had made it that night, I'm certain there would have been other opportunities.

We faded. Hearts weren't as invested as they were only a year before. Gigs were going through the motions even as our writing was maturing. In early 1983, at a nothing gig, in a broken-down ballroom with a wind tunnel money-giveaway machine as the main attraction, Tony came off the stage and said, "I'm done." In the two years since New York, the road had beaten us up and taken its toll. What had seemed like a meteoric ride ever upward had languished and frayed, starting a spiral in the wrong direction. My ever-increasing alcohol consumption was a contributing factor to the tension and anxiety. After six years filled with adventure and promise, Chaser was over.

23. (I'VE HAD) THE TIME OF MY LIFE
(Franke Previte, John DeNicola, and Donald Markowitz)

TIMING IS EVERYTHING. During Chaser's time together, we fought hard against the Urban Cowboy craze, disco, new wave, and punk for the attention of the music industry. We were a little too late for the glam of the mid-seventies and just a little too early for the hair band era of the mid-eighties. Although we had punk and new wave elements to our music, we were called dinosaurs. And we had much more substance musically than a large percentage of the acts that found success with radio, MTV, and massive album sales in the mid-eighties. A painful lesson that is hard to learn is if you're emulating something current, you're too late. To conform to what's happening and not be true to yourself becomes inauthentic and contrived. After Atlantic, we found ourselves trying to write a hit for radio that would open up the rest of our catalog, to the detriment of honest emotion.

Rick coached me extensively to be the best front person I could be. Many nights, I'd walk off the stage thinking I had done well, only to receive a litany of things I did wrong and what I could do better. Tough love, but he made me a compelling performer in the mold of Jagger, Tyler, and Bowie. "You didn't sing very well. You sang too well, without an edge. Lose the vibrato. You need to sing with more expression. Throw away the vocal; make it an afterthought. Your movements were predictable. Your movement was contrived. Your movement was erratic. You didn't communicate with the audience well enough. You talked too much." It was a constant lesson. Slowly, these seemingly contradictory critiques started making sense, and I felt the power and confidence of a seasoned performer take root. I worked the stage and the audience from the downbeat to the encore, constantly on the move and reaching for outrageousness in every show.

But if I'm being brutally honest with myself, I'm not the greatest singer. I can hold my own with the best of them in a certain vocal range, but most of our material, written around rock riffs on open guitar strings, was painfully out of my sweet spot. I made up for my shortcomings with live energy. I concentrated on being more visual than aural. All these years later, I lament that my live presence and performance likely helped further our career, and my weaknesses ultimately sunk it.

Smoking cigarettes and drinking my face off certainly didn't help in the vocal department but fueled my raucous stage persona. From my performance attire to various levels of makeup to prowling the entire stage, every show was a wonderland with new barriers to break. A transparent plastic raincoat over no shirt, orange silk pants with suspenders, and a New Year's Eve party hat was a memorable outfit. Other wardrobe choices pushed similar boundaries. Hanging by my knees from scaffolding, sometimes thirty feet high off the stage, was a move that made the band nervous, especially if I'd been imbibing, which I always was. Snarling and strutting my way across America helped to disguise my vocal deficiencies and always left people talking, negatively or positively; it didn't matter. Any press is good press. This was an era where every rock star would raise a bottle of Jack to thunderous cheers in arenas every night all over the world. Whether it was food coloring or the real thing depended on your level of professionalism or addiction. Being outrageous was almost a prerequisite to rock and roll, and I lived it on and off stage.

My friend Ron Goodrich tells a story of a burly biker challenging me to a contest, drinking shots of whiskey. After all, I was just a skinny, pretty boy. After matching the big guy pour for pour for a few rounds, he held up his hand and said he'd had enough, and it was my turn to start chiding him.

After he slunk defeatedly out of the bar, Ron says I was hardly affected. I had another. Alcohol in your twenties, especially in the upper Midwest and particularly in Wisconsin, is a different animal. The amount we collectively drink is astounding. In a 2022 study, out of the twenty drunkest cities in America, ten are in Wisconsin, down from twelve just a couple of years previous. It is our birthright. Heavily settled by German and Scandinavian immigrants, the habits were brought here and perfected. I made it an art form.

    I had consumed alcohol every day since I got in the van for the first road trip. Some days were worse than others, but there was constant intoxication to varying degrees. I wasn't drinking around the clock yet, but it's safe to say I never stepped on stage, regardless of the time of day, without liquid fortification. In many shows, my performance was inconsistent and substandard because of it. It's hard to say how many opportunities didn't materialize due to my drinking. Still, it's safe to assume a record label would be hesitant to invest time, effort, and money in a project fronted by a loose cannon. Though being fucked up was rock and roll, music at the heart of it was still a business.

24. GO YOUR OWN WAY
(Lindsey Buckingham)

I HAD A SOFTER MUSICAL side than Chaser. There had been many songs I had written and brought to the band that just didn't fit. Some were modified, and we made them up-tempo successfully, but I had a penchant for writing ballads that never found a place in our repertoire. I started booking solo gigs and discovered I knew nothing about the minutiae of the business, which Rick, GMA, or Tony C. had always handled. Off the strength of Chaser and my reputation, the early gigs were promising, but I struggled to find continuity, and my shows tended to be a little sleepy with all of the music I had always wanted to play and now did. The crowds started waning, contrary to my level of drinking.

I went to work selling cars for my father. While it was hardly a career choice, it afforded me the luxury of my own apartment, and I loved living alone after all those years of being married to five guys on the road. That's what a band is, a marriage with multiple spouses. I got a place in a complex called Nob Hill on the south side of Madison, overlooking a lush valley. One of the side effects of working in the car business is hard drinking. Beer time was still five, and we had a fully stocked refrigerator in the shop. Even though we were open for business until nine some nights, we started early. It became a social club, and on any given day, we'd have three or four people stopping on their way home from work to join us. Sometimes customers joined us while conducting a transaction. After closing time, we'd all head down the street to a bar, and nine times out of ten, we'd be there when the lights came on. Living alone also allowed me to drink without anyone looking over my shoulder, and I poured myself into bed just about every night.

I continued to write and play solo gigs. Some were received very well, when I kept it together enough to put on a good performance. While I wanted to explore different directions musically, I sorely missed the energy and adrenalin of rock and roll. I was floundering with no direction. As '83 faded into '84, Prince released "Purple Rain," and I couldn't get enough of the song. It made me feel. It triggered something internally like music hadn't in so long. I badly wanted to write a song like it and succeeded in writing "Tell Me Tomorrow." My friend Michael Blum had recently moved to Chicago and was working to help rebuild Pierce Arrow Studios in Evanston after a flood. I was able to play the song for him when he visited Madison, and he really wanted me to come down and record it with some studio musicians associated with Universal Recording Corp. I grabbed Tony C., and he and I took the trip and came away with a beautiful recording. On a subsequent trip, I had coffee with Michael and a friend he brought along, Patrick Leonard, a fleeting brush with greatness. Patrick went on to work closely and prolifically with Madonna, Pink Floyd, Elton John, Michael Jackson, Fleetwood Mac, and more.

Not long after that, my old pal Tony Cerniglia called me and asked, "How's the solo career going? Do you wanna be in a band?" It seems I wasn't the only one missing the power and adrenaline of rock and roll.

25. MY KIND OF TOWN
(Sammy Cahn)

BOYS IN WHITE was less a Chaser sequel than an attempt at modernizing. At its outset, we were embracing everything new about the mid-eighties fashion and sound. Rod Ellenbecker on bass and Brian Kroening on guitar were Wausau guys transplanted to Madison. Brian was and is a gifted, creative musician, and Rod has an incredibly beautiful tenor perfectly suited for harmonies. We also added Mike Ripp's brother Paul on keyboards to become a five-piece. We came out of the gates fast, capitalizing on Chaser's popularity while simultaneously distancing ourselves from it.

In August, Tony's Ludwig Drums endorsement brought him an invitation to participate in the company's seventy-fifth-anniversary photo shoot. All of its highest profile endorsees were going to converge on Chicago to shoot a giant promo photo. He asked if I'd like to come along. We were vacationing in a cabin on the Wisconsin River in Boscobel and set out for Chicago. Talk about culture shock. In four hours, we went from fishing surrounded by nature to residing in the Hotel Barclay in the River North neighborhood of the windy city.

We checked into our rooms and were invited to the hospitality suite, a room dedicated to making the world's most famous drummers happy. It succeeded. It was a smorgasbord of every beer, wine, and liquor available to man, hors d'oeuvres to please any palate, and a room full of people most often seen on the pages of magazines worldwide. The most social of rock and roll drugs was also prevalent—cocaine. At first, Tony and I were more than a little anxious, trying to reconcile our presence in the company of so many musical dignitaries, but after a few refreshments, we were chatting everyone up. Queensryche drummer Scott Rockenfield and I had a long laugh-filled conversation. Every time you turned around, you'd see another famous face. Yes, drummer Alan White, Don Brewer from Grand Funk, Tony Brock of the Babys, and Rod Stewart, to name a few.

Then we heard someone say in a wild recognizable baritone, "What are you guys doing here?" The voice of Budokan and Cheap Trick's road manager, Kirk Dyer, towered above us. We'd known "The Wheel" for years, and it was a fun reunion. He went to retrieve Trick drummer Bun E. Carlos from his room to join us in the festivities. At one point, Kirk disappeared into the Rush Street night and returned with more goodies, including a bag of McDonald's for Bun E. We traded stories, thunderous laughter, and consumed profuse amounts of alcohol and food. Bun E. was a gracious and amiable participant.

A downtown Chicago hotel populated by Ludwig drummers. It was madness. It was wild, luxuriant, demented, and surreal. A cacophony of spirited conversation filled the room and spilled down the hallway. The photo shoot was scheduled for nine in the morning, very early by famous drummer standards, so the suite was starting to dwindle by one in the morning. Tony and the Cheap Trick contingent went to their rooms to ostensibly retire for the night. Hell, I didn't have to. I wasn't gonna be in the photo. I'm just a singer, which many of the attendees held against me. I was in heaven—an endless supply of booze for a not-so-closeted alcoholic!

In my most memorable interaction of the weekend, Kiss drummer Eric Carr and I bonded over a bottle of Crown Royal after the majority of folks had called it a night. We solved most of the world's problems, taking turns pouring the amber liquid. I think we said our goodbyes around four in the morning. Eric didn't make it to the shoot. He was listed on the poster as "Not present due to schedule conflicts."

The hotel lobby was chaotic the next morning, with some of the world's most accomplished percussionists wandering around in various states of tux disarray, precisely what you'd expect with the people involved. Untucked and unbuttoned formal shirts, crooked bowties, dangling cummerbunds, and bloodshot eyes were everywhere. We took a deranged bus to the warehouse where risers and lighting were stationed for the shoot, and it took a while to herd the cattle to their places and try to get wardrobe and attitude adjusted. After a short time, the hangovers abated enough to become the raucous event it promised to be. I'll never forget it. During the festivities, I excused myself and walked around the industrial area in the West Loop in search of a bar for a pick-me-up, but that was par for the course. I found a dingy, small, windowless rectangle, weeds growing through the cracked parking lot, not nearly nice enough to qualify for dive bar status. Desperate, weathered people occupied every tarnished chrome stool. I did two shots and slammed a beer, enough to end my hangover and take me through the rest of the shoot. Seeing the shadowed faces in the darkened bar saddened me, and I was among their ranks.

26. STARMAN
(David Bowie)

WE WENT TO WORK writing new songs while continuing our day jobs. Brian and I didn't get along too well, and I suspect it was partly due to a clashing of egos, but I'll take the blame for that. I was an arrogant, entitled ass who thought the things I had accomplished gave me license. That winter, we arranged "Little Drummer Boy" and closed our always successful Christmas show with it. We recorded it live and got substantial airplay for years around the holidays.

Brian left the band in the spring of 1985, and we called on our brother-in-arms, Michael John Ripp, to replace him. Ripper's style changed the band's flavor slightly, adding his brand of snarling guitar, and we were happy with the reunion. The most significant talent show then on television was *Star Search,* hosted by Johnny Carson's sideman, Ed McMahon. They were holding auditions at a local television station, and we decided to do it for laughs, not really expecting anything. After a tight, polished audition, we realized we must've done something right because we were chosen to appear on the show. We spent much of the summer preparing for the trip, writing new songs and recording. We needed to record one minute and thirty-second instrumental versions of the song(s) we were to perform. The band would be synching, but Rod and I would be singing live.

We flew to L.A. on September 16 to tape the show. We checked in to the Hyatt on Sunset and freshened up. Mike Ripp and I got on the elevator, and in a surreal moment, Little Richard greeted us with a smile. He got off on the third floor, but he sure liked Mike. He looked him alluringly up and down for three floors. We had dinner with Rick the night we arrived at Marix Mexican restaurant and had a photo op with comedian Elayne Boosler outside. The next day we went shopping on Sunset Boulevard and bought stage clothes to wear for the show. I found a beautiful sweater in a shop and checked the price tag, $130. I thought, "That's a steal. If we win our show and stay to tape another, I'm gonna come back and buy it." I stopped in a little later to see it again because something just didn't seem right. It was actually $1,300. Oops.

The night before the taping, we had dinner at Barrymore's on Sunset. Pam Dawber and Mark Harmon were canoodling at the next table. I had smuggled a bottle of brandy in my luggage. I promised myself I wouldn't abuse it, just use it to take the edge off, and I kept my promise. I didn't hide it from the guys, but they weren't too happy about me having it. The morning of the taping, I woke up and barely made it to the bathroom before I puked my guts out. Maybe it was nerves, but I'd never been prone to nerves. Of course, I had never sung live in front of twenty-seven million people before, either.

After a morning full of logistics and rehearsal at the Aquarius Theatre, we broke for lunch. I went through the buffet line with Hal Spear, one of the comedian contestants. When we got to the beverages, I asked if there was any beer. The person behind the counter laughed and said, "The only beer here is in Ed McMahon's dressing room." I looked at Hal, and he at me, and we silently bonded. We left the theater and walked down Sunset and found a bar. We slammed a couple of shots, had a beer, and headed back to kick some ass.

During rehearsals and soundcheck, Ed McMahon was in a surly mood. He came out after most of the run-through was finished to get his bearings, but we still hadn't sound checked, so we began our song with Ed on stage. He started waving his arms and yelling, and we stopped. He said, "Turn it down! That's way too loud. I've got a headache on top of my headache!"

Somebody in the crew said later not to take it personally. "He's always like that."

MORE

The stylist who did my hair and makeup for the show had just come off the road touring with Tina Turner. Looking at those photos today, I think she thought she still was.

In big moments throughout my life, I've had the sensation of being outside myself, watching. We waited with electric anticipation for our introduction, and when the rotating television stage set started turning into the lights, I floated up and out of my eyes and watched the band kick it. Although detached, I can still feel the shiny stage and see the theater audience. We lost our first show, a "quarter star" short of Moment's Notice, a band of formidable studio musicians from Nashville. They were pros, through and through, and genuine, sincere people, but it didn't make the shared shuttle ride back to the hotel any less uncomfortable. All the lovable losers from that episode involuntarily developed a kinship and took over the Hyatt bar. Johnny Carson's Tonight Show Band piano player, Ross Tompkins, happily conceded the stage to us. I was playing the piano, and we were all singing our disappointment away. It was a fabulous wrap to an exciting yet frustrating day.

A bit of advice to all the performers reading this: You know that phenomenon where you always think your latest song is your best? When you fall in love with that new groove or melody and feel like it's better than anything you've ever done before? It's usually not. Trust me. Give it some time before you profess that opinion to the world. Our song choice, the newest we had written, was an upbeat pop song with a catchy melody, but I believe it is ultimately what cost us the competition. We had many songs with more depth, musicianship, and a better vocal range that would have served us better.

27. SPINNING WHEEL
(David Clayton-Thomas)

WE WENT BACK to work writing. In January 1986, we went to the Ripp family cabin in northern Wisconsin, rented recording gear, and made an album while the Bears demolished the Patriots in the Super Bowl. We called the record *Tamasha*, named after the cabin. Stevie Johnson engineered and mixed. One song off the record caught the attention of our old friend Jonathan Little at Z-104. We decided to release it as a single and had Butch Vig do the mix for the 45—yes, seven-inch vinyl. Tony and Paul wrote the song, and it was loosely directed at me, hoping I would get my shit together. It is a wonderfully melodic, keys-driven up-tempo pop song with Michael John Ripp's signature guitar edge giving it power. "Help Me" went top twenty on Z-104 in requests and sales. In that era, radio was king. With our profile raised, we sent the album to Michael Goldstone, our biggest L.A. supporter from the Chaser days, who was now A&R at Chrysalis. Michael was kind, but it wasn't his cup of tea. He said, "Give me something to sign. I want to sign you." He was more into raw talent, visceral rock and blues, timeless music that could speak to you and make you feel, while we were into the production, layers, and all things eighties. We would continue to send him new songs after we wrote them. We wore out our welcome. He was in more and more "meetings" when I called.

MORE

On Memorial Day, after a night of heavy drinking, I found myself on my girlfriend's second-story balcony. As only a bulletproof drunk can justify, I decided it would be easy to climb across the side of the building to my balcony, on the same level, with just one apartment in between. There were brick outcroppings for my feet and a handhold—piece of cake. Against my girlfriend's wishes, I made it to a window at the halfway point with no trouble until the young woman who lived in the middle apartment started screaming because there was a man on her bedroom window ledge outside the building at two in the morning.

It scared me just enough to lose my grip.

As I saw the window falling away, I distinctly remember my body relaxing during the downward flight before impact. I lay there looking at the sky, trying to breathe and wondering if I was hurt severely. I looked to my right and saw a five-foot studded steel T-post about ten inches from my face. It didn't register until later how close that brush with death was. Dawn came running down and, after some speculation and checking of extremities, helped me up. We limped around to the front of the building as police rushed past us to the scene of the crime. I was a little sore that night but couldn't move without acute pain when I woke. X-rays the next day revealed two compression fractures to vertebrae and two broken transverse processes on my spine. I recovered miraculously quickly and just shook it off, the immortality of the young, drunk, and stupid on full display. The Darwin Awards spared me that night, and my next-day apology to the young woman for my idiocy was not well received.

I still firmly believe I would have made it safely across without the complication.

We did a live showcase at the Coliseum for Z-104 called Beat of the City. Seven bands played the show, and the radio station recorded it live with a mobile truck. We chose the band's version of "Tell Me Tomorrow" for the live album. It also did well for us on the radio. The intro of the recording featured teenage girls screaming "Michael," and I had a hard time living that down.

That fall, we did another demo of a new batch of songs. Tony and Paul had been experimenting with the then-new concept of writing some of the parts on a computer program, and the music was unique and intricate. When we added bass, guitar, and vocals, it became a powerful sum of its parts. We went into the original Smart Studios in a converted factory across the street from the iconic building that would become home to Nirvana, Smashing Pumpkins, and Garbage, and Butch Vig engineered and mixed. We sent the demo to Goldstone. Again, he was kind, but it wasn't what he was after.

The other thing that happened during this time was that my father fired me from my job as manager of his satellite used car lot. He was consolidating his business, which, coupled with my woeful lack of production, resulted in being let go. I was lost. I realized I'd had a safety net for everything I tried to do, and now it was gone. I put some feelers out, and Mike Ripp's youngest brother Jim worked at a music store at East Towne Mall that specialized in pianos and was hiring. Joe Johnson was the manager and is still a great friend today. When Joe was younger, he was in a band that covered Chaser songs, so that might have helped me land the job. The staff at Forbes-Meagher was a combination of high school students, performers, teachers, and administrators that were like a family. All of them are dear friends even now. As it turned out, my parents did me a huge favor by changing my path. Not only did they finally force me to become self-reliant, but the experience opened the door for what came next.

28. DON'T GIVE UP
(Peter Gabriel)

THE GREATEST THING that ever happened to me in my life occurred in March 1987. I met Robin Valley.

At Forbes-Meagher Music, part of our job was called front pumping. We would play one of the organs, keyboards, or pianos in the front of the store to bring in customers. There was a young woman who would walk by the store and smile on her way to work. A mystery girl. I felt that intangible flutter in my stomach every time I saw her. On more frequent occasions, she started taking her lunch breaks out in the mall to listen. One day our coworker, Duane Vee, walked up to the front of the store, raised his hand in a wave, and said, "Hi, Robin!" and she replied with a congenial, "Hi, Duane."

My jaw dropped, my fingers hit the wrong notes. I got up from the piano, took Duane by the arm, headed toward the back of the store, and said, "We need to talk."

It turns out Duane rode the bus to East Towne most days with Robin, and they'd chatted a few times. I enlisted Duane on Robin reconnaissance. He was to ask her discreetly if she was single. To be clear, Duane was about five feet six inches tall, weighed 280, didn't have the best personal hygiene habits, and was at least fifteen years older than Robin at twenty-three, so she was a little taken aback by what appeared to be Duane hitting on her. Being Robin, she diplomatically said she had a boyfriend, but her interest was piqued when she found out the blonde guy who worked at the music store put him up to it. She walked into the store the next day, March 25, 1987, where I was at my usual spot behind the piano, extended her hand and introduced herself. I was thrilled and tongue-tied. Knowing she took the bus to work and finding out she worked at Peck and Peck, an upscale women's boutique, I called and asked if she'd like a ride home. She accepted.

At closing time, I walked down to the front of her store, and the mesh gate was at half-staff. Robin waved me in and had a few last-minute duties to end her day. She introduced me to her manager, Laura, and I shopped around the store for a few minutes, patiently waiting. As we walked to my car, I was silently in awe of her. Her classic beauty, tall, lithe frame, and elegant, stylish attire perfectly complemented a congenial, ready smile, quick wit, and charming intellect. I was enraptured. We stopped at Danny's, a pub on the east side and sat in a booth with our beer, negotiating the dance of early exploration. Those beautiful moments of discovery only happen once in a relationship as you trade questions and answer carefully, wanting to put your best foot forward. It was easy, warm, and comfortable, and underneath was more than a spark; it was an electric current. We finished our beer, and I gave her a ride to her Rutledge Street apartment and walked her to the foyer. We agreed it had been a lovely time and that we would see each other soon. She turned to go inside and looked back one more time with that smile.

I went to my parents' house after I dropped her off and told my brothers that I had just met the woman I was going to marry.

Right away, it felt different. Robin was one of the few people I'd dated outside of a music or bar situation, and she was different. I had been casually dating multiple women during this period. I didn't want anything serious, and there were no secrets. In Robin, I had found all of the individual strengths and best qualities of everyone I'd ever been involved with, rolled into one person. She combined compassion, humor, intellect, and beauty and oozed sexuality in one incredible package. The others simply faded away romantically though they all remain friends today.

Peter Gabriel's album So is a masterpiece. There is one song, "Don't Give Up," which he duets with Kate Bush, that became and remains magic for us. In Robin's apartment one afternoon when her roommates were away, that song came on, and we met eyes. They locked. For the entire six minutes the song played, the world ceased to exist. No words were spoken. It was like we were frozen in place, internalizing the lyrics and emotion of the song and juxtaposing it with our lives. Tears welled up in our eyes, and the telepathic bond was impossible to ignore. Love blessed us. When the song faded, we met in a tender embrace of mind, body, and soul. I am back in that moment whenever I hear it.

Due to my history of promiscuity, I wanted to wait before we got physical. I wanted to know everything about her. I wanted to linger in passionate kisses. I wanted to hold her hand. I wanted to laugh, to feel, to fall in love.

Although Boys in White's live version of "Tell Me Tomorrow" was on Madison radio, and we'd had a local top twenty single with "Help Me" the summer before, Robin had never seen me perform outside the music store. I was excited for her to see that different personality of mine but a little worried as well. That flamboyant performer was different from the piano salesman she had been getting to know. We played a good show at the Shuffle Inn, a fabled club in Madison, and the ice was broken. A late-April snowstorm descended on Madison that night, and I don't remember which of us suggested that I not drive her all the way home to the east side after the show. I lived closer, so we were just being safe. She spent the night. It was worth the wait. As unexpected as an April snowstorm, Robin Valley had melted my heart.

29. FALLING APART

(Emily Massey, Henry Stoehr,
Alex Julian Leeds, and Teddy Matthews)

MEETING ROBIN was the best thing that ever happened to me, but other facets of my life were starting to stress and crack. I wasn't making enough money to keep my apartment at Nob Hill and had to move into a garden apartment on the east side. Robin had also lost her roommates and was looking for a place. I did not want to just move in with her. I wanted to be old-fashioned and take it slow. She moved into a twin apartment to mine in the same building, where the only tenant was her cat. She never slept there once. After throwing away a few months of rent, we decided that economically we should live together, considering we already did anyway. The cat didn't mind.

I started working a second job landscaping during the day and scaled back my hours at the music store to accommodate. I also started drinking more heavily. A physical dependence was sneaking in to replace the desire to drink. I didn't know it until years later, but my landscaping boss and I were both hitting the bottle in the morning before we went to work. (What could possibly go wrong with shovels and axes and chainsaws?) Then I would have a bracer when I got home, shower, and head to work at Forbes. It was a brutal schedule, but I was young and immortal and had alcohol to prop me up.

And things were getting worse with the band. I started bringing bottles with me to shows. Because of our immense popularity on CHR radio, every high school within fifty miles wanted us to play. They actually changed the scheduled dates of their proms to get us. Outside Stoughton High School, I was sitting in my car drinking out of a brandy pint when a local police officer pulled up alongside me and asked what I was doing. I said I was getting a little courage to perform, not even thinking that what I was doing could be perceived as wrong. He said, "You can't do that. You're on school grounds, and if your keys are in the ignition, I could cite you for OWI." They weren't, thank God. I apologized, said I didn't know, and went inside.

A couple of weeks later, I brought a bottle in with me to Verona High School, and I had just a bit too much. My performance was disjointed and inadequate. I remember opening the show in the back of the gymnasium with a wireless microphone and working my way up to the stage. There were forgotten lyrics, bad vocal notes, missed keyboard cues, and an unfocused movement that was highly amateur. The band was furious. We took a break, and Tony yelled as he came into the dressing room. "What the hell is going on? You're all over the place!" I splashed cold water on my face and retreated into a meditative state in an effort to sober up. Here I was in a makeshift dressing room, drunk, playing for a high school prom, but in my mind, I was still one small step from rock stardom, a lucky break from greatness. I finished the show and was a little better the second set, but serious damage was done to my standing with the band.

Not long after, we were scheduled for a rehearsal on the day my brothers and I had long been planning to see a movie premiere. I thought I had made it clear. When I went to leave rehearsal early to meet my brothers at the theater, they asked where I was going. I reminded them of my previous engagement. As a result of a building resentment due to my waning enthusiasm, substandard performances, and increasing alcohol abuse, they said if you walk out that door, don't bother coming back.

I said goodbye.

I loved those guys, but there had been a departure musically from what I preferred to be doing, and playing to audience after audience of high school kids had taken a fatal toll on my desire to be involved. Once again, I was adrift, but a huge positive was that I had Robin in my life.

30. REWRITE
(Paul Simon)

IN THE SUMMER OF 1987, I sent "Tell Me Tomorrow" to the National Academy of Songwriters in L.A. to get a review. A creative consultant, Lara Cody, whose role was to screen submissions for pitches, recommend collaborations, and critique songs, contacted me and said she really liked the song but could see some lyric rewrites. I told her to have at it, thrilled that someone thought enough of the song to take a closer look and at the prospect of having a co-writer on the West Coast.

My lyrics were dark, inspired by a news story about a murder-suicide, and I took creative license with the back story. It's a beautiful melody that belied the content. Lara set out to make it more mainstream and accessible.

> TELL ME TOMORROW—Mike Massey ©1984
>
> *Johnny cried when his woman left home*
> *She told him, she told him, I just can't take it no more*
> *Johnny tried but he couldn't take no*
> *They told him, they told him, boy you better learn the score*
> *When will the rain stop falling down*
> *Tell me, tell me tomorrow*
> *Annie lied to her lover next door*
> *She told him, she told him, I promise you I will reform*

MORE

Annie's eyes had a certain rapport
A vision, decisions she never had to make before
When will the rain stop falling down
Tell me, tell me tomorrow
When will a smile outweigh a frown
Tell me, tell me tomorrow
Are you really gonna take a look at yourself
Are you really gonna take a look in the mirror
Annie's flight was Johnny's reward
They found them, they found them, lying beneath the porch
In Johnny's eyes was love he had found
He told them, he tried to tell them, now they can't ask him anymore

TELL ME TOMORROW—Michael Massey and Lara Cody ©1987

Johnny cried when his woman left home
She told him, she told him, you better stop your foolin' around
Johnny tried, didn't want her to go
But something inside him stopped the boy from settling down
When will the rain stop falling down
Tell me, tell me tomorrow
Annie tried. Made mistakes of her own.
Her dreams of a new love to rescue her and take her away
Annie cried when she decided to go
She loved him, but something inside of her had started to fade
When will the rain stop falling down
Tell me, tell me tomorrow
Washing away all truth we found
Tell me, tell me tomorrow
Dying expectations building up all around them
Guess they were mistaken that their dreams would never end
Johnny lied, said he couldn't care less
He told them, he told them he was better off than being alone
Annie's life turned out little success

But pride was the prime cause that kept the girl from going back home.

Lara did a lovely job putting a more poetic spin on the song. I felt it had lost its edge, but I came to embrace the change, especially if it increased the chances of getting heard by more people. It had already had a pretty good run on local radio with the Boys in White live version, but I thought the song was musically strong enough to go further. Lara and I developed an amiable dialogue. She sent me some of her lyrics, and I took a shot at putting them to music. My first attempts weren't what she was looking for, but I was game to try again. If I have a strength, it is being able to compose melodies. They are all around us. You pick one out of the air. We made plans for me to formally visit L.A. to meet and cultivate this budding collaboration.

31. THE IMPOSTER
(Elvis Costello)

IF THE HOUR WITH WARHOL is the one I wish I had back, this is the week. The entire trip was a series of missed opportunities due to my drinking. I was so incredibly excited to be going back to L.A. I hadn't been there in a couple of years and was hoping this would be the trip to make that a more regular occurrence. I was going to meet Lara in person and hopefully solidify that friendship, meet up with Michael Goldstone, a rising star in the record industry, and connect with Pam, Orly, and Ambrose.

On a sunny October morning, I took the shuttle into Hollywood from LAX and checked in at the modest Fairfax Motel, a lovely mom-and-pop not too far from Santa Monica Boulevard. Lara and I were to meet at a restaurant within walking distance for me, and we hit it off. We made plans for later that evening, and Lara said she'd pick me up and that she had a surprise. I had a couple of hours to kill and went to find a liquor store. Perhaps it was nerves, being alone in L.A., or my blossoming alcoholism that made me drink too much again. By the time she picked me up, I was sloppy. The surprise was a BoDeans show at a theater in Hollywood. They were a Wisconsin band doing big things and were about to tour with U2. I had never seen them live but truly enjoyed their melodic roots rock. My memory of the show is mostly me overreacting and hooting and hollering like a school kid. As the night wore on, Lara became increasingly put off by my behavior, becoming distant and telling me to knock it off at one point. I was oblivious in my entitlement and drunken stupor to the impression I was making on my host. When we got back to the car, I asked if she could drop me at a bar close to my hotel. She nodded, and the ride was tense and quiet.

She stopped on a bustling Santa Monica Boulevard and said, "Here you go," driving off immediately after I exited. I walked into the club, past happy revelers on the sidewalk, and wandered through the comfortable haze to the bar. After slamming a shot and chasing it with a few swallows of beer, I turned to survey my surroundings. In the dim light, there were beautiful people as far as I could see, and I noted with amazement that there were large screens on all four walls with videos of nude women! It was good to be back in L.A.

I struck up a conversation with the woman standing next to me, and she bought me my next beer. I told her I was in town to meet a possible songwriting collaborator, and she told me she was an attorney. I excused myself to find a restroom and made my way across the room. As I got deeper into the crowd, it gradually became apparent that all of these beautiful people were women. I stood in the middle of the room as if underwater and realized I was among them in disguise, clean-shaven, having applied a small amount of makeup to look my best and wearing a loose-fitting jacket. The awareness slowly bloomed in my alcohol-soaked brain. Not wanting to be found out, I chugged my beer and slunk into the starless city night. I was embarrassed by my lack of perception. I was in the club for a substantial amount of time before my senses caught up with the moment. It's easy to find humor now, but later that night brought only shame.

Robin and Lara had talked a few times on the phone during our collaboration. Lara called Robin and told her of the evening. She also said that she had had a bad experience with an alcoholic and wasn't about to enter into another relationship with that albatross surrounding it. My initial indignation resulted in the philosophy that we just weren't compatible and that it was best we found out now. In my denial, I blamed everyone but myself for anything negative.

    Lara Cody bears no responsibility here. It was me alone that sabotaged my relationship with her. Who knows? Maybe nothing would have happened from our partnership, but the other possibility is that it might have resulted in a fruitful and creative collaboration for years to come. Maybe we would've snagged that lightning bolt and found magic. It is a major regret I didn't allow us to find out.

32. NICE TO SEE YOU AGAIN
(Michael Massey)

MICHAEL GOLDSTONE was a teenager, working at Chrysalis Records, when we met him. Everyone loved Michael, and he loved Chaser. He came to as many shows as he could when we were in L.A. He was warm, genuine, and sincere, personality traits in relatively short supply in the music industry. That astute, observant teenager was drinking in knowledge of the business and how it worked every day and would become enormously successful.

I had scheduled a breakfast meeting with him the next morning at a different restaurant within walking distance from the Fairfax and looked forward to seeing him again. All of my convenient excuses were there, and I hit the bottle for fortification before I left. You're living in dangerous territory when a shot from a bottle of eighty-proof liquor in the morning settles your stomach, alleviates a headache, and calms your nerves. I underestimated my time to walk there and was late even though I half ran. I was sweating by the time I arrived. I smelled like a distillery—at breakfast.

Michael excitedly talked about Charlie Sexton, whom he had signed to Chrysalis, and a band he was working with from Seattle that would become Mother Love Bone. He said they had the raw power of early Chaser. And when I should have shut up, listened, and learned from a man cemented in the middle of the cutting edge of the music business, I talked about myself. He was gently alluding to a cosmic shift that was coming in the music industry, and I didn't get it. Things were going to change from the synth-driven, mechanical eighties and head back toward organic, emotional power, what Chaser was in the beginning.

Boys in White had inundated him for the past couple of years with demos and copies of our singles. We were privy to all the secret codes that got your music past the record label's front desk and into the decision-maker's hands. If you wrote "Glimmer Twins" on the package with the cassette, it would go directly to Michael's office and bypass everyone else. Sitting in our bubble in Madison, we were churning out synth-pop that sounded like what was charting on our Top forty radio stations, and that is where the tragedy of not being true to yourself as an artist hits home.

If you emulate or conform to what's current in the music business, you're too late. We should have just continued to write from the heart. Michael was a fan of Chaser at its most raw, most visceral. He was polite through our eighties offerings because he knew what we were capable of, not because of what we were giving him. And then I show up after not seeing him for years, with bloodshot eyes, surrounded by alcohol fumes at breakfast. I'm lucky he didn't get up and walk out when I arrived.

By all accounts I have read, Michael Goldstone is still genuine and warm after meteoric success. Tragedy struck Mother Love Bone only days before the release of their debut album, losing their singer, Andrew Wood, to a heroin overdose. Michael eventually signed the remaining members with a new singer named Eddie Vedder and a new name, Pearl Jam, to Epic.

He went on to sign Rage Against the Machine, Buckcherry, and Regina Spektor, among others.

33. BAD REPUTATION
(Freedy Johnston)

I SPENT THE REST of the trip in a fog. I replenished my bottles with a fifth for the hotel room and pints for traveling. Pam and Orly came to pick me up for a thrift shopping excursion. I found it interesting that chrome and Formica dinette sets, like most of my peers and I grew up with in Wisconsin, were now garnering premium prices in L.A. Orly found a bookcase and had the idea to spatter-paint it. My years as an auto detailer for my dad came in handy. I made it sing. Then Pam announced she had tickets to a Def Leppard show that night.

Among the myriad of successful things Pam has done is manage The Bangles. Besides other guidance, she was instrumental in getting the band to cover Paul Simon's "A Hazy Shade of Winter." It peaked at number two on Billboard's Hot 100. Bass player Michael Steele, "Mickey," was going to join us for Def Leppard. You can write the ending to this paragraph. By the time they picked me up, I was headed toward sloppy again, gave Mickey a terrible first impression that precluded any hope of getting to know her, and ended the night with Pam pissed off at me as well. A trifecta of glory. I never expected to become best friends with Mickey, but I could've at least been companionable if sober and myself. And to alienate my longest L.A. friend was just bitter frosting on the cake. I vaguely remember asking about the climactic last note on one of The Bangles' biggest hits, "Eternal Flame," telling Pam it should have been more forceful. That was the last straw. After subjecting her to an evening of drunken false bravado and unjustified opinions about a business she knew infinitely better, Pam stopped at the Fairfax and told me to get out of her car. I stumbled up the stairs to my room and drank myself into unconsciousness.

Walking back to the Fairfax alone from Rick's late one night on Santa Monica Boulevard, I had to politely turn down overtures for sex from men in Mercedes and BMWs. The first time surprised me; the second time, I just laughed. If their wives, family, and country club buddies only knew. Almost back to the hotel, I encountered a man whose only belongings were in the shopping cart he pushed. He asked if I had any change. I didn't have much to spare, but I emptied my pockets of change and added a few bills from my wallet. I found a pawn shop the next day with broken cement steps and a cheap keyboard in the window and wrote the song "Hang On." It finally made it onto the Naked album thirty years later.

HANG ON

Walkin' the streets of the city alone tonight
Hands in my pockets, starin' straight ahead
The billboards say what's hip, what kind of clothes to wear
When all I'm worryin' about is tryin' to find a bed

Standin' on the corner got my world in my hands
And I'm so far away from home
If you had an extra quarter would you help me out
If I told you it would only be a loan

CHORUS
Hang on, hang on
Hear the children say
Did you ever feel like runnin' away
Hang on, hang on
Tomorrow will be a better day

MICHAEL MASSEY

Laughing in the shadow of the Hollywood sign
I stand here on my own
With God's grace, He's shown me a place I've left behind
It's the love and the life and the friends I have at home

Maybe next time I'll find this world I sought to pretend
Time just gives me more to say
It's a long, long road to travel but I'll find my way
You gotta keep I' stronger every day

34. (JUST LIKE) STARTING OVER
(John Lennon)

ON THE THIRD or fourth morning into my stay at NewStart, I awoke to an explosive sensation. The smell of bacon. It had been forever since my senses worked. I sat up in bed, and another distantly familiar sensation hit me—ravenous hunger. I quickly dressed, bounded down the hallway, and piled my plate high with eggs, toast, bacon, and sausage. Every bite was orgasmic. I drank coffee and orange juice, the flavors dancing on my tongue. I finished and went back for seconds. That morning, I made eye contact with the counselors, took notes in class, and kept my eye on the clock for lunch break, my body craving nourishment beyond hunger.

I started regaining mental and physical strength, was contributing to the group, actually smiled, and began completing my assignments with ease. My vision was clearing. I could feel the good soreness that tells you you've been working your muscles. I felt lighter. My goal was to gain one sit-up and pushup per day. By Friday, I did ten and ten more before I went to sleep.

That weekend I was furloughed. I could go home, sleep in my own bed, and attend a Halloween party at the Alano Club, a dedicated AA building on Madison's north side. Robin went with me. I have been behind the rock and roll curtain and been to naked and wild parties. With a brain still foggy while negotiating unfamiliar sobriety and out on bail from lockdown, it was quite possibly the most surreal event I have ever attended. My perception of two hundred recovering drunks getting crazy at an AA clubhouse, in costume, on Halloween, was like Stanley Kubrick on steroids.

I was able to get a good night's sleep, but Sunday, it was back to NewStart for another week. When Robin dropped me off, I had to take a piss test to prove I hadn't used while I was away. It would be grounds for immediate dismissal from the program. That out of the way, I went back to my room to get settled. I was just finishing unpacking when a knock came on the door. "Pack up your things. You're outta here!" What? I answered the door, and they said I was being discharged for dirty urine.

I said, "That's impossible!"

They said, "Science doesn't lie." I pleaded with them and maintained they were wrong somehow. There must be a way trained therapists can tell if you're being less than truthful because they believed me after more strong-arming and my refusal to budge on my innocence. But the truth of the matter is I actually had dirty urine. Ten days after my last Valium in the hospital, it was still present in the test!

I threw myself into treatment. I did, however, break the rules. I intellectualized. That was a cardinal sin. At this early stage of sobriety, counselors told us that it's easier and more effective to accept what they were saying and not try to overthink it. "One Day At A Time." "This Too Shall Pass." I took to heart the parts of therapy and group that I felt were beneficial and dismissed the peripheral ones. I deeply analyzed myself and looked at the paths that were being laid out for success and found that while I agreed with much of it, there were things that didn't sit well. In myself, I had found the switch to flip that told me drinking was never again an option. The rhetoric and statistics in the classroom were enlightening but incidental. I kept my blasphemous opinions to myself and became a polite and eager student. It worked for me.

Let me be clear that I am not making light of substance-abuse treatment and its protocols. My point is that recovery is a profoundly personal journey. Everyone has their abyss to cross, and the procedures in treatment are scientifically designed for the best chance of success. My hat is always off to the people who pledge their lives trying to help others. But finding your internal switch is the best chance for a new life.

MORE

Twenty-eight people were in that residential treatment with me. Ninety days later, only two of us were sober, and one was dead.

35. WORKIN' FOR A LIVIN'
(Huey Lewis)

AS 1987 ROLLED into 1988, I found myself mired in a routine for the very first time in my adult life. Much of that year is a blur. I was a person without a band and no real prospects. Forbes-Meagher Music was a fabulous place to hang my hat, but I suffered withdrawals from adrenalin, the most addictive of drugs. I did an occasional solo one-off gig, but I was facing the reality that I was nothing more than a hack singer making a buck on covers. I tried hard to become a good salesperson, but something unseen was holding me back, standing in the way. I believed there was something more out there. I was missing a window to create and be an artist. The truth is, I was living in the past. I thought I needed to be an artist 24/7 to succeed. I existed in a dream world, thinking that the next song would be the one to rescue me and put me back on track in the music business. And alcohol was creeping deeper into every cell in my body, luring me into a physical dependency that I didn't see coming.

Robin and I made a home in the small garden apartment on Gorham Street. Garden apartment is an attractive euphemism for the basement. It was small and not very nice, but I was in love, and her presence made it a beautiful place. The longer we were together, the more remarkable she became. Her compassion for others is astounding. Robin exudes a warmth that precedes her into a room. You can feel her. She can converse with strangers and leave having made a new friend. She will see someone she met at a party two years ago and call them by name. She made me better just by being with her.

One day while working at the store, I had to do a double take at a guy browsing our harmonicas. I thought I was looking at—no way! But it was. Pop music legend Donovan was standing in our little store! I knew he was in town for a show at the Barrymore Theater that night, but I never thought I'd see him at East Towne Mall. I had been a fan of his hits growing up, and Chaser had covered "Hurdy Gurdy Man." I walked over and introduced myself, and he said he'd like a G harmonica. I went to the manager of the accessory/band side of the store and introduced him, saying, "Let's give Donovan a harmonica if he signs something we can hang in the store." I got a blank look and a no. I was confused. Didn't he see the value of having an autographed album framed and hanging behind the counter? Nope. He said he had to account for inventory, and he couldn't go giving it away.

I bought Donovan's harmonica for him. I went to a record store in the mall, got *Donovan's Greatest Hits*, and had him sign it for me. I still have that vinyl.

Despite thinking I needed to be living an artist's life to create, I had a prolific songwriting year, many of which I still play, and some are on my *Naked* album. I was around music and musicians every day, and playing was what drove sales. I did, however, have to split time between playing piano and playing cheesy, recognizable, beloved, classic melodies to try and sell the keyboards and organs to an older clientele. "Somewhere My Love," "The Girl From Ipanema," "Beer Barrel Polka," "Spanish Eyes," and "Reveille" were just some of what we used to front pump. The other side of coin was that I could play some of the beautiful grand pianos and digital models that were incredibly inspirational. I would play for hours, pulling melodies out of the air that eventually became songs.

I signed on for landscaping again that spring. It was a three-season job, paid well, and still allowed me to work the music store. Like the year before, I scaled back my hours at the store and worked days outside and evenings at East Towne. I was late getting to Forbes ninety-nine percent of the time. I was still hitting the bottle first thing in the morning before

I showed up at the landscaping job and again before I left for work at the store. I was terrible at sales. I was out of my element, still dressing and acting rock and roll in a store designed to sell to middle America. It didn't help that I was exhausted by the time I got there and, while not visibly drunk, probably smelled like I had just left a bar half the time.

A delightful musical project that came from Forbes-Meagher was The Keys. Being in a band defined me for most of my adult life. Being without was a hollow condition. I loved my coworkers dearly, and they were all musicians. We decided to put a band together to play my songs. Ted Wingfield was a six-foot-eight-inch Rastafarian on bass. Ted taught guitar and bass guitar lessons at Forbes. He was one of the greatest people I've ever had the honor to know on this planet. Sadly, Ted left us way too soon. He was gentle, soft-spoken, immensely talented, and smooth. His musicianship was effortless and velvet. I miss his friendship and presence, as do so many. Joel Rogers was the drum instructor at the store and a hell of a drummer. Joel and Ted had been accomplished touring musicians before the road took its toll, and finances dictated a turn to teaching. My boss, Joe Johnson, was on guitar, Jim Ripp was on guitar and keys, and Stephanie Virchow handled backing vocals, and we had fun. We learned a set of my songs and played gigs, under-rehearsed and raw. It didn't matter. I was playing music that neither of my bands ever played, and it was mine. The Keys were short-lived but endearing to me and everyone involved. It was an escape from the real world, there was camaraderie, and it provided a platform for great times and creativity. It also rekindled my desire to play full-time. I felt lost working two jobs in the real world. I needed to play again. I needed to find purpose

36. ON THE ROAD AGAIN
(Willie Nelson)

MICK WHITMAN was a talented pianist, singer, and songwriter. We had played together in the high school band, Legend. Mick had a gig at a club on the west side, and I started regularly hanging out and sitting in. Our harmonies could be transcending. We hatched a plan to put a show together and tour. We landed an agent out of Minneapolis, Joe Ferraro, bless his soul, and he immediately had us on the road playing hotel lounges and resorts. Joe's company was called Oakwood Productions, and he had a roster of ten duo acts that traveled the country. For us, it was bliss. Starting in April 1989, we attacked every lounge show like it was an arena, and for us, it was. We were playing, and we were making money. It didn't occur to me how far removed I was from just a couple of years ago and brushes with legitimate avenues to success.

Initially, Robin was supportive of this endeavor because she knew how much I needed to play, but when it started becoming one constant party, her enthusiasm justifiably waned. She had taken a job with our friend, Dr. Chris Kammer, a dentist who was also a promoter of concerts, record collector conventions, and closed-circuit boxing matches. It was exciting, varied, and interesting work. Chris also produced a variety television show for the Fox affiliate in Madison. Robin was assistant producer, did on-air promos, and had the occasion to interview traveling artists as they came through town. She also took a second job, again in women's high-end fashion, because I was drinking up my profits, and we were struggling financially.

Mick and I were good together musically, but we fueled the inner child in each other and felt and acted like we were twenty again. We performed in Green Bay, La Crosse, Madison, and Wisconsin Dells in Wisconsin; St. Paul, Brainerd, Owatonna, and Alexandria in Minnesota; Sydney, Montana; Columbus, Ohio; and Ames, Iowa. The road was our playground. Mick and I drank ourselves across America and into Canada, enjoying a months-long bacchanal. We were drinking most of the time, all day, every day. Once in a while, we'd go to the club and rehearse new songs, but we didn't work that hard, instead relying on our charm to carry us through. We were unattached and free, deluded that we were stars and acting the part. There were many mornings when the previous evening's show was fuzzy for one of us, or both. It didn't matter. In our minds, we were bulletproof, above the law, and beyond blame. Joe Ferraro made many calls to me to tell us of a new booking and admonished me for drinking too much on stage. These calls were commonplace. We had really good nights, really bad nights, and many nights when our alcohol consumption overshadowed what we were trying to accomplish musically. When the bad started outweighing the good, it was the beginning of the end.

In June, we were playing Fort Dodge, Iowa, in a great club attached to a hotel. It was a fabulous time, and the mythical radio jock, movie star, and voice of *The Midnight Special*, Wolfman Jack, came in one night and caught our set. He was in town to officiate the grand opening of a Ford dealership. Ah, the fate that awaits aging legends. The Wolfman sat with us during our break and regaled us with tales of his life in that storied gravel baritone. He told us he loved our act and took a demo tape with him, saying he would pass it on to some people he knew that could further our career. Mick and I weren't just playing covers at our shows. He was a prolific songwriter in his own right, and we had dozens of our own songs woven into the show. Wolfman took his leave, and we continued with the night after doing a couple of shots to celebrate.

37. MARRY YOU
(Bruno Mars, Ari Levine, and Philip Lawrence)

I HAD HEARD THROUGH the grapevine that Robin was unhappy. That if I didn't commit to some semblance of a future, she was going to have a hard time waiting for me at home while I sailed across the country on a party boat. I went to a small mom-and-pop jewelry store on the square in downtown Fort Dodge in search of a ring. I was going to propose. I knew without a shred of doubt that I wanted to spend the rest of my life with Robin Valley.

The jewelry store was a throwback to the 1950s. Glass display cases presented the wares, and the weathered hardwood floor creaked with every step. I told the kindly old shopkeeper what I was looking for, and he brought out some diamonds to see. The first couple were beautiful gems but light years out of my price range. After a couple more swings and misses, he asked me what I had to spend. When I told him, he looked over his glasses, perched halfway down his nose, and sighed. I was going to spend my entire week's earnings on the ring. That amounted to a measly $450. To me, it represented hard work and sweat. To the owner, it was below the barest of minimums, but he had a kind heart.

He brought over a wooden box lined in navy blue velvet that housed a potpourri of miscellaneous jewelry, including some rings with smaller diamonds. He helped me pick out a lovely, elegant ring where the setting gave the appearance of a larger stone. It was perfect. And though the price was much more than I had, he let me have it with a smile and a wish for good luck. There are still good people in the world.

On June 18, there was a centennial celebration at the farm in Barneveld, Wisconsin, where my father grew up, and my grandparents still lived. It was on our route home from Iowa to Madison. It would be my immediate and extended family and all of the locals partying to celebrate a family legacy. Robin was going to meet me there, and every mile seemed like a thousand. It was about a four-hour drive, and we arrived mid-afternoon. Before I said hello to anyone, I grabbed Robin's hand and practically dragged her behind the barn. I found out later that half the party thought I'd been away so long that I just wanted sex. Geez.

On the driftless prairie, where I was the fourth generation of Masseys to stand, she answered yes to the most monumental question I'd ever asked. As we embraced, I felt a profound love, deeper than I previously knew existed. We rejoined the party and gleefully announced our engagement. Everyone was delighted! I think my family loved Robin more than they did me—still do.

38. BORDER SONG
(Elton John and Bernie Taupin)

THE END OF JULY found Mick and me at the absolutely beautiful Radisson Arrowwood Resort in Alexandria, Minnesota, for two weeks playing six nights a week. We were given a cabin for accommodations. It was fantastic! Two Olympic-size swimming pools, one indoor, one outside. The outside pool had a swim-up cabana bar. Yes, you could order food and drinks while swimming, and we did—every day. We'd go up to the pool around noon, order a couple of beers and then a couple more, and we'd head back to the cabin around five and take naps. Get up, shower and shave, head to the show, play from eight to midnight, head back to the cabin and drink until dawn. Wake up, rinse and repeat.

Mick's wife, Karen, and Robin joined us for the weekend. We scaled back our debauchery so they wouldn't think we were what they knew we were. When they departed on Sunday, a day off, we made up for lost time. The following week we hit it even harder. The staff at the club had been happy and amiable the first week, but they became increasingly distant as the week wore on. We didn't care. We had monster egos, and we thought we were stars.

We packed up and slept after our Saturday night show. Stupidly, we decided to stay at the Arrowwood an extra day to party on Sunday. It was so beautiful, and one more day in paradise appealed to both of our devil-may-care natures. We'd have plenty of time to make our drive to Red Lake, Ontario, the next day. Red Lake is where the road ended—literally. There was a little chain with a red handkerchief suspended in the middle stretching across the highway, and the only way you could go farther north in western Ontario was by seaplane.

Monday was my thirty-first birthday. We stopped to get beer for the drive up and discovered that the gas station only sold 3.2 percent alcohol beer, a uniquely Minnesota thing, so we filled the cooler, popped the tops, and headed north. We woefully misjudged the distance not only to Red Lake but to the Canadian border. Minnesota is a huge state. We were scheduled to start playing on Monday night. What we thought was a six-hour drive was nine! The scale of our maps was off, and now we were in trouble. We got to International Falls and crossed the bridge into Canada. We knew we needed to stop and get a temporary work permit to perform within the confines of our northern neighbor, so we went into the border office, filled out the necessary forms, paid our eighty dollars, and got back in the car to try to make Red Lake and our show that night, except we hadn't cleared customs yet.

They took our money, said thank you, and sent us on our way ... for about 100 feet. Beer, consumed all the way from Alexandria, was likely creating a cloud of fumes surrounding us. They said to pull the car over to the side and park. They asked us to step out of the car and proceeded to inspect it with a fine-tooth comb. After all, we were musicians. They found a single pot seed. One seed. Who knows how long it had been hiding in the carpet. It could've been years. I had stopped smoking weed way back in the Chaser days because it raked my voice, but Mick indulged, and he had about an ounce of weed with him. I was the co-title holder of the car for financial and legal reasons, so I was complicit with anything that happened here. This was way before weed was legal in Canada, not to mention smuggling it across an international border.

They ripped the car apart. Seats, door panels, and the contents of our trailer were strewn on the tarmac of the bridge. The weed was tucked in the excess cloth of a needlepoint hoop. It was sitting right on top of a canvas bag. If any other Border Patrol searched that bag, there might have been increased scrutiny of the hoop, but the woman picked it up with her left hand, held it next to her ear, and rifled through the contents of the bag with her right. Then she placed the hoop back down on top and said, "Clean." I realized I hadn't taken a breath for the duration.

They separated us into two small rooms. Two border guards accompanied me, and when the door was closed, they simply said, "Remove your clothes, please."

After I was completely naked, one of them said, "Now let us see the bottoms of your feet."

They found no drugs, but they did find Mick's 410 gauge shotgun he "forgot to declare" stuffed underneath the spare tire. They found a box of magazines my partner liked to travel with, some of which the Border Patrol deemed unacceptable to bring into the country. We had to drive the rifle back to U.S. customs and leave it with them to retrieve on our way back. They left a depleted cardboard box of pornography among the carnage. They put the seats back but left the rest for us to clean up and put back together. The thing that still astounds me is that we could have smuggled pounds of drugs that day. They had no dogs and never opened any of the cases with our instruments.

39. SMOKE! SMOKE! SMOKE! (THAT CIGARETTE)
(Merle Travis and Tex Williams)

DURING THE FIRST FEW DAYS of treatment, when I had been catatonic and lost, the laughter and animated conversation that came from the kitchen were annoying. I would shut the door to my room and try to tune it out. After I had revived, the informal smoking club would become as important to my recovery as the classroom. Strangers thrust together under common but less-than-ideal circumstances can form a powerful temporary bond that mimics good friendship. When sent their separate ways, the fragility of that connection is exposed, but bond we did.

One of us would light the first cigarette on the electric coils of the range (we weren't allowed matches or lighters), and we would share cherry to cherry until we were all fired up. A dozen packs of cigs lay in disarray at obtuse angles around the communal table. From then on, someone would always have a cigarette going, and we would piggyback that fire until lunch break was over or lights out at ten. We watched wild turkeys strut their stuff on the prairie through smoke-filmed windows as we created our Marlboro cloud.

We got to know each other through stories of wild exploits, heartbreak, and pain. A crash and a DUI, embezzlement, lost marriages, jobs, and relationships. We gave advice freely to those who sought the opinion of our flawed company. It was easy to see who among us was going through the motions and who was taking the quest for sobriety seriously. There weren't many in the latter camp, and as I learned of the forced treatment to satisfy court injunctions for some and the general apathy of most, it strengthened my resolve to make a change in my life.

We shared secrets, partially because of the power of our newfound friendships and partly because we'd likely never see each other again. At admission, one of the first rules imparted on us was, "No hooking up!" Romance was strictly forbidden, for good cause. The vulnerability of someone undergoing treatment is immense, and initiating a relationship under those circumstances is almost always doomed to failure. We were privy to one couple who was skirting the rule. We kept their secret, but the counselors weren't stupid. They know what's going on in their insulated world. The clandestine couple made it a week but was unceremoniously dismissed from the facility when the evidence became insurmountable. They didn't last a week together on the outside.

I looked forward every day to the time spent together. Two weeks after my discharge, NewStart instituted a no-smoking policy in the building. I'm so grateful for that timing. I learned as much about myself during the informal smoking club as in therapy.

On my last night there, we were in our usual positions around the table when a counselor poked his head in the door and said lights out was in five. He was treated to the usual groans at the news. But then he said, "Just kidding. You've got another hour. We turn the clocks back tonight!" A thunderous cheer quickly replaced the groans. That gained hour was the sweetest feeling. Although I was anticipating going home the next day and moving on with my life, a part of me had grown attached to these intimate moments with a ragtag group of strangers turned friends. I would miss this fellowship of the lost.

I had changed the direction of my life, and NewStart had given me the foundation to be successful. Most of the classroom lectures fade in memory, but not the feeling of community, of reawakening, of hope. The greatest thing I carried forward from treatment is that anything is possible.

MICHAEL MASSEY

I was a broken human, hanging on to the slimmest of threads when I walked in the door. I was leaving the facility small, vulnerable, and fragile but alive. I had nowhere to go but up, and I looked forward to the climb.

40. THE PIANO HAS BEEN DRINKING
(Tom Waits)

THERE WAS NO WAY we were going to make it for our first night in Red Lake. We had very little money because when we went to settle up in Alexandria, we owed THEM money from our two-week bender in paradise. We called Ferraro and the venue and said due to circumstances beyond our control, we would not be making it tonight. We pooled the last of our money and got a hotel room to lick our wounds and regroup. We had just enough left to grab a few beers in the hotel bar. When we started talking to the locals and told them our sob story, the drinks started flowing. Friendly, those Canadians. We didn't buy another drink all night and managed to get shit-faced. We were nothing if not charming.

It was another half-day drive to Red Lake. It was the only trip we bungled our travel time so badly, and we almost didn't make it in time for our second night. Canada. Gravy on fries is awesome. I drank cases of Labatt's Crystal Ale. Making it back to my room after the show just in time to hear "Oh Canada" on the small black and white TV before the CBC turned to snow. And finding out there was a luxurious community shower at the end of the hall on our last day there. We had languished in bath water for two weeks. Our alcohol consumption pushed new boundaries, even for us, but it didn't matter how fucked up we were; the audience was in worse shape. We were rock stars to them.

We stumbled through the rest of August into September, and October found us in Columbus, Ohio. We were watching the World Series in the club when the earthquake hit San Francisco. We played an abbreviated set that night. Everyone was subdued and in disbelief.

Depending on who you were talking to, Mick's family thought I was a drunk, mine the opposite. The truth was, we were both drunks. We hadn't played a sober note in months. After the earthquake, I felt Mick had a really bad week. I was not an angel, but he was missing cues and singing badly. Another act in Oakwood's stable had a night off, and we were traveling through, so they looked us up. Our set was horrible. I knew how good we could be and occasionally were, but we made fools of ourselves in front of our peers. That night when we got back to our room, Mick was really hammered. With unfocused eyes, he looked into mine and said, "If you ever do anything to fuck this up, I'll break both your legs." Mick is a big guy. He saved my ass more than a few times on the road. I was badly shaken by the threat, and even though he acted as though nothing had happened the next day, I called Joe Ferraro and told him I was done after our gig in Ames, Iowa, in December and not to book any more shows. Things fizzled to a natural end after that.

Pressures were mounting at home to come off the road and act like adults, so I didn't have to confront him with his threat and that I had called it quits. In November, we were in Green Bay, occasionally partying with members of the Packers. The kid in me was in heaven. I'd been a huge fan all my life and still am. We were at the sports bar Coaches Corner the day Don Majkowski threw the "instant replay" touchdown against the Bears. We had been drinking at our hotel with a couple of players the night before. December was Ames, and we played out the two weeks, sharing a few moments of brilliance before we turned the lights out for the last time. It had become more work than fun. Fun was a casualty of what was becoming full-blown alcoholism. Robin was both relieved and worried I was calling it quits.

41. VIDEO KILLED THE RADIO STAR
(Bruce Woolley, Geoff Downes, and Trevor Horn)

I CAME HOME adrift, again. I didn't know what I wanted to do with my life besides play, which hadn't worked out so well. It occurred to me to try radio. It was part of the music business, and I had done my share of interviews and seen the airplay side of things. Maybe there was something there.

My name recognition got me a job in sales at a progressive station. Sales? It was a foreign concept to a person who looked at radio simply as a means to get my music to the masses. I hadn't even thought about the fact that, as a business, they had to actually make money. It was difficult selling "air." Rejection was a daily occurrence. I found the most success on the creative side of radio advertising. I was good at writing copy and composing music for the spots, but while it got me a few clients, I wasn't bringing in the numbers to be considered successful.

I was drinking early in the morning, before sales meetings, finding out later I wasn't the only one. When you start drinking in the morning, doing it around the clock soon follows. When you come down from that first jolt, you basically have a hangover and need periodic boosts to stave off nausea and the shakes. It began a three-year period of maintenance drinking and attempting to hide it.

I didn't know how the world worked. Since I was a teenager, I'd either traveled playing music or landed somewhere I could coast for a while. The concept of radio sales at first was counterintuitive. Radio was music. It was a magic feeling, not a business. I quickly learned what was expected and tried diligently to comply. But after having repeated doors slammed in my face, the honeymoon was short-lived. I would leave the station after the morning meeting to "hit the streets," where I would end up drinking their booze and watching TV at my parents' house. I'd make a couple of calls to set up meetings and basically give up for the day. I was doing just enough to appear to be making an effort. It is a testament to my boss, my potential, and our friendship that he kept me around.

And painfully, my relationship with the on-air people, most of whom I'd known as a recording artist, was deteriorating. I couldn't understand why until I had a candid conversation with a friend who explained that successful sales staff usually made more money than the product they were selling. We represented the talent, years in the business, and hard work of the people whose likeness, personality, and music curation were the product. After that revelation, I had an even harder time reconciling my role. But I soldiered on, doing my best while my substance abuse ramped up.

One morning at 10:00 while raiding my parents' liquor cabinet and pouring myself a healthy dram of brandy, my father snuck into the house silently. As I was downing the high-octane liquor straight from the glass, I heard from behind me, "what are you doing?" Shaking and coughing from being caught in the act, I slowly turned to face him. Red-faced and ashamed, I didn't know what to say. Neither did he. He just as silently left. We never spoke of it again.

42. GET ME TO THE CHURCH ON TIME
(Frederick Loewe and Alan Jay Lerner)

APRIL 21, 1990, dawned 75 degrees and sunny. Weekends on either side of it for weeks were cold and rainy. I took it as a sign of wonderful things to come. The wedding party did shots before the ceremony at the Ohio Tavern, a block away from the church. There was also some homemade moonshine being passed around, but contrary to my nature, I didn't over-imbibe.

It was a fabulous day. Four hundred people attended the ceremony at St. Bernard's Catholic Church. It is a venerable, beautifully ornate stone building that is a towering icon in the east side neighborhood where I grew up. Robin was from a good Catholic family, and her mother insisted our day would be in a church. I had written, orchestrated, and recorded our processional at Smart Studios with Steve Marker. It was a breathtaking moment when I saw my imminent bride appear in the narthex, poised to walk into the future with me. During the ceremony, I left the altar to perform a song I had written for the occasion. It was the only time I've performed it. I had never felt more confident and secure than in saying "I do" to the woman I loved.

My father was a vintage car collector. After the wedding, with the help of members of his car club, his gift was to create a parade of beautiful antique and unusual cars adorned with the wedding party for a trip through the city to circle the Capitol Square. Robin and I sat on the back deck of a white 1975 Cadillac Eldorado convertible with bright red interior, waving to onlookers in our nuptial finery. We made quite a sight!

Our reception was at The East Side Club on the shore of Lake Monona, with a sprawling lawn down to the lake, dinner for four hundred, and a live rhythm and blues band. The golden sunset over the lake was magnificent. It was a day that matched my love for my bride in beauty and magnitude.

If you're waiting for another implosion story, I did not get sloppy and ruin the day. I had too much respect for my wife to even consider it. Sorry, not sorry to disappoint.

Thirty-two years later, the depth of my love has grown far beyond anything you can imagine on your wedding day. It bears repeating that Robin is the best thing that has ever happened to me. Every day I wonder how I deserve her.

43. THE BOYS ARE BACK IN TOWN
(Phil Lynott)

CHASER WAS PLANNING a reunion. The radio station got behind it, and I abandoned all pretense of trying to sell and concentrated on performing again. We got into rehearsals. Ambrose joined in the fun, and we played two sold-out nights at a club with massive promotion. My maintenance drinking got a little out of hand. I was good at being lucid, energetic, and perfectly normal while keeping a certain amount of alcohol in my body. But if I exceeded that level, even just a tiny bit, my memory would disappear, and I would be smashed. Not long after, Ambrose and Tony unveiled the master plan of changing our name and evolving into a working, current entity. The new name was to be "Someone Like You." Rick had whipped up an impressive new logo, and we were going to give it another go with a fresh attitude and renewed purpose.

After a rehearsal, I was driving home, and a car pulled out in front of me. Plenty of time to slow down, but I only had front working brakes, slid on wet leaves, and plowed into them. Sitting in the back of the squad car, I remember thinking, "If they breathalyze me, I'm screwed." They didn't. I got away without even a traffic ticket.

We were booked to open for Mick Taylor, former John Mayall's Bluesbreakers and Rolling Stones guitarist, in a club in Madison. In the middle of our set, I was to say the big reveal, "Chaser is Someone Like You," but I couldn't remember where I parked my car. Nothing felt right. I struggled to remember the lyrics, and my feet felt like cement. After the show, my bandmates were distant and quiet. They'd given me the benefit of the doubt all these years and couldn't do it anymore.

There is a video cassette of the show. I tried to watch it once in my early sobriety and started crying and had to turn it off. Of all of my missed opportunities, this is the one that would have the most concrete of far-reaching implications. I had sabotaged the project's future before it had a chance to grow and let everyone down.

44. I AM THE WALRUS
(John Lennon and Paul McCartney)

ROBIN AND I LOOKED FORWARD to a vacation in May 1991. We were going to borrow my dad's conversion van that got eight mpg and drive to L.A., seeing the country on the way out. We set out in good spirits, looking forward to our adventure, then ran into gale-force winds and drove through tornado warnings in Iowa. We should have taken it as an omen and turned around.

We made it to Denver and were going to spend the night and depart early the following morning. A freak May 18-inch snowstorm closed the mountain passes, so we had to stay an extra day. In Utah, while assuming the driving duties at night, Robin had to negotiate hundreds of mule deer on the side of the highway. Sheer cliffs were on both sides of the road, giving the deer no recourse but to share our path. Driving across the Mojave, the turbulent Santa Ana winds buffeted the van and reduced visibility. The unending adversity almost became comical. Almost.

We drove into West Hollywood and went to the Fairfax Motel. They didn't take reservations, first come, first served. Though my '87 trip was a disaster, I still enjoyed the motel, and it was cheap. But they didn't have a room, and the woman behind the counter remembered me, not in a good way, shooting daggers out of her eyes as she turned us away. I feared that more had happened on that trip than I remembered. Now what? There used to be another nice, reasonable place on Santa Monica Boulevard, and we searched but not before stopping at a liquor store with bars on the windows to grab a bottle of brandy. (I didn't think Robin knew about the hidden one I had stashed beneath the driver's seat, but she had just chosen not to confront me.) We found a place to stay, although the area had severely deteriorated since my days there a decade earlier. The neighborhood had a menacing feel, or maybe it was just me. After settling in, we went for a walk to find some takeout to bring back to the room.

I don't know if the bottle I got at the dingy liquor store was laced with acid. I don't know if it was a foreshadowing of my hallucinations in withdrawal. I don't know if it was some sort of psychotic break, but I became convinced with every fiber of my being that gang members were out to get us. I made Robin hide in the closet with me, crying out and shaking with every noise that filtered into our room. I remember being in it. I've never, before or since, been more terrified. I wouldn't allow us to leave the closet and forced us to urinate in our pants to not risk detection from our assailants. After a painfully long imaginary siege, my angelic and very worried wife managed to calm me down, and we emerged from the closet. I couldn't stay there. There was residual fear that the villains would return. Robin didn't know what to do, so she called Rick.

He came over and read the riot act to the front desk, reacting to what little Robin had conveyed on the phone. They must have thought we were all crazy. He invited us over to his apartment on Fountain, where I relayed the wildly fabricated series of events we had just lived through. With a nervous laugh, he said it sounded like a bad TV movie of the week, and I could tell he thought I had lost it. He was not wrong.

Ambrose was undoubtedly relieved when we left to find another place to stay. We ended up at the Kings Inn on Wilshire, a seedy motor inn, but it was a room. We got settled and realized my ankles were swelling to a concerning extent. Whatever had caused my psychosis was still wreaking havoc on my body. Robin finally got me to sleep. The next day, the swelling had diminished a bit, and my state of mind was tenuous at best. My wife was wondering what the hell she'd gotten herself into.

To try and salvage something good on this trip, I suggested we go to the beach, so we made the trek down Wilshire Boulevard to Santa Monica State Beach. We staked out a spot and laid on Kings Inn towels in the sand. The sun just barely made an appearance. Robin excused herself to walk over to the public restrooms, and I lay listening to the waves. She returned and was repositioning her towel when she realized in a panic that she had left her purse in the bathroom with every cent we had! We ran back to find, not surprisingly, that it was gone.

After everything we'd been through, how could it get any worse? Distraught, we returned to the motel to figure out a way forward. Robin had left the receipt from the motel in her purse, and miraculously, we got a call from a family who said they had found it in a trash can on the beach. We made arrangements to go to their home and pick it up. Enormously grateful, we couldn't thank them enough for recovering her driver's license and personal effects but couldn't offer them a reward because the money was gone. We called Robin's mom, and she wired us enough money via Western Union to drive straight home.

45. LIVING IN MY MOM'S BASEMENT
(I.D.F.K.)

TO PAINT OUR MARRIAGE as all gloom and doom is doing it a disservice. I adored Robin, and it was the most natural thing in the world to be married to her and share our lives. But I was keeping secrets. She would mark the glass liquor decanter where the brandy resided to monitor how much I was drinking, but I would add water to keep the level manageable until the color became pale and supplement it with pints. I was pretending to work all day when, in reality, I was hanging on by a thread.

I had two high-profile music accounts, The Crystal Corner Bar and The Barrymore Theater. The Crystal was a prominent blues bar, and I wrote the copy for David Day, a co-owner, to read on air for his commercials. The Barrymore was a neighborhood east side theater that did a fabulous job booking current and legendary touring artists. I would spend an inordinate amount of time at the theater because I loved the people in charge, Terry Spilde and Richard "Sich" Slone. My slide was becoming evident to everyone. When even these mainstay accounts suffered from my obvious alcoholic detachment, I started getting reprimands and stern warnings from my boss, Jerry Goeden. Jerry was a former on-air radio personality and one of the best in the business when it came to sales and promotion. He was my friend first and boss second, which I'm sure was

MORE

extremely difficult when all of his efforts to get me to improve were futile.

I was doing so poorly earning commissions that we struggled to make ends meet. We decided to move into Robin's mom's basement in Janesville to save money and right the ship. We did our best to dress up the room, but the only light was the two tiny windows at the top of the wall.

I had my usual bottles hidden and started to sneak out to neighborhood bars after everyone else had gone to sleep. Now my commute to the radio station was forty minutes instead of fifteen. In the same week, I got the only two speeding tickets of my life, driving to work and a promotional event. I was lucky there weren't breathalyzers involved.

Jerry let me go that autumn. I'd stretched his patience to the breaking point, and I was becoming a liability.

Robin quit drinking in September. She had never struggled with alcohol like me, but when she did drink, she had a penchant for over-imbibing. After my old friend Mark Davini's wedding, she called it quits, partially because she didn't like getting out of control and mostly to be a silent example for me.

Her sympathetic sobriety for all these years is a supremely powerful kinship and affords me a great source of foundation and comfort.

Feeling trapped, I started exploring my options to get back on the road. I figured my being gone would improve Robin's mental well-being. I promised I would clean up my act and take it seriously this time. It was my best route to providing income. I called Joe Ferraro in Minneapolis and asked if he'd consider taking me on again if I re-surfaced with a different partner, and he said yes. I guess I hadn't burned all of my bridges.

46. THIS IS AMERICA
(Donald Glover, Ludwig Göransson, and Young Thug)

I TAPPED JIM RIPP, my coworker at Forbes-Meagher and Michael and Paul's younger brother, to see if he wanted to join me in the endeavor. He was twenty-seven years old and had never traveled playing music. "It would be a blast," I said. Jim and I got into rehearsals and came up with a diverse, fun playlist of covers sprinkled liberally with Mike Massey songs. Not only would I be playing again, but I would be playing my songs. We called the project Circle Park after the neighborhood park we grew up with. We took promo photos and sent all of the material to Joe, and bookings started coming in almost immediately.

Before we hit the road, Robin and I would take a trip to New York for the wedding of Robin's lifelong friend, Susan Tessmer. We stayed at the Mayflower Hotel on Central Park West and Columbus Circle. I was thrilled to be back in the city. After getting settled, I snuck over to the deli on Broadway and slammed a shot and a beer, something I would frequently do on this trip. They got to know me fast.

It was a great trip, highlighted by the stunningly beautiful wedding on Long Island of Susan and Mark Fried and reconnecting with New York radio legend Marc Coppola and his wife, Elizabeth. Marc had gone to college in Madison, worked in radio, played Chaser songs on the air, and sat in with us on guitar numerous times. We went to see him perform in an off-Broadway play and had a late dinner. The only time I was ever on top of the World Trade Center was that trip with Marc. I'm so grateful we had that opportunity and have photos. Ten years later, the towers were gone.

The first show for Circle Park would be in Pine Bluff, Arkansas, at a club attached to a Holiday Inn. As Jim and I were fond of doing, we chatted up some of the hotel's staff and invited them to the show. They just laughed and said they were not members. I didn't understand. Members? Of what, a Holiday Inn? They said it was commissioned as a private club. That's how they kept undesirables from coming in. It took me a minute for the implication to register. Growing up on Madison's relatively diverse east side, I had been sheltered most of my life from some of the uglier sides of human nature. While it's obvious we have light years to go in the battle against racial inequities, I'd never been slapped in the face with such blatant racism and unjustified supremacy. I couldn't stand being there.

There was a big, sloppy caricature of a racist buffoon who held court at the bar every night. A wealthy man, he expected everyone to cater to his every whim. We didn't. He wanted country. We didn't play much country. When he yelled things at us, we yelled back. We contemplated quitting but decided making the asshole mad and uncomfortable was a better path. Besides, getting fired unjustly looked better on our resume than quitting. It gave us street cred as opposed to not fulfilling a contract. Knowing the prick held an inordinate amount of sway with management, we did everything we could to annoy him and make that happen before the contract was through. We succeeded.

47. A HAZY SHADE OF WINTER
(Paul Simon)

WE WENT HOME to lick our wounds and were booked for a return trip to Owatonna, Minnesota, where Mick Whitman and I had enjoyed a good run. We had good friends there, and it would be a great place to get our feet wet. Knowing all of the staff at the Western Inn in Owatonna gave me an unjustified feeling of familiarity and entitlement. On one of our first nights there, I went into the bar after hours and helped myself to a couple of beers, planning to pay the next day. I didn't latch the door on the cooler tight enough, and the next morning, it was discovered that the beer was warm and some perishables had to be discarded. I confessed. It was a serious black mark and one that I never fully recovered from. My relationship with the management was forever damaged.

A noteworthy event was a record Halloween blizzard in Minnesota. It shut everything down. The state averaged 28.5 inches, with 36.5 in Duluth and a whopping 45 in Superior, Wisconsin. We didn't care; we had a captive audience! No one could leave, and the credit card system was down. One high roller decided to spread the wealth around, buying numerous rounds for the entire bar, eliciting cheers every time. He bought us dinner, saying, "You should get anything you want." It was a raucous night, ending with the entire bar standing, swaying, and singing to Billy Joel's "Piano Man."

The next day wasn't so rosy. The man was gone, and when the system came back online, his card was declined.

Being in Arlington, Texas, in December reprised the feeling of freedom I had enjoyed during the road days of a decade past. I loved everything about the road. Seeing new geography, meeting new people, but especially the catharsis and release of playing music. Jim wrote a great song about the road entitled "I'm Free," and we debuted it the first night. Unfortunately, we weren't the right fit for the club, being more pop than they'd like, but we made the most of it, did the best we could, and had fun. Jim even got a ten-gallon hat and, I must say, looked damn fine in it.

My drinking was out of control. In Pine Bluff, I had gotten into a car with a couple of strangers who said they could take me to a liquor store. Later, I realized what a risk that had been. I searched for a liquor store in Arlington only to find out it was a dry town. No carryout eighty-proof liquor was sold, only watered-down facsimiles, and I was a pro. Half-ass shit wouldn't suffice. I ended up winding my way to Fort Worth to find a store where I could replenish my stash. These days, I was never without a bottle. I would make that circuitous trip many more times during our stay.

While in Texas, we got a call from Ferraro. We were booked on a cruise ship in the Gulf of Mexico for eight weeks in January and February!

We returned home for Christmas and started preparing logistically for the cruise. We'd need to drive to Galveston with our gear to get on the ship. On the eve of departure for the drive, Ferraro called and said, "This is the hardest call I've ever had to make. The cruise is double-booked, and it ain't you."

48. MASTER OF PUPPETS
(James Hetfield, Kirk Hammett, Cliff Burton, and Lars Ulrich)

I HAD BEFRIENDED a man in treatment. Jeff Kincaid and I had connected over a love of music and sports. When we were finished with our stay and released, I reached out to him in an effort to keep both of us clean. My parents offered their remodeled, comfortable basement to host a party to watch the Badgers in the Rose Bowl, the first time the team had been there in thirty years. I brought my TV from home, we stocked up on soda and snacks, and Jeff came over to hang out and watch the game. I sensed he was different and asked if he'd been using. He said he hadn't, but I had my doubts. Jeff was suffering from a dual addiction to alcohol and painkillers, and while I would be able to smell alcohol on him, I'd have no way to know if he'd gotten some Oxy.

I kept up my efforts, and after a time, Jeff stopped answering his phone, and his demeanor reverted to the surly, slurry guy I met when we first entered NewStart. I went to his apartment a couple of times and found him passed out. One day, I walked in to overhear a phone conversation with his doctor, Dr. Ken Felz. Hearing one side of the conversation, it was readily apparent to me that Dr. Felz felt compassion for his patient. He was doing all he could to gently nudge Jeff in the right direction.

MORE

I had my own history with the good doctor. In 1990, I went for a checkup and was assigned Dr. Felz randomly. He did the exam, and when I got home, he called me and asked how much I was drinking. Doctors know that you will answer approximately half of what is happening when they ask a question like that. He said my liver enzymes were alarmingly high, and I needed to stop drinking. I pulled the old alcoholic indignation trick and hung up on him, pissed off.

A few days later, Jeff overdosed. We went to visit him in the hospital. He said, "I guess I fucked up, huh?"

I said, "Yes," but it wasn't too late to turn it around, so he could start again. I could see in his eyes and body language that it was a losing battle. He just slowly shook his head. Dr. Felz had come in while we were there, and again, I was struck by his direct but gentle, no-nonsense approach to Jeff's disease. He was doing all he could to help.

With regret and sadness, I had to disassociate myself from Jeff out of concern for my own sobriety. Not long after, I would hear he had died from a lethal combination of OxyContin and alcohol. Jeff Kincaid was dead at thirty-seven.

After seeing Dr. Ken Felz tend to Jeff's illness with deep compassion, tough love, humor, and a twinkle in his eye, I sought him out as my primary physician, which he continues to be decades later

49. LAWYERS, GUNS, AND MONEY
(Warren Zevon)

NOT ONLY WERE WE despondent about missing out on the cruise, but now there was a hole in our schedule and income that you could drive a truck through. Joe assured me he would work overtime to try and fill the void, but that's not how the entertainment business works. Gigs are booked months in advance. He got us a gig in South Beloit, Illinois, at a club/restaurant called Shabani's, right on the Wisconsin border, for mid-January. It was a twenty-minute drive from my mother-in-law's basement in Janesville, so it would work out great. I wouldn't need a hotel room. It wasn't going to make up for our deficiency, but it was a gig. The next day, Mr. Ferraro called me and said Shabani's had a cancellation and we could go in a week early. Things were looking up! We played a really good week, getting along marvelously with the staff and having a great time. On Sunday, Joe called and said they wouldn't need us for the second week. I was confused. We had just finished a week we had no contract for, played well, and now we were being fired? We had a contract for the following week! I was just indignant enough to take them to court for lost wages, against the wishes of our agent, who said, "These things usually don't turn out well for the artist." We secured an April court date, and I was confident the law was on our side.

We didn't play again until the first week in March, when we headed just as far north as you can go in the contiguous forty-eight states, shouting distance from the Northwest Angle in Minnesota, the town of Baudette, at the Sportsman's Lodge. March in Baudette is smack dab in the middle of their busiest tourism season for ice fishing. They have it down to a science. Heated shanties with gargantuan holes cut out of the ice, miles out on Lake of the Woods, bombardiers to get you there, and lunch delivered to their clientele. It was magnificent. Our brand of pop, rock, and country hit the nail on the head. It was a constant, wild party! It wasn't noticeable how much I was drinking because the audience was right there with me. We had a raucous week with full houses singing along and cheering every song. It was just what we needed to build our confidence back after the cruise and Shabani's. Entertainment director, Shelley Phillippe, booked us to come back in August.

April arrived, and with it, our date at the Winnebago County Courthouse in Rockford, Illinois, with Shabani's. Our first mistake was representing ourselves, but we went in armed with a signed contract and the assurance of some of the staff that we had performed well for a week and had been let go due to no cause of our own. Nick Shabani's slimy, slicked-back lawyer approached us and offered a meager settlement to keep it out of court, and we refused, confident justice would prevail. And it usually does in a court of law unless perjury becomes your defense. I don't know if Nick gave his employees a bonus or threatened their employment status, but he had clearly coached them as we watched a parade of staff members take the stand and answer, "I don't recall," to every question asked. We asked if they could see our performance while they worked. We asked if the audience had responded favorably to our music. I exasperatedly asked if they remembered us at all!

"I don't recall."

Not a good look, Winnebago County. The dirtbag lawyer and the judge exchanged smiles more than once, not even bothering to hide their amusement.

We walked away with nothing. Perjury absolved Nick Shabani of breach of contract. Justice dropped her scales.

50. HANG ON SLOOPY
(Wes Farrell and Bert Berns)

WE STEPPED OUT OF the courthouse, got in the van, and went directly south to Lancaster, Ohio, about thirty miles from Columbus. I included this trip for a couple of reasons. First, it was where Jim met Anita, who would become a significant part of his life, and second, I had never before experienced state-run liquor stores. I made my usual scouting journey to find the best and closest place to keep myself in booze and couldn't find any eighty-proof liquor. It was all knock-off cheap shit with half or less than half of the alcohol content. Growing up in Wisconsin, I had never seen liquor that wasn't full strength. It just doesn't exist. We don't fool around.

I asked where to find the real stuff, and the clerk told me, "You have to go to the state store for that." Ohio's liquor stores are controlled and regulated by the state, as are the fuel and restaurant oases on the interstate. I finally found one, and it had closed at six. I was caught without a stash. A pretty rare occurrence. The thought of it threw me into a state of anxiety, knowing it would be a long, restless night without the calming effects of brandy.

I eventually made my way to the store the next day and stocked up. These days I was supplementing my public consumption with a constant, measured private use, and I thought nobody knew. Drunks may be cunning, but they're also really stupid. There's no way I could be getting as drunk as I was with the few drinks I would have at shows. Jim was slowly starting to sense that something was rotten in Denmark.

The upstairs flat had opened in the house where Jim lived with his sister, Meg. It was just a few blocks from where I grew up on the east side. Robin moved out of the basement in Janesville and took up residence in the comfortable, familiar neighborhood. She also changed jobs, pivoting to working with Chris's father, Dr. Jack Kammer, founder of the American Academy of Cosmetic Dentistry. Robin was an administrator and director of marketing and produced the national conventions for the AACD set in different hotels around the country. She also kept her second job.

As our tour continued, we had very good nights and not-so-good nights, usually but not always due to the amount I drank. Like my marriage, our time on the road wasn't all disastrous. Jim and I had some transcending musical moments during that year. We had audiences applauding and asking for more. We shared a deep and abiding friendship that was crumbling because of an insidious disease called alcoholism. When we returned to Green Bay in May, I was ready for a break and really wanted to try and get the drinking under control. I found and attended AA meetings. I stopped drinking. Robin came up and spent the weekend, and we had a wonderful time. I made it about a week until I stopped at a liquor store, returning to the hotel from a meeting. I didn't go back.

51. HEAD
(Prince)

ON A SUNNY MORNING in Green Bay, Joe Ferraro called me and said he needed to discuss a delicate matter. He haltingly told me I needed to be more discreet. I panicked a little, thinking he was on to my secret drinking. I asked him, "About what?" He said I was seen in the hotel's parking lot engaged in a sexual act.

I knew I hadn't been that drunk.

I told him there must be some mistake. He said no, and that a staff member had seen one of the guys in the band getting head in a car not far from the front door of the hotel. I looked at Jim, covered the phone, and asked him if he'd had a good time last night. Surprised, he looked at the floor and confessed. I asked Joe why he would automatically assume it was me, somewhat offended but comically so. He apologized profusely. Through his stuttering and stammering, I told him not to worry about it, and he directed his ire at Jim, saying, "Tell him not to let it happen again!" Now it seemed our mild-mannered agent had two provocateurs to worry about. We were making him earn his fifteen percent.

Another instance of note in Green Bay started innocently enough. Dawn was the bar manager at the Embassy Suites. We had a great relationship rooted in good humor and mutual respect. I had known her since the 1989 residency. I was in the office one day to ask for our check. Dawn wasn't in, and the office manager said it hadn't arrived yet. As I turned to leave, I saw my name on a letter in Dawn's mailbox. The check was peeking through the window in the envelope. The mailboxes were an open grid, and everything was exposed. I turned to the office manager and said, "Here it is. Please make sure Dawn knows I got it," not thinking any more about it.

Dawn was livid when we got to the club to play that night. "How dare you take something out of my mailbox!" She felt betrayed and hurt. Although it was innocent, and I thought our relationship was evolved enough for it not to be an issue, she was absolutely right. I shouldn't have overstepped my bounds, but I still don't think the offense was egregious enough to warrant the reaction. Dawn and I never recovered. We had an icy rapport for the rest of our stay.

It wouldn't be the first or last time in my life I thought a friendship was deeper than it actually was. There are a few examples of thinking I was developing a lasting connection and assuming other people felt the same, only to find I was mistaken. As much as that hurt, I would still rather err on the side of reaching out than not try at all. Most times, it's worked out just fine.

On to Springdale, Arkansas, a suburb of Fayetteville. I decided I was going to try vodka for my drink of choice. Supposedly, its odor wasn't as conspicuous on your breath, and God knows I wanted to avoid detection at all costs, but that misconception is bullshit. Alcohol, especially when seeping out of your pores, smells like alcohol. I got a 1.75-liter bottle of cheap vodka and hit it hard. I have fleeting memories of the club, our shows, and something to do with an office chair on the dance floor while doing "Piano Man." My biggest regret, and Jim and I still laugh about it, was not being able to take advantage of the incredible all-you-can-eat buffet because of a lack of appetite caused by all my drinking.

I also called Linda, my high school sweetheart, in a vodka-induced haze. I told her we were coming to Owatonna in a couple of weeks and that I would drive up to her suburban Minneapolis home and say hi. I never did make good on my threat, but those and subsequent drunken phone calls finally killed any hope of future communication.

52. MERCY, MERCY ME
(Marvin Gaye)

I ABANDONED MY vodka experiment in Owatonna and resumed the brandy habit with a vengeance. After a particularly bad show, Jim immediately walked off the stage, quietly packed up his guitar, and returned to his room without a word. It was very unlike him. I knocked on his door and asked what was wrong. He said, "If you show up drunk one more time, I quit. I'm done playing with you." Of course, the reflex response for a drunk is indignation. I went back to my room in silence.

The next day, I knew I'd better keep everything in check. Jim would cool down. He had been mad before, and it always passed. I only drank a little through the day and had a bigger hit after showering and getting ready for the show. We hadn't spoken all day, and I knocked on Jim's door. He opened it, and I said, "You ready?"

He took one look at me and slammed the door in my face. Through the door, he said, "I told you I'd be done!" Defensively, I said I'd play the show alone. I'd done it for years. I'd show him.

I died a slow and painful death during that abbreviated set.

The regulars and staff knew something was wrong, and the rest of the audience was disengaged as I floundered through a set and never found rhythm or flow. I told the audience I was going to take a short break and went back to Jim's room. I begged him and pleaded with him to finish the night with me. On the verge of hyperventilation and panic, I felt the weight of all my deceptions and guilt. He relented. Later, he would say he's never seen me as humble and gracious as that night. He saved me from me. They all say a drunk needs to hit their bottom before they can change. That this episode wasn't my bottom shows the sheer power of denial and the all-consuming disease of addiction.

I was going to drive home Saturday after the show to attend a wedding with Robin on Sunday. It's a four-and-a-half-hour drive. I had a pint with me as I left at bar time. I made it as far as a wayside in Wisconsin, pulled over, and passed out in the back of the van for a couple of hours. I woke up disoriented, still drunk, and got back on the road. We made it to the wedding. I slept at home Sunday night and returned to Minnesota on Monday, getting another bottle as I skirted out of town. I was fighting the battle of hiding my alcohol consumption while appearing sober. I won most of the time, but Robin was able to tell. I asked her how, and she couldn't define it, just that she knew. She said I was a little too animated. That there was a subtle shift in speech patterns and demeanor. It would be nearly impossible for anyone except those closest to me to detect my blood alcohol content was far north of legal. I overdosed on Listerine breath strips and mints and drank profuse amounts of non-alcoholic beer in an attempt to disguise my secret. In my profound denial, I was killing myself, one day at a time.

53. ALL MEN ARE LIARS
(Nick Lowe)

LATE AUGUST brought us back to Baudette. The water was no longer frozen, and pristine northern air and cloudless blue skies accentuated the breathtaking beauty. I much preferred this to March! We played the last week in August to an equally festive summer crowd and cultivated friendships that have survived decades. Then we were to have a week off while Jim met his brothers and dad in Canada for their annual musky fishing trip before returning to play September 7-12. I drove Jim into Ontario to meet up with the boat that would take him miles up the lake to meet his family. Funny thing, when your diet is predominantly brandy, it goes right through you. When you have to go, you have to go—now. After dropping Jim off, I got a few miles south and started feeling cramps. I knew I wasn't going to make the border and pulled over on the side of the road. No doubt you've heard the expression, "Does a bear shit in the woods?" Well, I can tell you an alcoholic does and then hopes he's not using poison ivy to wipe.

I had found a cheap flight out of International Falls and flew home for the week Jim was in Canada. To this day, I still feel funny getting close to that bridge from the ill-fated Red Lake trip. The week passed without much incident, and I tried relatively successfully to keep my drinking to a dull roar and hidden from my wife. We attended the annual Taste of Madison festival, and I delighted in telling friends and acquaintances I was flying back to a gig the next day. It sounded so much more glamorous than it actually was, and I was still deluded that I was a rock star. I got a bottle, hid it in my carry-on, and Robin took me to the airport. I hit the bottle as soon as we were in the air and continued through my layover in Minneapolis and onto the puddle jumper that would take me to International Falls, where the van was parked, waiting to take me seventy miles west back to Baudette. By the time I landed, I was hammered, knowing that I wouldn't have Jim to contend with. The drive back to the lodge was dicey at best. The dark, moonless night and the meandering Highway 11 along the Minnesota-Ontario border would challenge a sober driver, and I did it smashed. Completely inexcusable. I got back to the lake and went down to the Wigwam, another lodge that had live entertainment, to see Al and Lorelei, a fantastic married duo of musicians we had easily befriended. My memory deserts me after I arrived. People told me later how exceedingly drunk I was.

Jim's family dropped him off the next day, and we picked up right where we left off, playing to receptive, generous crowds, but my shenanigans had finally taken a fatal toll. Jim was done with me after this gig. Anita had moved to Madison from Ohio to be with him, and that, coupled with the prospect of a constantly inebriated partner, wrote the end of another chapter. Joe Ferraro canceled the remaining shows on our calendar. Circle Park was grounded indefinitely.

54. CHASING PAVEMENTS
(Adele and Eg White)

I CAME HOME TO Center Avenue and once again searched for a direction and purpose. The radio station wasn't an option; I had burned that bridge. I answered a classified ad in the Madison newspaper for Murphy Music, went to a job interview, and hoped for the best. Rick Murphy was a venerable radio star in Madison. He had curated and hosted his own program on Radio Free Madison, WIBA-FM, an album-oriented rock station in the 1970s. Rick had a jingle company, writing and recording music for advertising. My job would be to sell his services to clients ranging from mom-and-pop advertisers to huge corporations. But what really made me want the job was the use of the studio. Rick went home at five, and the room was mine until he returned at an unspecified time each morning. I slept in my office many nights because I was too trashed to drive. I still truly believed that it would only take one hit to open up my catalog of hundreds of songs to the world, so I spent long hours writing and recording.

Rick's studio was housed in a larger complex, Concept Productions. Concept was a top-notch commercial studio with a beautiful, large live room and another supplemental editing suite with a voiceover booth. It was buzzing on a daily basis, with major clients coming and going in a flurry of activity. The people at Concept took note of my efforts, and there was a growing mutual respect. It would ultimately be reciprocally beneficial in the long run.

And I worked my ass off. Georgia Roeming, another occupant of the studio complex and CEO of the GEO Group, loaned me a book of contact info for all of the major corporations in Wisconsin. I wrote hundreds of letters with follow-up phone calls soliciting Rick's services. It was a disaster, and the crushing onslaught of rejection destroyed my self-confidence. Later it would be clear it wasn't my lack of salesmanship but the weakness of the product I was selling that resulted in the failures. While I had done a little composing music for clients when I was selling radio, I was new to the advertising music business and didn't know how it worked. I couldn't know that the brand Rick was selling was dated and mediocre. But that year, I worked extremely hard at my job and new songs and made very little money. I was paid $1,500 for my part in a series of pieces for Oscar Mayer and received a few random incentive checks, but I contributed just about nothing to our household income and living expenses.

Later that September, I attended an intensive outpatient treatment program for alcoholism. At Robin's urging, I gave it a shot. I went for a month, four nights a week, three hours a night. I think I made it a week before I was drinking during the day and coming to treatment at night and saying all of the right things with a blood-alcohol content over the legal limit. It is why I often advise against outpatient treatment as an option for people who are struggling. There's no policing it, and alcoholics are the smartest people I know at concealing their truths. It may work for some who are ready to make the change and need a gentle nudge, but for professional drinkers, it's a way to appear as though they're making an effort.

I limped through the program and came out the other side, pretending to be sober. I would not drink in public, or to anyone's knowledge, ever again. I kept my consumption manageable for a time, thinking I was successfully hiding the fact that I had relapsed. Robin was suspicious but wanted to give me the benefit of the doubt. It didn't last long. I fell into a self-destructive pattern of leaving for work in the morning, heading into the studio to bang my head against the wall, and trying to sell jingles until Rick would leave for the day, and I would take over the studio. It was what I was living for.

I would head out, get a pint and some beer, come back, and create as long as I could hold my head up, sometimes coming home after Robin had gone to bed and occasionally crashing in my office chair. A few good songs came out of that time, most notably "Get A Life," which got extensive airplay on 105.5 Triple M in Madison years later from the *Attack of the Delicious* album. But for the most part, my writing was starting to take a decidedly darker turn. Alcohol was beginning to fuel my every day.

The winter dragged on as the calendar turned to 1993. The good things were our cozy little apartment and my saint of a wife. The bad was the volume of my drinking and everything that went along with it. It was becoming alarmingly challenging to maintain a façade of normalcy.

55. HELP
(John Lennon and Paul McCartney)

WE HAD DECIDED we were going to try and get pregnant. When we got married, we both were of the mind that if we had kids, great; if not, great. It wasn't a priority, but we weren't against the prospect. That mentality slowly changed, and I believed that if I had a child, I would be forced to clean up my act once and for all. I knew Robin would be the world's greatest mother, and I thought I had a lot to offer as a dad. We vigorously threw ourselves into the business of making a baby, enlisting fertility specialists when our efforts weren't fruitful. Looking back, it was a blessing in disguise that my besotted seed careened around and didn't find an egg. I wouldn't have been much of a father. I couldn't even care for myself.

I had bottles hidden in the sofa, in coat pockets in the closet, under the driver's seat of my car, in bushes outside, and anywhere else I thought they would be safe from discovery. I had a bottle in my office, and when the stash was cashed, I would wait at various liquor stores at nine in the morning for them to unlock the door. I started hitting it in the morning after Robin left for work. I went to work until around ten when I would go for a drive on rural roads west of Madison to give myself a belt to keep it smooth. I'd head out again around two in the afternoon for another pick-me-up and start for real when I had the building to myself after five. It was a vicious cycle that seemed innocuous to me at the time but was threatening my marriage and everything I knew.

I got involved in numerous musical projects to broaden my horizons and scrape a few dollars together to feed my habit. Code Blue was a good R&B band fronted by one of the Forbes-Meagher family, Michelle Grabel. I had always loved blues and Motown and really enjoyed the opportunity to play them. Plus, it was a good and different feeling to play keys and not be the front person for a change. Code Blue played a number of gigs at hotels, resorts, and clubs around southern Wisconsin, and I welcomed the income and the fun. There was a fluidity of members in the band, with Jim Ripp sometimes filling in for our old pal Ted Wingfield playing bass guitar. Michelle and I would later play as a duo for many years. Harvey Briggs, Bruce Geiger, and I joined forces with drummer Jimmie Nahas and formed Bent, a band that concentrated more on writing and showed promise, rehearsing in the Nahas basement. We would end up playing just one opening set at the Crystal Corner.

In April, Circle Park got a gig at the Sheraton in Madison, and I was so drunk I fucked up the opening song, Bob Seger's "Hollywood Nights," even though I had played it hundreds of times. Our families were there celebrating our wedding anniversary, and there was a murmur through the crowd. Although they loved me, they were all too familiar with my ongoing battle with the bottle, and that day, the bottle was winning. Jim went into one of my songs, "Jeannie," thinking it would ground me and get me back on track. I sat down on the front of the stage, the walls crashing in and tears in my eyes. I couldn't remember the lyrics. The words wouldn't come. There was nothing except a blank slate. I could feel my heart racing and my face flushing. There was a roaring in my ears. Jim brought the intro around again, hoping it would trigger the song I had written from my heart, and still, there was nothing, a void growing darker by the second. His surprise slowly turned to anger, and Jim said we were going to take a break and angrily left the building into the parking lot. Disappointment filled Robin's usually supportive eyes. I was a mess. Tapped. Lost. I wished I was invisible to steal out of the room undetected. It took all of Robin's power of persuasion to get Jim to return and finish the gig. It was a moment that tested and found a chink in the armor of my powerful denial.

The year is a blur, with incidents and accidents dotting the memory landscape. I was spiraling down so gradually that I didn't even notice the degradation of my skills, but my edge and timing were disappearing. I remained living in that delusion of grandeur fueled by my youthful adventures that told me I was still a heartbeat from stardom, still relevant, still healthy.

56. WALKING ON A WIRE
(Eric Lowen and Dan Navarro)

THE KEY WAS KEEPING the balance. I was becoming skilled at maintaining a level of booze in my bloodstream so that I didn't appear intoxicated but remained above withdrawal. I never had a hangover. I'd get the morning shot in, fifty percent of the time, not vomiting it back up, but even when I did, I had ingested enough to quell the shakes and nausea so the next one stayed down.

To maintain that balance, I had a million excuses to run an errand or forget something in the house after we were already in the car to come back in and hit my stash. It was mentally exhausting scoping out a bar I could escape to or a place I could sneak away and hit the bottle in my pocket, but I made it work.

Most of the time, I thought I was presenting myself well as a self-assured musician on the cusp of success with a type A personality. The only problem is that I was none of those things.

Alcohol had created that persona since those high school dances. At best, I was an extroverted introvert. At worst, I suffered from deep anxiety in everything I did. Drinking numbed it and gave me the courage to overcome these tendencies.

The other side of the balance equation was ugly. If I tipped the scale, even the smallest amount, I would become sloppy drunk, and my memory would disappear. I was lucky most of these episodes occurred away from Robin while I was alone in the studio, but on some of these occasions, I drove home.

One of the aspects of alcoholism that I don't think gets enough attention is the crushing guilt that accompanies it. It is fuel to continue the deadly cycle. Since I resumed drinking during the ill-fated outpatient treatment, I started having psychic conversations with myself. I would tell myself I was going to quit drinking tomorrow. Between intervals of around-the-clock imbibing, I struggled internally. On countless nights, my resolve would get stronger, and I'd feel the optimism of the possibility of a life without this pain. I would work up to it, finish whatever stash I had before I went to bed, and convince myself that it was my last drink—ever. I'd get up the next day, get ready for work, and the shakes would start, along with a queasy weakness that was too familiar. I told myself, "I can get through this," and headed down the road. Countless days, I pulled into the liquor store parking lot, got a fresh pint, guzzled a mouthful, and as that warmth spread to my fingertips, the guilt would be debilitating. Despair was my constant companion. I would cry resigned tears, even as the drug killing me temporarily made me feel like all was right with the world.

57. PAINT IT BLACK
(Mick Jagger and Keith Richards)

MY FRIEND FROM CHASER, Stevie Johnson, married Brenda Allen. They had their reception in the beautiful barn twenty miles north of Madison, where Chaser used to record and rehearse. Robin and I attended. I brought along a plastic flask filled with brandy and hid it in the bushes under the windmill on the farm so I could sneak away and maintain my balance, my party-going veneer. It worked until it was time to leave. I couldn't retrieve it with Robin walking with me. Around midnight, we got in the car and went home. Robin drove. I thought I had a bottle in the closet, so I would wait until she went to bed and have my nightcap. It was empty. It was too late for last call at the bars, and liquor stores wouldn't open for another eight hours. I decided to drive back to Stevie's farm and get the flask, which still contained a few belts. Driving out there in the moonless, pitch-black night, I parked down the road so no one would see my car and floundered around in the bushes, unable to find the flask. Some stragglers were still at the party. A couple of times, I had to hide from them. I couldn't go into the barn and get a drink because I hadn't been drinking publicly for a year, and besides, we had already left. Why would I have returned? I got back in the car, drove home, and spent a restless, shaky night hardly sleeping until I could get up and wait in the parking lot for the liquor store clerk to put their keys in the door.

Robin was working for the American Academy of Cosmetic Dentistry.

She oversaw the promotion and organization of a national convention at the Four Seasons Hotel in Chicago and left earlier in the week to get things going. It was meant to be a fabulous weekend surrounded by opulence like I had rarely experienced. I went down on Friday and quickly scoped out a bar across the street where I could sneak away to find the balance. I couldn't hit the minibar at Four Seasons prices; I would have dropped a few hundred dollars without breaking a sweat. Robin would be busy most of the time, providing me with ample opportunity to wander. Our room, on the twentieth floor, was adjacent to and had a breathtaking view of the Hancock Tower and would afford a lovely time together in between my forays for alcohol.

I had a gig in Madison with Code Blue on Saturday night, so I reluctantly had to return. After a quick pick-me-up across the street, I thought I had left ample time to make soundcheck without thinking about Chicago traffic. I sat at a dead stop on the Kennedy Expressway for more than an hour. When I finally made it out of the city, I drove over eighty mph. Thank God I had my bottle stashed under the seat for fortification. My anxiety over being late resulted in a few too many visits to the brandy. I tipped the balance, and when I arrived at the gig, I was shit-faced after driving 150 miles on the interstate, twenty mph over the speed limit. I remember the sideways, angry glances from the rest of the band and the drummer, who was a dick under good circumstances, reaming me a new asshole afterward.

Labor Day weekend, Code Blue was scheduled at the Taste of Madison, a massive annual festival held on the Capitol Square. My life at this point was like hanging on to the caboose of a speeding train, careening down a mountain with no brakes. I played the gig with Code Blue and was dangerously close to tipping the balance. I strutted and preened, overcompensating to act sober. I was too animated for a sideman playing keyboards, but in my borderline psychosis, it felt right. I was oblivious to the concerned looks and whispers behind my back.

Jim and I were booked back in Baudette for the next week in September. We had good friends up there who wanted to give me another chance to recreate the euphoria of our first couple of visits. Robin was nearly at the end of her rope with me, and I was hoping the trip would bring me clarity and calm and a renewed effort to kick the monkey off my back. It did the opposite. I fell into a deep depression, only eased by Windsor Canadian whiskey. I didn't accompany Jim fishing. I performed lackluster, mediocre shows, losing my voice the first night of five and never really recovering it. People were asking Jim what was wrong with me, a fun, outgoing, energetic performer only a year before. Most of the time, I stayed in my dark lodge room, with the curtains drawn, only surfacing to do a show, sparingly eat, or run into town to get more Windsor. I finished the week in a daze, and when I returned home, Robin had finally had enough.

58. THE SOUND OF SILENCE
(Paul Simon)

WHEN I WAS RELEASED from the facility, I was subdued. Robin came and quietly retrieved her sober, chastened husband, a completely different human than she had taken to the hospital twenty days earlier. Instead of bravado, there was humility. In the place of expansive laughter, there was reserve, with a tenuous hold on reality. I had started to relearn how to be myself. It was a process only I could facilitate. I spent much of the time staring into space, lost in faraway thoughts of how I came to be here, in this moment, and how I could get better. The only thing I was certain of was my love for Robin Valley-Massey. There was nothing I wanted more than to reward my lovely wife with the partner she deserved.

I'm one of the fortunate ones. I've been so incredibly lucky in my life, and sometimes I wonder when the other shoe will drop. I didn't have cravings for alcohol. In twenty-nine years, I can count my cravings for a drink on one hand and a couple of fingers. While frighteningly powerful, thankfully, they were fleeting. I've heard stories and talked to people who have tried and failed to get sober, and they describe constant cravings. That would be the cruelest brand of hell.

Here is as good a place as any to say without hesitation that I believe Robin saved my life. To support me unconditionally while I faced my demons and continued the internal wrestling match gave me hope. It gave me a foundation to crawl back to. It gave me a comfort that is nothing less than lifesaving and life-changing. Her belief in me was my source of power to make the change.

But Robin was worried. In my quietude, I was different. Was I the same man she had fallen in love with and married? Or was I changed? Would she like the change?

I needed direction and a job. I had no skills. I sometimes joke about playing the piano as the only thing I know how to do and that I'm otherwise unemployable. It's really not a joke. The only thing I could somewhat fake was selling something. Forbes didn't have a position, and I was lost as to what might interest me in the real world. I've always been interested in interior design, so I thought maybe I could get involved with a furniture store. I went to work at Leath Furniture in February.

I was terrible. My knowledge of the vast array of inventory was sparse, with no real motivation to improve. I figured it would come with repetition. But in the meantime, I floundered. Because my income level had been day-to-day all my life, I equated others' incomes to my own and never tried to sell expensive items. I couldn't wrap my head around people spending that much money for furniture—not a successful philosophy if you're in sales. But to be honest, I was still recovering, making everything more difficult. I was wading through quicksand. I was watching a movie about my everyday life with the main character being played by someone who looked like me. The store manager put me on probation for selling far below my quota. I was a lost puppy, a far cry from my boisterous youth. It got so I would cringe at the electronic bell signaling a customer had just walked in the door.

I get it. Nobody wants to talk to a furniture salesperson until they've decided what they want. I'm the same way now. But facing that animosity day after day was exhausting. A couple of my powerful cravings happened in those early days, driving home from work in the snow, seeing the warm glow of neon in the windows of the bars I was passing. I never stopped, but I thought hard about it.

Thanks to my friend Billy Erickson (he who sat upon my dresser during those withdrawal hallucinations), we heard of a small bungalow for rent on Erie Court next to his mom. It was a lovely home, filled with sunlight that made the beautiful golden woodwork glow. And it was affordable, even for us and our uncertain future. We moved on May 1. To have this comfortable home to call our own felt heavenly. It was there that I truly started living again.

59. HERE COMES THE SUN
(George Harrison)

EARLY ON, Robin and I went to a party. Thankfully, being in proximity to alcohol didn't bother me. I didn't expect the world to stop drinking around me. After all, this was Wisconsin! We mingled and laughed, and after a time, I asked where the restroom was and was directed upstairs. As I returned, I stopped at the top of the open staircase and looked at the steep incline. I started down the stairs, took my hand off the rail, and slowly descended. All these years later, I still vividly remember the overwhelming emotion that followed. Something we take for granted every day, an act so common as to be subconscious for most people was, in that moment, a triumph of spirit, a victory so satisfying, I fought back tears. The simple act of completely controlling my balance, my countenance, and my input in a conversation was an epiphany. It was a clarity and a feeling I hadn't had in perhaps more than a decade, giving me a new sense of power.

I started a pattern of sitting late at night in our raw concrete basement, with my cat Abby in my lap, smoking cigarettes and self-analyzing. A comfy chair and lamp from someone's trash, a rug from somewhere, and it became my sanctuary. Sometimes I'd sit in the dark. I opened folder after folder of data in my mind, deleted what felt self-destructive or inhibiting, and saved the positive and affirming. I analyzed my past and my present. My self-administered treatment continued throughout the next few years, and my recovery continues even now. Much of what I write here is saved from that internal hard drive of 1994.

I had been advised to stay away from bars, so I couldn't book any gigs right away. We set up a music studio on the sun porch. It was warm and bright and inspirational. I started fresh, playing for myself from deep inside. The keys felt like an old pair of jeans found in the back of the closet. Soft and familiar yet somehow forgotten, the memories of countless days triggered by their touch.

I dove into practicing. I was getting my chops back, and I was writing. The sun porch inspired most of the instrumentals on my *Be Careful How You Say Pianist* album. Robin and I had an emotional experience watching the movie *When a Man Loves a Woman* with Meg Ryan and Andy Garcia. The film follows Ryan through her descent into alcoholism and treatment. We both ended up in tears, holding each other tightly. Inspired by that shared moment, we co-wrote a song called "Julia's Escape" that hasn't yet made it on an album. I'm waiting until I capture a vocal performance befitting the power of the message.

JULIA'S ESCAPE

You
Come to me
Silent

I
Feel your sorrow
Do you mourn

The rustle of linen
A shadow of doubt
A candle burns slowly
Flickers out

She walks into the dawn
Tears dried upon her face

She'll be high tonight
That's Julia's Escape

You
Stand in the corner
Painted in

I
I can't
I can't help you
You're on your own

A sign at the crossroads
A lingering shame
Desire washes over the pain

She walks into the dawn
Tears dried upon her face
She'll be high tonight
That's Julia's Escape

    I went to the Concourse Hotel, which had a piano bar, and asked if they needed anyone. I set up an audition and played well enough to get a gig. I would be on the list as a sub and work my way into a regular slot. It paid a hundred dollars. Getting my feet wet at the Concourse also opened other doors, and I had a few inquiries about playing elsewhere. The furniture store paid two hundred dollars for a forty-hour week, plus commission. I never earned any commission. I was on probation for most of the time I was employed. I went to my beautiful wife with a question. The answer held my life in the balance. I asked, "If I could maintain the income I was making at Leath, could I quit and become a full-time musician?"

    There was no hesitation. That "yes" was beautiful and affirming. I could become myself again, a better version of myself. Robin's trust and belief in me and my abilities were immense and a driving force in making every day better than the last. I gave my notice at the store, and I was free. In

MORE

May 1994, Mike Massey Music was born, a sole proprietorship of a diverse amalgam of musical projects, ideas, and performances. For the first time, I was taking things seriously and looking at music as a means to create a life instead of chasing waterfalls.

60. OSCAR MAYER WEINER SONG
(Richard Trentlage)

IN THAT FIRST YEAR of recovery, I was walking on thin ice. I was rediscovering some things, reevaluating others, and generally hanging on. At the end of my darkest times, I started playing with Jimmie Nahas, Harvey Briggs, and Bruce Geiger. We called the band Bent, and we rehearsed in Jimmie's basement. I hadn't seen them since I was in a world of hurt, living on Simpson Street and driving drunk all of the time. Now those guys emerged again and provided me with a foundation to repair my performance skills. They brought me along slowly, and it was just what I needed.

We were writing songs. It was a time of healing and working in new ways. Importantly, Harvey was a partner in an advertising agency. One day he casually asked whether I made advertising music. I said yes, though I had only dabbled in music beds for the radio station as a value-added product for my sales clients and just scratched the surface with Murphy Music. I didn't have a clue how to navigate that world. With his guidance and support, I began to explore the possibility. Harvey gave me the first of many opportunities, enlisting me to score a thirty-second television commercial for Unity Health Plans.

I discovered that I had an innate talent to maximize thirty seconds. It was like writing a pop or rock song with a memorable melody or theme that had to scream "hit" in that abbreviated space. Melody has always come easily to me. I could rattle off ideas in whatever direction I was given, often in just a few hours or overnight. The new technology that was emerging gave me the ability to write and record ideas by myself in my home studio, bringing musicians into a real studio for the final product. A new facet of my career was born, thanks to Harvey. The Unity score resulted in the first of many ADDY Awards for music that I would ultimately receive in the next decade.

At Concept Productions, Murphy Music was gone, and they welcomed me back into the family. Dan Geocaris, Rod Barelmann, Doug Schoebel, and company gave me free studio time, and I recorded a batch of songs I had written during my Murphy Music days. It was a redeeming catharsis that boosted my self-esteem and solidified those friendships for life. I repaid their generosity and warmth with loyalty in a competitive business, forging a partnership with much of the ad music I produced.

Concept became a home away from home and familiar in a more intimate way than when I was a lackey for Rick Murphy. Good people surrounded me, and I was slowly regaining a place in the world.

61. THE TIMES THEY ARE-A-CHANGIN'
(Bob Dylan)

THERE HAD BEEN CHANGES in that magical place on the Minnesota-Ontario border. The manager at the Wigwam Resort, Joel Jackson, knew of my situation, and I called and asked if there were any opportunities to come up and play. He created a happy hour show for me. It wasn't much money, but I would have accommodations and food. It was an extremely generous gesture. I had given my notice two weeks prior at Leath, and now I was on the road again. Not long after I returned from that trip, he called me and asked if I was available to come up to play the main gig for the weekend because he'd had a cancellation. Jim was living in Massachusetts with Anita, and he was out, but I called my friend Robert J. Conaway and asked if he'd be into a trip. Robert is a fabulous, prolific singer-songwriter and performer. We called ourselves Bobber and Pike, the Fishin' Musicians. We pooled our song lists and rehearsed for an hour. An hour! Then we headed north to play three sets a night. That's how good Robert is. And that's how good a person Joel Jackson is. I credit having those gigs, some of which he created for me, for strengthening my resolve and growth. It was becoming evident that I was getting better and hadn't lost my creativity in sobriety.

Baudette was magic. It was exactly what I needed. Going back there allowed me to breathe again. I was able to compare, with the same audiences, performing sober to being trashed. I felt a lucidity that had escaped me for years in my performance and my thoughts. It gave me latitude, and it gave me time for introspection in the crystal-clear air. Bobber and I would go back two more times that year, each as therapeutic. Robert did, however, catch the biggest fish.

Later in the year, I stopped participating actively in Alcoholics Anonymous, AA. I felt strongly that at that point in my recovery, I wanted to dwell on the positives I was feeling more than reliving the past. The last AA meeting I attended was in a smoke-filled basement of a business on Monona Drive. You could smoke at meetings, and everyone did. Cigarettes and coffee were the substitute drugs of choice. I settled into the table and was by far the youngest attendee at thirty-six. The older, whiskey-voiced men took turns running through some of the most agonizing stories: "I hit and killed a four-year-old girl," said one. "I beat my wife to within an inch of her life," said another. "I lost it all, all of my money and my family." "I wrapped my car around a tree and walked away without a scratch."

I finally couldn't take it anymore. I got up from the table, and as I was walking out, said, "You guys make me WANT to drink," and didn't look back.

I recently had a conversation with Kathryn Ripp, a lifelong friend, sister to the Ripp brothers, a psychotherapist, and a drug and alcohol counselor. When I recalled this story to her, she laughed and said one word: "crocodiles." She said she tells her clients that if they find themselves at a meeting with crocodiles, don't go back. Find another meeting. Really good advice.

I want to be completely clear here that I am in no way trying to invalidate the good that AA has brought to the world. They gave me a direction and purpose in my earliest days of sobriety when the world seemed vicious and cold. The organization has saved the lives of countless thousands through the years, and I have nothing but respect for those results.

I have carried one chip in my wallet all these years—my red one-month chip. It was in those thirty days that the surrender, revelation, and hardest work changed my life.

I believed then and now that celebrating victories, no matter how small, and enjoying clarity as your new high is much more beneficial than getting stuck in a Groundhog Day of revisiting the hell of the past.

Simple things, enjoying a clear mind and self-control, all add up to powerful equity in your recovery and ongoing sobriety. I started inhaling those moments, the uncomplicated moments, and looked forward, not back. It was then that the weight began to lift from my shoulders.

A tenet of AA I disagree with is the unclear references to making amends. The eighth step reads: "Made a list of all persons we had harmed and became willing to make amends to them all." The ninth step: "Made direct amends to such people wherever possible, except when to do so would injure them or others." Who are we to assume anything about the people we've hurt? I understand saying you're sorry for the small shit, but in most cases, people you have wronged, sometimes in awful ways, have moved on. They have dealt with the psychological damage we've caused and resolved it so they can feel better equipped to thrive. I think for us to come along and apologize and make them relive their darkness simply for our own personal, cheap absolution is arrogant, tone-deaf, and self-serving. That being said, there are people I wish I could talk to and let them know I'm ashamed of how I was, and I'm so sorry for the grief and pain I caused them. My penance is living with the guilt until the day I die rather than making them face it again.

One year after the "Boot Camp" essay, I returned to the journal and added one last page:

MORE

10/24/94

One year has passed since my last entry. I have dreamt alone, and I have moved within a delicate world. But I have not been alone. I have been blessed and supported by people who care, most of all by the woman heaven provided me, my loving, compassionate, beautiful wife.

Without Robin, I would have had no reason to change, no reason to succeed. I only hope I can adopt more of her philosophies and principles in my dealings with life. I am truly blessed.

And I will try to help others through situations I am familiar with in any way I can. There is so much to say and a lack of printable words to express it. I am not now, nor have I been journeying alone. I have a soulmate holding my hand through this cosmos.

I spent 1994 slowly healing. I had been as low as a human could go, on the edge of death from poisoning my body with alcohol. I would spend the next two years clearing up late notices from collection agencies about bad checks written in liquor stores in three counties. But now, as the gray gradually dissipated, I could see the sun burning through the haze. My purgatory was fading, and the world was coming into focus.

MICHAEL MASSEY

Lucifer at St. Bernards – L to R: Mark Davini, Rick Paulson, Mike Massey, Ron Hoffman, and Michael John Ripp

Early Chaser – L to R: Rob (Fish) West, Mike Massey, Michael John Ripp, and Pat Hynes
Not pictured: Tony Cerniglia

MORE

Chaser – L to R: Tony Cerniglia, Stevie Johnson, Michael John Ripp, and Mike Massey

Jethro Tull backstage at Chicago Stadium – L to R: Ian Anderson, Tony Cerniglia, Michael John Ripp, and Mike Massey

MICHAEL MASSEY

Mike and Andy Warhol, Atlantic Studios, New York

L to R: Rick Ambrose, Michael John Ripp, Tony Cerniglia, Stevie Johnson, Andy Warhol, Roger Probert, and Mike Massey

MORE

Chaser at Headliners 1980

Ludwig Drums seventy-fifth anniversary poster

MICHAEL MASSEY

Boys in White, Star Search Green Room – L to R: Paul Ripp, Mike Massey, Michael John Ripp, Tony Cerniglia, and Rod Ellenbecker

Boys in White Beat of the City

Circle Park. Photo by Paul Ripp

MORE

Mike and Robin, April 21, 1990. Photo by Scott Duckwitz

Mike and Emily at Randy's Recording

MICHAEL MASSEY

Francie Phelps and Anna Massey at Woodland Montessori

MORE

Mike and Genevieve Custer-Weeks, An Evening of Romance – photo by Andrew Weeks

The Renfields – *Dracula: A Rock Ballet*

MICHAEL MASSEY

Chaser Reunion, Joey's Song 2014 at the Majestic Theater

The Masseys in the Alps 2014

MORE

Steely Dane at The Pabst Theater, Milwaukee, WI

Robin gets her master's degree

MICHAEL MASSEY

The Furious Bongos – photo by David Yates; L to R: Mike Massey, Christopher Huntington, Vince Szynborski, Lo Marie, Lou Caldarola, Conrad St. Clair, Randall Harrison, Matt Peters, and Scott Gendel

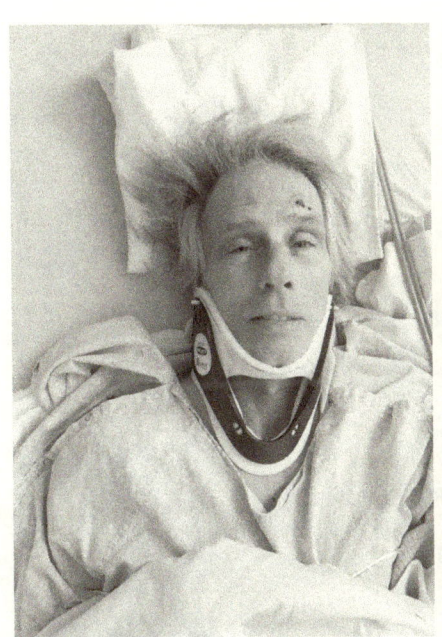

Mike, UW Hospital, March 2, 2020

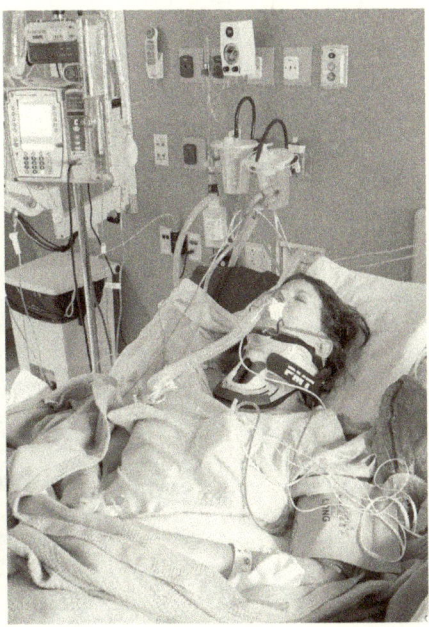

Robin ICU, UW Hospital, March 2, 2020

MORE

The Masseys at UW Rehabilitation Hospital

Emily and Mike recording vocal tracks for Moveys

MICHAEL MASSEY

Massey Valley

MORE

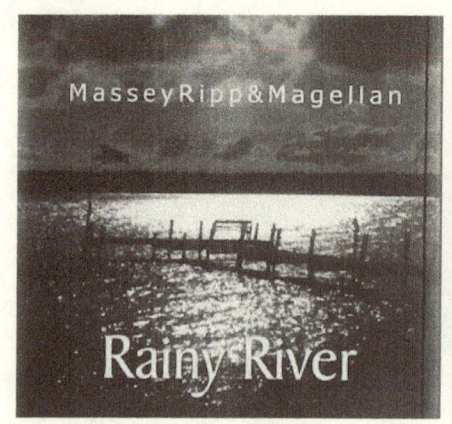

"Rainy River" EP Massey, Ripp, and Magellan

Be Careful How You Say Pianist, photo by John Urban

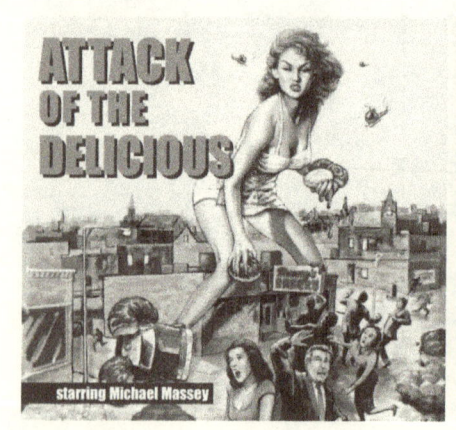

Attack of the Delicious, artwork by Glenn Fuller

The Present, photo by John Urban, present wrapped by Lisa Grainger-Briggs

MICHAEL MASSEY

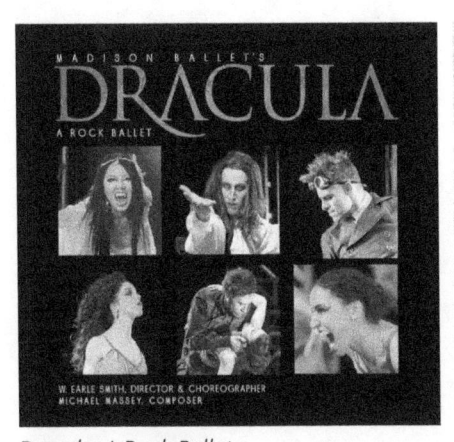

Dracula: A Rock Ballet, photos by John Urban

Stop the Clock, *Gifted at the Hula*

Naked, original artwork by Kristina Zengaffinen

Jack's Bootleg, cover art design by Rick Ambrose and Jim Ripp

To listen: www.mikemasseymusic.com

62. TAKIN' CARE OF BUSINESS
(Randy Bachman)

ROBIN AND I HAD TRIED earnestly to have a child in 1993. In retrospect, we likely weren't successful because my sperm cells were so drunk they couldn't find the target. In mid-February of '95, Robin presented me with a greeting card that contained a positive pregnancy stick. We were thrilled! And then shortly after that, Robin being Robin, accompanied my brother Scott on a medical mission to Haiti. Scott had been going down for years and had taken the lead as a physician assistant. He and his then-wife had also adopted a son, James, from Haiti, so Scottie was well-versed in the protocol. Robin came back from the trip profoundly impacted. She wasn't herself for quite some time. The combination of the constant militaristic presence of guards armed with machine guns, abject poverty, the likes of which is incomprehensible to most Americans, and the patience and joy of the people themselves while receiving medical care was menacing and humbling. It took a while for her to recover.

As for me, clarity was starting to become my new normal. Stopping drinking was only the tip of the iceberg. After the change, it took more than a year to regain my sense of self, and my musical skills were still rusty. It was like the neural pathways from the brain to vocal cords and fingers were foggy, although as the fog lifted, I wrote some of the best songs of my life. It shattered my deepest fear and biggest obstacle to getting clean, that my creativity would stop in sobriety. Inspiration is sharper and more defined with a clear head. If you have aspirations of making a life with your art, it will most likely not happen if you're struggling with substances. When one is suffering in the claws of addiction, the amount of concentration, hard work, and perseverance it takes to succeed as an artist isn't even on the radar screen.

Professional artists do what they have to do to become successful and maintain it. You can't lie around wasted and wait for the songs to appear out of thin air. You can't let your mind and body get out of shape if you want to compete in the breakneck music industry. At best, you'll be a flash in the pan, more likely just left behind. And now, in my burgeoning sobriety, I was seeing things differently. Song structures, chord progressions, and lyrics felt deeper and more coherent. When I wrote "Tears Disappear," it became the bar. The best song I had ever written became the benchmark for everything that came after. And with a clearing mind and healthy body, I could keep it all straight and work on improving every day.

And that is another way my vision changed. I was seeing a long-term future for the first time in my life. A pervasive philosophy in the rock and roll days was to live fast and leave a beautiful corpse. I almost did. But now I had a child on the way, I was thinking clearly, and I had a partner in life that made every day a joy.

63. WISH YOU WERE HERE
(Roger Waters)

I PLAYED AS MANY GIGS as possible, usually five or six days a week. After our child was born, it was unknown what my schedule could or would be, so I was getting in as much as possible.

Bobber called me one spring day and asked if I was available to fill in for him at a little club in Wisconsin Dells, Giada's. I took the gig and walked in to find Sharon Olson, a striking older (to me then) woman behind the bar. She said, "Who are you?"

I said I was filling in for Robert and then asked, "What's that?" pointing to the grand piano under a cover on the stage.

She said, "It's a piano. It was delivered an hour ago."

"Can I play it?"

She said, after a beat, "I don't know, can you?" With that joke, delivered with impeccable timing, a long and lasting friendship was born. I set up on the cozy stage with the serendipitously delivered grand and got ready for the gig. The owner, Todd Nelson, and his extended family, all came in to see this guy who was playing their new piano. I had a great night. I felt in my element and comfortable. The synapses were starting to click into gear. I booked two months at the club the next day, three, sometimes four nights a week.

MICHAEL MASSEY

Memorial Day evening, I picked up Robert and his gear from a gig at bar time, and we headed back up to Baudette, playing the Sportsman's Lodge this time around. Our friends from Colorado, Al and Lorelei, that fantastic duo, were down the road at the Wigwam, and Donnie Bell, a singer-songwriter from Nashville, was around the corner at another lodge. We had a fabulous two weeks in paradise, all getting together with our intermingled audiences after our respective gigs on various front porches on the river and singing until dawn. I was quite literally the only person not drinking. It didn't matter. I was high on life and clarity.

One memorable night, a raucous poker game came to the trailer we were given for accommodations. At about three in the morning, with everyone but me hard-drinking all night long, Al and Bobber suddenly got serious and started betting in earnest. After their pockets were empty, Al put the keys to his boat in the pot. Robert countered with his van keys. When it came time to call, Al laid down his cards—full house, aces high. Robert looked calmly at the cards on the table for a moment and laid down four of a kind. The air was tense and still for a moment, and then Bobber said, "Aw, take your keys. I ain't gonna take your boat." Al hugged him, and all was right with the world, and they did the sideways walk out into the sunrise.

We spent our days hunting northern pike on the Canadian side of Fourmile Bay, where McGinnis Creek empties into Lake of the Woods. And we spent our nights amidst laughter and song, cultivating friendships that I'm happy to say remain today. For them and our snapshot in time, I wrote "Friends Forever," one of the favorite songs of my career between the Memorial Day trip and a late-summer excursion with Jim Ripp. It was a joy to come back later that year and play it for them.

Cindy Wangerud, Shelley Westerlund Phillippe, Lynnie Eaton-Svihel, Jess Jackson, Sheila Berg, Michael Fox, Joel Jackson, Jody Hasbargen-Tessier, Ellen Gross, Maxine Wangerud, Michael Hovde, Lisa Phillippe-Borg, and Sherry Wangerud are just some of the people I've kept in touch with through the years. In fact, I've made the trek to Minnesota to perform the music for several of their weddings. Baudette, Minnesota, in that summer and fall of 1995, was yet another instance to prove to me how sweet life can be sober.

MORE

FRIENDS FOREVER

Are you thinkin' about me as you draw the shade
Do you ever think about me, so far away
I miss you most of all when lyin' awake and waiting for the dawn
It's been so long
Do you remember when our souls touched
I left a piece of my heart, keep it safe
Do you remember friends forever
Innocent magic that can't be explained
I've been thinkin' about you when I light a cigarette
I've been thinkin' you were different, you chase the sunset
I keep your letters in a drawer
And read them every once in a while
They make me smile
Do you ever think about me
I've been thinkin' about you
Do you ever think about me
I've been thinkin' you were different

Giada's was a burgeoning scene. There was live music six nights a week, and I played a large percentage of it. In August, Wayne Jandula, a regular patron and friend, invited a young woman to "come see this kid who's playing down the street." Mare, one name is sufficient, like Cher or Madonna, had recently returned home to Elroy from a good degree of success musically in Las Vegas after a bad marriage breakup and was working at the upscale steakhouse, The Del-Bar. She came down and sat in, and there was instant chemistry. She started coming in regularly after her shift to do the last set with me, bringing a significant percentage of the Wisconsin Dells service industry with her. Giada's became a destination. Mare and I would perform as a duo for many years in central and southern Wisconsin.

64. DOCTOR MY EYES
(Jackson Browne)

IN '94 AND '95, I spent a lot of time at Randy's Recording with Randy Green. Randy was a phenomenal, accomplished musician and had added a studio to his home. I spent hours with him, recording each new song as it was written and, more importantly, healing. Randy was my unofficial therapist, a musician with a psychology degree, and our sessions were sometimes more soul-searching than recording. The hourly rate was ten dollars when I started hanging out. I think he eventually raised it to fifteen much later on. His experience level in writing, performing, and recording was vast. I learned so much from him.

We would get tracks recorded and come into the control room to listen and invariably get sidetracked on a conversation that could be so left field, so convoluted, that we'd go on for an hour, smoking cigarettes and exchanging remarkable dialogue. It always circled around and ended in a valuable lesson. When it came time to settle up, he would always adjust the time for "distractions." Randy didn't drink, and he was a major cheerleader of my sobriety. It helped me to see someone I looked up to, firmly entrenched in music, that didn't need the crutch of alcohol to thrive. I'd often call him out of the blue at odd hours of the night, and if he didn't have a session, I'd drive over and hang out, effectively saving his exorbitant therapist's fee.

MORE

We talked about music. How a good song needs to make you feel. We talked about composition, structure, melody, countermelody, the importance of message, and the best way to arrive there. But more importantly, we talked about life. We talked about relationships, overcoming adversity, and how it can make you stronger. We solved political and global socio-economic problems all from the muted, comfortably charming, smoke-filled control room, him leaning back in his command chair, shirt tails perpetually out.

Randy mentored many artists, including some who are successful at the highest levels of the music industry. Why is it that good people leave us way too soon? I am forever indebted to his insight and wisdom.

65. TAKE ME TO THE RIVER
(Al Green and Teenie Hodges)

AFTER AN EXHAUSTINGLY busy summer of playing around southern Wisconsin, Jim and I returned to Baudette in September for another two-week engagement, my last road hurrah before the October arrival of our baby. It was another two weeks in paradise with all the good friends from the earlier trips, and we cherished every moment.

I was looking forward to our child for many reasons, but I also had flashes of strong self-doubt. What's next? Would I be a good father? I was taking time in this most meditative of locations to self-search and reconcile the impending event. Very soon, life as I knew it would never be the same.

Sheila Berg's family owned a cabin with a dock on the Rainy River, the border between Ontario and Minnesota that flowed into Lake of the Woods. After leaving one of our boisterous bar-time jams, I was walking her home, and the pier was just across the road, so we decided to head over for a cigarette and sit on the bench for a moment to look at the bright moon hanging in the sky.

The water was softly lapping on the shore, and the full moon stretched from Canada to Minnesota across the mirror that was the river. I tilted my head back and blew smoke at the billion stars in the desolate sky. Sheila and I were easy friends and didn't need constant conversation to be comfortable. The silence was soft in the darkness. It started dimly, just a couple of flashes, and then the most fabulous aurora borealis bloomed and spread across the sky.

Curtains of green shimmered and danced, infusing the night with an incandescent glow. The full moon sat muted gold and cuddled in the folds of light, and it was all echoed on the glass-smooth water. Earth and sky, connected by green fire. I couldn't breathe. We didn't speak. I was on the edge of the world, about to fall up into oblivion. I've never felt so insignificant in the grand scheme. The vastness of the universe overwhelmed and suffocated me.

It was an incredible display of Mother Nature's power and an amazing revelation. My doubt was erased. I knew in that moment I would do the very best I could as a father and a husband, and that's all I could do. My best would be my very best, with a clear heart and an open mind.

In the next few days, I wrote another of my favorite songs, "Rainy River," to commemorate the night and my newfound confidence in tackling the next challenge.

RAINY RIVER

Here I am, I stand before you
I'm just a man, alone and scared
And then you offer me a gentle hand to hold
You stop my shiver, give me shelter from the cold

CHORUS
Moon over the Rainy River, come and take me home
Night covers the Rainy River with phantom streaks of gold
Roll on you Rainy River, come into my soul
Carry the piece of my heart to deliver I left here long ago

Here I stand, my shadow falls below me
I'm feeling small, my life's beyond control
I'm just a man who tries to live with virtue
One step away from the haunting river's call

MICHAEL MASSEY

Each and every day, the sun goes up and down
And with every choice we make, our world can turn around

CHORUS
And when the moment comes, we have to say goodbye
Hold me closer dear, teach me how to fly

66. I HOPE YOU DANCE
(Mark D. Sanders and Tia Sillers)

I WAS PLAYING. I was healthy. I was clear. And I was about to become a father.

I was scheduled with Michelle Grabel at the Concourse Hotel for a gig around Robin's due date. This was before casual cell phone use, so I had a pager on my person in case the blessed event transpired during the show. Jim Ripp was in attendance at the show as an emergency backup. Sure enough, about an hour in, my pager went off, Robin's water had broken. Jim stepped up, took one for the team, and finished the night so I could retrieve my wife and get her to the hospital. We had chosen not to find out the gender of our unborn child, opting for the surprise factor. If it was a boy, he would be William Massey V. If it was a girl, she would be Emily Marie. Although Emily was the number one girl's name in America that year, we chose it in memory of Robin's sister, who died at birth. Marie was my maternal grandmother.

I was secretly hoping for a daughter.

Emily Marie Massey came into this world after twenty-two hours of labor at 19:19 p.m. on October 13, 1995.

Exactly two years since the date I relinquished alcohol in my life!

The immense display of nature's beauty in Baudette and the synchronicity of the calendar led me to believe that the universe was smiling on the decision to change my life. And the thought occurred to me then, as it does from time to time even now, that none of this joy, the life we've created together as a family, nothing that happened in our world since, would have been the same, would have been possible, if I hadn't made the change.

I would have been a statistic.

Emily and Anna wouldn't exist, and Robin would have moved on, forever scarred by my selfish demise.

It needs to be said that for the next decade of my life, regardless of musical accomplishments, my primary vocation, my most prized role, would be as a stay-at-home dad. I would have the privilege of watching my daughters grow and, along with Robin, be their first teacher. I'm going to continue with the story of my journey but do not forget that above it all, I was Dad.

67. OUR HOUSE
(David Crosby, Stephen Stills, and Graham Nash)

I HAD SPENT MY teen years and early adulthood chasing a deluded version of rock stardom with plenty of flash and no substance. I escaped that fantasy that drove me to the brink by tearing myself down to bones and shreds of flesh.

Life—real, tangible life—began to seep into my existence for the first time. I was no longer living in the past. I wasn't on the outside looking in, watching myself perform on stage and off. I had a family. I had a wife I adored and an infant daughter who was the most priceless of gifts. My days were spent caring for Emily in our comfortable, sunny bungalow, making lunch for Robin, and walking Emily in the stroller to meet her mommy as she came home from work. Afternoons would be spent in the park across the street and then home for a shared nap to rest for a gig that night. We'd wake after about an hour, and I would usually have dinner ready when Robin came home for the day before I would shower and depart for a show. I loved every moment. But it should be noted, the juxtaposition from my earlier life to the new one I was embracing now. My life was no longer a page-turner, but the protagonist wouldn't meet a ghastly, early demise, either.

MICHAEL MASSEY

Thanks to Harvey Briggs and his faith in my abilities, I was developing a reputation as a go-to guy for advertising music. During the second half of the nineties, I composed dozens of pieces of music for ads, perfecting the art of thirty- and sixty-second time restraints. It helped my songwriting immensely by molding ideas into a more concise and pure form, free of redundancy and streamlined. It was a marriage of creativity and commerce. I was working with several advertising agencies and individual clients, able to do a lot of it from home with Emily by my side. Back when that was a rarity, I had dial-up internet and email from home.

Harvey and Bruce invited me to join their band, Johnny and the Nakomans (there was no Johnny). It was a band comprised of advertising executives, attorneys, a U.S. congressman, people in finance, and me. Throughout my life, doors have been opened because of music. I've experienced things I would never have done or seen if I wasn't a performer. Now, I was playing music with this group of guys who were respected and revered in their fields. It started giving me confidence that I hadn't known I was lacking.

An early major piece I did for Lindsay, Stone, and Briggs was a sixty-second music bed for a television spot for UW Hospital and Clinics. Before I had state-of-the-art equipment of my own, Rod Barelmann and Dan Geocaris at Concept allowed me to go into the studio after hours to use their freshly acquired and hottest new technology, the Ensoniq ASR-10 keyboard. This was before you could bring video into your computer and score a piece of music. I had to play the video cassette and compose it in real-time manually. I sequenced the piece internally on the keyboard, working with trial and error until it synched perfectly to changes in the scenes. The spot won numerous ADDY Awards, including musical score.

Some of the clients I created music for in those years of revival included Wisconsin Power and Light, UW Hospital, New Balance Stores, Research Products, Mercury Marine, United Way, Michael's Frozen Custard, Fiskars, Farm and Fleet, Verlo, CUNA Mutual, GHC, The Janesville Gazette, Country Kitchen, Metra, and many more.

MORE

One of the perks of being a stay-at-home dad was watching the Wisconsin State high school basketball tournaments on TV. I love the pure passion of the game at that level. We got a Fisher Price hoop, and Emily and I played ball while we watched the tournaments. As I was getting into advertising, a personal goal became having an ad that I score appear during the tournament. Many years later, quite by accident and due to the longevity of some of my pieces, I sat with surprise and a divine sense of accomplishment, tipping my hat to my younger self, as the entire three-minute commercial break during the championship game was ads with music I had composed and produced.

A memorable incident involved a thirty-second piano piece for Meriter Hospital. Nancy Mayek, creative director of Meriter's media, called me and said, "I need a thirty-second lullaby for a gorgeously filmed black and white birthing center spot. I envision a mother singing to her infant." I thought for a second and told her I had composed a piano piece just the night before that might be perfect. I would, of course, do whatever the project called for, but I hoped she'd give this a listen first. I recorded it on a cassette and dropped it off at her office. It ran for eight years and remains the single most beautiful commercial piece I ever did. Nancy and I would team up for many more projects through the years.

68. GO! YOU PACKERS GO!
(Eric Karll)

MY EDITOR ASKED how the following anecdote connects to the larger arc of this book. Although it does nothing to further the story, I want to include it anyway because it is an important part of my history, and it fits chronologically here:

Thanks to friends Stephanie Stender and Rob Lux, I had the opportunity to go to Lambeau Field for every Green Bay Packers home game during the 1996 season. Stephanie and Rob had inherited season tickets on the forty-yard line, twenty-two rows behind the Packers bench. It was heaven. I had been a rabid fan throughout the dismally mediocre seventies and eighties and had suffered with the rest of Packer Nation. As a state, Wisconsin would be grouchy for a couple of days after a Packers loss but never lost faith and never waned in its loyalty. People wear Packers jerseys to church, and sermons are cut short if it's going to interfere with kickoff! We were rewarded with the arrival of Brett Favre and Reggie White to lead Titletown back to the promised land. In 1996, the Packers led the league in most categories, offensively and defensively. The team was a juggernaut created by mastermind Ron Wolf. That year was thrilling and a revelation.

After the Packers won Super Bowl XXXI in New Orleans, there was a victory parade through the snowy streets of Green Bay. The players sat in buses with the windows down and waved to their adoring fans, and I wept like a baby—not a tear trickling down my cheek but flat-out, blubbery sobbing with snot running out of my nose. Sixteen-month-old Emily was confused and asked Daddy why he was crying. I said that they were happy tears. Enduring all those years of mediocrity and disappointment came out in a wave of emotion that astonished me and was amazingly cleansing. Mixed with my sports allegiance was the sense that perhaps I was winning as well, and the overwhelming passion pouring out was also expelling doubts that I was capable and deserving of success. Since that day, the Packers have been just a football team, not an obsession.

The only game I didn't attend in the Lux/Stender seats was with a friend from Milwaukee I had met in the Dells. His soon-to-be-brother-in-law had a friend who owned a sporting goods store in Green Bay, and Brett Favre was going to be doing an autograph session at the store on Saturday. Tony asked if I'd like to come up and act as security for the session! I was immediately twelve again.

My job was keeping people in line and ensuring they had their tickets ready, but during a break, I was walking around the back room and chatting with Brett Favre!

After the session, I asked if he'd sign something for me. My father had given me a limited-edition football commemorating Brett's 1995 MVP award, and I tossed it across the room to him. He signed it with a gold sharpie and went to throw it back to me. I said, "No, don't throw it. It'll ruin your signature!" He got a mischievous look in his eye. So, I have Brett Favre's autograph on a limited-edition football, smudged from when I caught a pass from him.

69. WHAT A WONDERFUL WORLD
(George David Weiss and Bob Thiele—as "George Douglas")

I GOT INVOLVED with Harvey and Bruce's annual Nakoma neighborhood play, *Twelfth Night*. I provided part of the musical accompaniment along with the accomplished and fabulous Crellin Johnson. We put on a remarkably good production every year. I also befriended a bunch of new moms, and we had lovely playdates with the kids. One particular friend, Amy Kruger, and her daughter, Anna Kay, joined Emily and me at an east side ballet studio for their "Big Feet, Little Feet" program. It was an idyllic time, and Amy and I got into better shape, stretching and dancing with the budding ballerinas.

I would practice piano, and Emily would dance among the slatted shadows of my sunny studio, no doubt honing her learned skills from ballet class. She had a doll inspired by the PBS series *Big Comfy Couch* and would spin in lazy circles with "Molly" while I played. I composed a piece for the occasion, "Molly's Dance," which leads off my *Be Careful How You Say Pianist* album. I can close my eyes and see her diminutive, blonde form pirouetting even today.

We enrolled Emily at Woodland Montessori Preschool. Our good friends, Jim and Ann Stanger, had two kids attending the prestigious school, and their daughter Margot was Emily's best friend from birth. It was a fantastic social and learning environment for Emily, and I also found a kinship with other parents and created lasting friendships with the staff.

Natasha Kassulke, a writer for *The Capital Times*, one of Madison's newspapers, did a feature article on me. It delved into my alcoholism, ongoing recovery, and musical rebirth from the edge. One of the photos that ran with the article was Emily sitting on my lap in my sunroom studio with headphones on. I was getting there. I was rediscovering the best of myself and leaving the worst behind.

My life was far from what I had pictured it would be ten years previous. I was the farthest thing I could be from being a rock star, but I was generating substantial income with music. One day, it truly surprised me when I slowed down enough to take stock in what was happening.

I had the newest technology available in my music studio on the sun porch in our home. I was composing and producing pieces of music for radio and television that were creative and successful. I played at least four and sometimes five and six times a week at hotels, resorts, and clubs. Giada's was a packed house for almost every show. Mare brought along a wonderful coworker, Kimmie Vernon, who started joining us to create soaring three-part harmonies that made something fresh and exhilarating every night. I wrote songs with Harvey and played with him and Bruce in the newly monikered Mike and the Tall Boys. I played shows as a duo with my lifelong friend, Michael John Ripp. And every year, we'd make the pilgrimage to Baudette for music, friendship, and fishing. It was never the same lineup, but we always had a fabulous time. I played in some configuration up there at least once, sometimes three, four, and five times a year, for consecutive years from 1992 to 2002.

In October 1993, I had been close to death from substance abuse, and now just a few short years later, with Robin's love and support, I had a prosperous, blue-collar music career that wasn't what I had set out to do all those years ago but was fulfilling nonetheless. Our lives never turn out the way we planned, but a major key to happiness is embracing what we have and being grateful for every moment. None of this would be possible if I were still drinking. At the very least, I would be divorced and trying to scrape out an existence. More likely, I would be dead from liver failure.

MICHAEL MASSEY

Instead, I was a father, a husband, still a performer, and looking forward to improving on all of them every day.

I was no longer rubbing elbows with rock stars, wondering what ceiling I was looking at as I pried my eyes open in the morning. My life was no longer hanging on to that out-of-control train's caboose. I was learning how to live. I was learning how to love more deeply than I ever imagined. And I had sobriety to thank.

I'M LEARNING

I'm learning the difference between holding a hand
And chaining a spirit that I don't understand.
I'm learning that love doesn't mean hanging on
But framing a moment spent to cherish again.

I'm learning that kisses have no guarantee.
And presents aren't promises, the best gifts are free
I'm learning that rainbows, castles in the air
Fairy tales and dragons are hiding somewhere

I'm learning to build all my roads on today.
Tomorrow's never certain for the plans I have made
So tend your own garden, decorate your soul.
Realize the difference between lonely and alone.

I'm learning I'm someone worthy and strong
Greeting every sunrise, my heart filled with song.

70. THE MUSIC MAN
(Meredith Willson)

The Capital Times Thursday, May 8, 1997
Wisconsin State Journal

MUSIC MAN MASSEY VERY GLAD TO TALK ABOUT HIS RECOVERY
By Natasha Kassulke

Who's in rehab this week? Tabloid fodder, or a fact of life?

Michael Massey, 38, says stories of musicians turned alcoholics or drug addicts aren't as uncommon as they should be.

But what is uncommon is when a musician actually wants to go public with his story.

Massey doesn't want to preach, but he does hope that hearing about his personal hell will prevent someone else from taking his path.

"I lost my ego when I lost alcohol more than three years ago," Massey says. "And it's therapeutic to talk about it now."

Massey eases into the topic of his addictions at first. But then he starts to open up as Emily, his 17-month-old daughter, bounces between him and her Barbie doll.

Massey's life wasn't always as sweet as this scene in his tidy east-side home. "There's nothing wrong with alcohol until it starts controlling your life," he says. "And that's the story of my life."

Massey started drinking as an East High School student. A few beers before dances seemed innocent enough.

But as the pressures to perform got greater, he turned to the bottle more often. By the time he was in his 20s, Massey enjoyed widespread local and moderate regional success in two bands: Chaser and Boys in White.

Chaser was born as a hard rock band in 1977.

"It was a band that should have made it," Massey says. "It missed its timing. We were fighting punk, disco, power pop."

Atlantic Records took a chance on them, though, and spent $35,000 for Chaser to record a demo in New York.

"I thought we'd be signed," Massey says. "But we weren't. I beat myself up now, thinking that maybe it was because I wasn't as good as I could have been because of alcohol."

Massey said there were other opportunities to court labels in Los Angeles. "But I was the lead singer and the front person, so when I wasn't on, sometimes the record labels wouldn't look beyond that," he says.

In 1983 Chaser disbanded. Massey was playing solo piano when he was asked to join Boys in White.

"In Boys in White, I started drinking bad," he says. "I was showing up for gigs with pints of brandy."

Like Chaser, Boys in White had their chances. They even played "Star Search."

"Everyone was playing to the tape on 'Star Search' except me," he recalls. "I had to play live. Alcohol made me so arrogant; I wasn't myself."

In 1988 Massey left the band and slipped into self-pity and nearly empty bars. During what he now calls "the fog" from 1987 to 1993, he met Robin Valley.

In 1989, during a rare sober moment, he proposed. Robin accepted. But what she didn't accept was the alcohol.

"I wasn't a violent drunk," Massey says. "But I was an insensitive one."

Robin gave him chances to get sober, but when he settled on a quart of brandy a day, she kicked him out. Massey moved into a rough Madison neighborhood. He lived on brandy for breakfast, lunch and dinner.

"Then on October 13, 1993, I looked outside and saw people gathering around a burning car," he says. "I wondered what I was doing with my life and how I ended up there."

He called Robin and told her he was quitting. Although she had heard that before, this time Massey meant it.

He went to a hospital to dry out. He spent another two weeks at NewStart and six months in Alcoholics Anonymous.

Emily was born on the second anniversary of his sobriety.

Now more than three years after giving up alcohol, Massey is resurrecting his music career. He's part of a new and yet unnamed rock band that will include former Chaser guitarist Mike Ripp, plus bassist Jim Ripp, drummer Bill Erickson and singers Mare Petrowitz and Kimmie Vernon.

Massey also supports his business, Massongs, with radio and TV commercial work for companies such as Unity Health Plans and The Janesville Gazette. His work for them won him two ADDY Awards for best musical score. And he has a following for his warm, Neil Diamond-like voice at Giada's Pizza Pub in Wisconsin Dells, where he performs regularly.

Every now and then, Massey says he has a craving for alcohol. "But that temptation goes away when I think of the hell I went through," he says. "I want my epitaph to read: He kept trying to get better. Life is so sweet, sober."

71. 1999

(Prince)

IT WAS LATE SATURDAY NIGHT, and I was doing a vocal track to my song, "Tears Disappear," at Randy's Recording with Randy Green. I wasn't quite there on the delivery yet, and we were doing multiple takes when my baby pager went off to call Robin. She was due any day with our second child. She said her water had broken and that I should come home so we could ready ourselves for the trip to the hospital. I said I'd be right there and hung up the phone. I looked at Randy and said, "One more take."

That was the one.

Robin and I went to The Birthing Center at Meriter Hospital and settled in. Unlike Emily's entrance into the world, surrounded by family and friends, it was just us this time, calmly anticipating our new addition.

We walked slow, deliberate laps around the floor as Robin's contractions got closer together, a quiet time so deeply filled with love and a feeling of companionship that is only known through years together. Back in the room, she said she needed to use the restroom and, once there, told me I'd better call the nurse because "things were starting to happen." We helped her to bed, and it happened at light speed and slow motion, all at once.

On April 25, 1999, at 8:07 a.m., Anna Rose Massey, named after two of her great-great-grandmothers, entered the world in dramatic fashion.

The doctor was all smiles when she came into the room, and the delivery went quickly and smoothly, but I saw her smile turn to a guarded panic when our child, blue and unmoving, came into her hands. She worked feverishly, untangling the umbilical cord wrapped twice around the baby's neck, cutting the cord, and whisking my child away. Standing frozen and mute, I turned my attention to Robin and realized that a copious amount of blood was pouring from her. I asked the nurse if that was normal, and all of a sudden, there was controlled chaos in the room around me as I was pushed aside so the nurse could attend to Robin. In a state of surreal panic, I wondered if I would lose both of them as I stood back and watched, eyes darting back and forth like a tennis match. The conspicuous absence of a baby's cry hung over the room. After what seemed like an eternity, I was allowed to step up and hold Robin's hand just as Anna registered her outrage at being taken from the only warm, dark place she had ever known. Tears of gratitude and joy filled our eyes.

Faced with the unthinkable, I realized later that I had reacted with complete calm. First of all, I had no control over the situation, and getting hysterical certainly wouldn't have helped. Second, a clear head and the growing stability of my sobriety allowed me to grasp the gravity of the situation and answer it appropriately. I was living life fully, present in every moment.

We settled into having four people in the family.

It soon became apparent our perfect little bungalow was on the small side for a family of four. After Anna was out of the bassinet stage and into a crib, we would have to reconfigure things a bit. We talked about moving our bedroom into the smaller room Emily had acquired and giving the larger bedroom to the two girls. All of their toys—OMG, all of their toys—would have to be moved into the dining room.

"If we move our bed into Emily's room, it should fit sideways on the far end."

"I'll have to crawl over you every night to get into bed, but we'll make it work."

"The crib and Em's bed will have plenty of space in our room."

"And the rocking chair should work, too, unless we read to them in the living room and then carry them into bed."

"No, I want the rocking chair in their room."

"Okay, but don't forget about the changing table. We'll have to move the toys and the toybox."

"Where?"

"The dining room?"

"There's nowhere else?"

"No."

"Where are we going to put the dining room table?"

"It can stay. There'll just be toys around it and underneath and against the walls."

"What about the dining room chairs?"

"What about them?"

"Will they be functional?"

"There's no room for our dresser in the small room."

"Well, it will fit, but the door won't open all the way, or enough."

"Really? Will it fit in the closet?"

"No."

"Can it stay in the girls' room?"

"No."

"Is there room in the hallway?"

"No."

"Maybe it will have to be in the basement."

"I'm not having my dresser in that shithole of a basement."

"Oh, come on, it's not that bad."

"It is that bad. It smells like a musty ashtray."

"I'm sorry."

"No, it's fine, just not for my clothes."

"Maybe we can move my dignity to where I can have access."

This quasi-fictitious account takes the place of numerous conversations along those lines. We were amenable to making it work because our home was filled with love.

72. MONEY
(Roger Waters)

NO CREDIT IS WORSE than bad credit, and we had both.

While playing in Baudette for a week with Michael John Ripp in June, I got a call from Robin saying she had found a house. Through my sister Joni, we discovered that her lifelong friend Heidi's mother was selling her home, which hadn't been listed yet. What? My first thought was that we would never be able to get a mortgage. In those days, our credit was in the toilet. I wasn't that far removed from cleaning up my bad checks written for booze with collection agencies, and while we were doing modestly okay financially, we didn't have a financial footprint. Since we'd been married, we didn't have credit cards or any debt and had paid for most things with cash. It was a comfortable, stress-free way of getting on our feet

I went to see the house when we got back, and it was a beautiful home in a great neighborhood just two blocks from East High School. We set about trying to get the money to make it a reality and were turned down by two Madison banks. A friend of Robin's brother worked for Wells Fargo in Janesville, and we hoped a family connection would help. It didn't. We were too big a risk for a bank.

Kimmie Vernon (Lockwood) and I had become the best of friends after meeting at Giada's in the Dells, and through her, Robin and I met Kelly Maki (Gorton), a delightful, charismatic young woman who had marched in the University of Wisconsin band with Kim. Kelly's dad worked at M&I Bank and, after hearing of our troubles securing a mortgage, said she'd ask him about it. The next day she said to call her dad. No promises, but he thought he could make it happen for us!

We drove up to the bank, exhausted from being repeatedly rejected, with little hope of success. Dale Maki ushered us back to his office, and we sat down. Right away, his easy, laid-back demeanor felt different. After a few questions, he was aware of the difficulty of the task and set about looking at options. Dale worked hard at finding a program that would work for us and didn't quit, looking at file after file. We dared to hope. He opened a file, was about to put it down, and looked again. He opened it fully on his desk and said, "Here we go."

Thanks to the tenacious Dale Maki finding a low-income, first-time buyer program for us, we moved on July 31, 1999, the hottest day of the year, into the stone Cape Cod on Dayton Street that would be our home for the next twenty-two years. It had been less than two months since Robin had first looked at the house.

Most of the good things that have happened in my life are due to the singular nature of my wife's courageous intention. When she wants to make something happen, it happens.

73. ALL THE SMALL THINGS
(Tom Delonge)

YOU CAN'T QUIT USING for someone else. It has to come from within. And the desire to change has to be more powerful than the tendency to continue with the status quo. It's easier and more comfortable to stay in a world that's fuzzy around the edges than to be faced with hard reality. To get sober for someone doesn't get to the root of the problem. All of the best intentions to get clean for your loved ones are most frequently not enough, and then you are in danger of blaming them for failing to deliver on a promise—a vicious, destructive cycle.

When my brother Keith gently suggested I was going to need treatment, it was a course of action that hadn't remotely occurred to me. As I thought about it, internalized it, I began to feel like a weight was lifting off my shoulders. All of my failures to change in the previous years seemed like the preamble to a successful attempt. When I finished writing my short essay ending with the line, "I look forward with trepidation and excitement to embark upon this Boot Camp for Life," I looked up from the page a different person. I had flipped my switch. I felt my blood pressure relax. Drinking alcohol was no longer an option for me. It was just not an option.

It was that simple.

I was going to move forward, out of the prison of substance abuse. I had that power. You have that power. I was going to embrace this unknown path into treatment and therapy and give it my very best, but the overriding sentiment was that I was through drinking. I was done. Forever. And I was excited and happy about it. Flip. The. Switch. I don't believe this philosophy contradicts AA's "one day at a time" mantra. I believe it makes one day at a time easier.

I wish I could find it for everyone who's struggling. I'm certain it's different for each person, but it's there to be discovered. It is a calm revelation that unburdens the soul. It's not your fault you're an addict; you have a disease. A disease that affects your friends and loved ones as badly or worse than it affects yourself. But in that quiet, resolved mindset, you have the power to change, to heal, to love life again.

As the Valium gradually left my bloodstream and my appetite returned in treatment, the world came rushing back into the black hole I had created in the throes of my addiction. And with it came a craving to achieve clarity. I was bone-weary of needing alcohol to function, of a foggy consciousness, of chemically induced bravado. I began celebrating small victories, things a normal, healthy person takes for granted dozens of times daily. Things that, for me, symbolized an awakening, a rebirth, a consummation of rejoining the world after staring into the void:

Remembering clearly the events of the previous evening.
The smoky aroma of strong, fresh coffee brewing.
Stomach rumbling at the prospect of a hot breakfast.
Brushing my teeth without gagging.
Noticing a sunbeam pouring in the window, dust specks giving it shape.
Breathing a little more deeply.
Effortless balance.
Setting the alarm and rewarding yourself with a luxurious nap.
Sleeping more fully and deeply through the night.
Flavors bursting to life.
Feeling the sun on your face and the breeze in your hair.
Lingering on a good memory.
Not freaking out while being followed by a cop.
Finding the words and saying them rapidly, confidently, and coherently.

Reflexes and reaction times getting faster and more precise.
The "good sore" of muscles after stretching and working them.
Feeling stronger.
The sex. Oh, the sex! Vibrant nerve endings.
Being on time.
Not being able to put a book down.
Marveling at the wonder in the eyes of a child.
Driving with the windows open, singing at the top of your lungs.
Staying on task.
A kiss.
Skin a healthy, rosy hue.
Eyes clear and white.
Smiling.

Small victories carried me further down the path toward lasting sobriety.

I questioned the philosophy of reliving horrible events from your past as a deterrent to drinking and instead thought that positive motivation would be a much better way. This world is woefully devoid of positive reinforcement. Productivity in every industry, every facet of modern life, would soar if there was praise for a job well done instead of hammering on what was wrong. Correcting mistakes would be easier if there was constructive criticism mixed with kudos. It's no different with addiction. Counting your blessings with a clear mind and an open heart beats the hell out of constantly being forced to remember mistakes and lapses in character. Greeting each day anew and feeling alive is far preferable to recalling when and how many times the specter of death stopped just short of knocking on your door.

So, find your switch and flip it.

It really was that simple for me.

Flipping the switch takes the need for white-knuckle willpower out of the equation.

74. THUNDERSTRUCK
(Angus Young and Malcolm Young)

ROBIN AND I SPENT New Year's Eve 1999 at home. It was one of very few I hadn't performed somewhere for more than two decades. At midnight, just in case the world ended at "Y2K," we were naked in our hot tub on the patio of our new house, watching fireworks light up the sky from downtown Madison and creating our own.

Robin's good friend, Kay Drew, worked for Brad Bensman and Bensman Advertising, an agency for whom I had done extensive music production work for the past few years. She called and said they were looking for music for a radio and television campaign for New Balance stores. In my new Dayton Street project studio, we talked about tempo, energy, and genre, and I said I'd give it a shot. I hung up the phone, picked up a guitar, and started strumming. In one of those magical moments that songwriters hold so dearly, I literally sang their tagline on the first attempt. I ran it a couple of times and thought, "It couldn't be that good that easily." I called her back after fifteen minutes and said, "Listen to this." I put the phone down and played and sang it into the receiver. I put the guitar down, picked up the phone, and said, "Well?" fully expecting her to say it was nice but then give me some more direction to go back to the drawing board.

She said, "That's it!" It ran in thirty-three markets from coast to coast for many years, and Robin had a cameo in the TV spot.

MORE

The next few years were a whirlwind of life. My role as stay-at-home dad had expanded to taking Emily to Woodland Montessori Preschool a year earlier, but now I had Anna in tow. Emily attended the morning session, and noon pickup became a social event for all of us adult-human-contact-starved parents. When the majority of your conversation is directed at a toddler, intellectual stimulation is at a premium. We shared parenting tips and told stories of our pasts, making sure each other knew we weren't entirely defined by the bags under our eyes, our disheveled hair, and workout clothes wardrobe. There was a shared surrender of fashion and vanity, and we wore it well.

Robin went back to school to get her nursing degree. She had been an administrator in occupational healthcare and was unhappy in the job. She wanted to help people, which is what she was born to do. I was playing extensively at the Kalahari Resort in Wisconsin Dells to help fund the endeavor. In a series of calculated business successes, Todd Nelson, the owner of Giada's, had parlayed his nightclub and restaurant holdings into the Ramada Raintree Resort and then the world-class Kalahari Resort. I owe a debt of gratitude for Todd's support through the years. He provided a steady, well-paying gig to get Robin through nursing school.

Emily graduated from Woodland and entered kindergarten at Emerson Elementary School in 2001. The morning of September 11 dawned crisp and cloudless. There is a special shade of blue in September, somehow deeper and more brilliant than any other time of year. We excitedly walked Emily to her new school and mingled with the unbridled energy of the playground. After seeing that she got in the right line to be herded into the building, Robin, Anna, and I leisurely walked the five blocks home and I commented more than once on the beauty of the day.

When we arrived, I turned on the computer to see the first images of smoke coming from the North Tower on AOL's homepage. Speculation was that a small plane had crashed into it and conflicting reports abounded. To our horror, we turned on the TV just in time to see the second plane hit the South Tower in real time. Everyone remembers the anguish they felt when they saw the news. It is a day that transcends history.

MICHAEL MASSEY

My brother Kevin was a frontline worker for the American Red Cross. An ordained Lutheran pastor, he was part of a team that travelled around the country offering comfort to victims of natural disasters and mass casualty incidents. Following the attack, he found himself at ground zero, helping emergency responders and delivering blessings and last rites to the unfortunate victims of the disaster, many times just fragments of human remains.

After speaking to him while he was standing below ground level on a mobile phone amidst the abominable annihilation and hearing the sadness, conviction and resolve in his trembling voice, I wrote the song "Time To Go Home" to honor his selfless, heroic contributions and echo the emotions of a stunned nation.

Time To Go Home

Sometimes I look inside myself
Questions reaching to the edge of sanity
Walk blindly down the hallway
Outstretched fingers searching for the light

Time for the little one's lullaby
Oh it's time to find another lost soul
It's time to let the memory come back to me
Yeah it feels like it's time to go home

Grey days and broken sidewalks
I feel the scars of earth and sky and shattered minds
The world is cracked and reeling
I keep looking for the pieces to make me whole again

It's time to put a little road between us
Oh it's time to find a life o' my own
It's time to open up my eyes and learn to breathe
Yeah it feels like it's time to go home

MORE

Can you hear my thoughts
Do you know my number
Can you feel my heart beat
Do you know my name

I feel like another one got away
But I feel like I'm not alone
I'm feelin' strong and tall and I wanna say
I feel like it's time to go home

Time for the little one's lullaby
Oh it's time to find another lost soul
It's time to let the memory come back to me
Yeah it feels like it's time to go home

It's time to put a little road between us
Oh it's time to find a life o' my own
It's time to open up my eyes and learn to breathe
Yeah it feels like it's time to go home

75. BUTTERFLIES
(Kacey Musgraves, Luke Laird, and Natalie Hemby)

IN RAY BRADBURY'S STORY, A Sound of Thunder, also known as the Butterfly Effect, time-machine travel came with explicit rules not to stray from the path provided. One unfortunate soul strayed from the path and accidentally killed a butterfly, and the entire course of history was forever altered.

So it goes for all of us every day. Life is a series of decisions and events, each one affecting what comes next. In September 2003, I was enlisted by my friend and colleague in the advertising world, Billy Nahn, to contribute songs for a musical he was writing. The decision to say yes would have enormous, far-reaching implications, even years later.

Billy wanted to bring in an accomplished friend to help stage the show. W. Earle Smith was a world-class ballet dancer and had moved back to Madison to become the artistic director of Madison Ballet, a classical ballet company in the Balanchine tradition. Earle and I hit it off immediately and proceeded to block out the show. He brought in an accomplished East Coast singer-performer to take the lead female role, and we started rehearsals with yours truly standing in for the male role, a fish completely out of water. After a while, Earle reluctantly resigned from being an active participant in the show because life and growing the School of Madison

Ballet was proving too time-consuming. Emily would enroll at the school and dance for years. The esteemed performer Earle brought in found a well-paying theater gig and also took her leave. In January 2004, we started auditioning new female leads, and Billy brought in an incredibly talented young woman named Joy Dragland. She was fantastic! We offered her the part immediately, and she said she'd have to see if it fit into her schedule and that she'd get back to us.

Meanwhile, Anna had enrolled in Woodland. There was a new playground supervisor, a young woman recently removed from the University of California Berkeley. She had moved back home to pursue other interests. In the years since, it never ceases to amaze me how Francie Phelps and I were friends from the moment we met. There was an ease that belied our age difference, and a couple of days later, she asked if I wanted to see her friend in a cabaret show downtown at a new place called the Slipper Club. Little did we know that shortly after that, we would both be members of the troupe. Her friend Joy Dragland was the principal performer. It's a small world. We met at the show. It was a raucous romp, and we had a fabulous time. Joy came to a table read a few days later and said she was too busy to commit to doing the musical, but would I consider playing for her cabaret show? I couldn't say yes fast enough. Her talent was fascinating, and besides, I had been itching to branch out from my "piano bar in the Dells" mode. For eight weeks, I accompanied Joy on piano for her performances while the others in the ensemble sang to pre-recorded tracks. I had to take a night off to play a songwriter's showcase that had been booked for months, and when I returned the following week, Joy had recruited a full band. The Mad Cabaret would go on to sold-out Thursdays for three solid years, with the line to get in the building stretching around the corner.

76. CABARET
(John Kander and Fred Ebb)

OUR EMCEE IS the irascible Pierce Bottoms. He of acerbic wit, biting sarcasm, and timely progressive social commentary, usually adorned in blue eye shadow, a see-through aquamarine robe, and a speedo.

An average evening might go something like this:

Pierce opens the show belting out "Cabaret" with a quick segue into Elton John's "Bitch is Back," delivered with his unique brand of flamboyance, joy, and aplomb. The band, The Slingbacks, playing with reckless abandon, is comprised of John (don't call me Johnny) Velvet on guitar; Bongo Gigolo on percussion; Mr. Pickles on bass; Ronnie Beaver on drums; and yours truly, Fabrizio, on keys.

My character, created by Joy Dragland (Honey Lingus), is an Italian playboy who takes himself too seriously, wears an untucked tux that looks like last night's and slept in, accessorized with motorcycle chains instead of bling. I delight in putting on the guyliner and getting into character.

Pierce negotiates the production like the pro he is, offering his take on current events and problems of the day while introducing performers as they drift on and off the stage in a fabulous cavalcade. Klitzy Licious (she later changed her surname to Normus) handles singing the Disco; Ivana Getchakokov (Francie) smolders her way through The Go-Go's, Bangles, or Nora Jones; and Neil Mother Fucking Diamond (affectionately known as NMFD) gyrating to "Kentucky Woman," with very pregnant hillbilly women in straw hats and overalls smoking, drinking beer, singing backup, and getting into a fight over his attentions. Frank Sinatra flies us to the moon; Billy Idol officiated a "White Wedding;" and of course, the star of the show, Honey Lingus, tenuously appears onstage on roller skates singing "Brand New Key." Dancer Anita Johnson graces numerous numbers with accompaniment and appropriate costume changes, boxing gloves for "Hit Me With Your Best Shot," and sexy lingerie when the song calls for it. And occasionally, a guest artist's strip tease goes farther than planned and maybe too far for city ordinance.

It was mayhem. Elegant chaos. The band would go in early and learn six to eight new songs to be performed that night. The audience, the atmosphere, and the pheromones in the air were part of the show, and you never knew what would happen next. We had guest performers. Among others, they included The Dudes in Suits, Nyanyika, Olive Talique, and a traveling troupe from San Francisco that we had to give the hook to because they droned bad poetry on and on. The Slipper Club itself was a part of the show. With its curtained-off back room, it felt illicit to be there. It was fishnets, platforms, and makeup. It was wigs, fabric, and sex. The dressing room was light bulb-studded mirrors, costumes being flung to the corners during quick changes, and varying degrees of undress at any given moment. It was fantastic.

One negative that transpired from the show was relapsing on smoking cigarettes (you could still smoke in clubs in Wisconsin when the show premiered, and you could cut a block of it out of the air with a knife and hand it to someone at the Slipper Club). I had quit for four years. One night while performing, I noticed backlit smoke coming out of my mouth while singing. I came to the misguided conclusion that I was smoking anyway, so why not buy a pack? Robin was justifiably furious.

After the magnificent show had run its course, Francie Phelps and I would go on to perform as a duo to the present day, and she is one of my dearest friends on earth. We booked Thursdays at The Ivory Room, an intimate piano bar in downtown Madison just three blocks north of the Slipper Club, and held court for years. The Ivory Room became its own scene, with regular patrons adopting a family atmosphere. Bruce Geiger from Johnny and the Nakomans and Mike and the Tall Boys fame would join us to create soaring three-part harmonies as the audience sang along.

The Cabaret represented a personal rebirth as an artist. It was an official transition from the stay-at-home dad for very young children to stylish human. It energized me in a way that had been missing since my Chaser days. It was a reclaiming of youth, of being a part of something magical. It fueled my creativity and expanded my sphere of friends exponentially. I released my first album, *Be Careful How You Say Pianist*, with thirteen instrumental piano songs, recorded while living on Erie Court but only then mixed and mastered.

A composer's greatest reward is the knowledge that your creation has affected someone's life. I have gotten emails from all over the world thanking me and saying that the music on *Pianist* provided comfort in times of need. It is far more valuable than money. The most downloaded track on the album is my version of Pachelbel's Canon in D. It was titled "Apologies to Pachelbel," not only for the performance but also because it's in the key of C.

Concurrently with the Cabaret, I was starting to write a new slate of pop and rock songs with the hope of another album on the horizon. "Star" captures the feeling of our magical Thursday night escapades:

STAR

All alone in a crowded dressing room
Waiting for the show
Slow-motion voices echoing
(You gotta get out of this town, girl, if you wanna go far, if you wanna be a star)

Eyeliner and a borrowed lipstick
In a champagne glow
Feather boa wrapped around your instinct
It's time to go

MORE

Moonlighting on a one-way street
Recognizing faith is all you need

You stand outside yourself, watching every night
Twirl the microphone
Smoke and mirrors do a tango with the spotlight
Swirling vertigo

Moonlighting on a one-way street
Recognizing faith is all you need
Slow-motion voices echoing
Don't stop me, help me to believe

Rumor has it there's a record label guy
In the second row

77. I WAS LOST
(Anna Massey)

A PHENOMENON THAT BEARS scrutiny here is Anna Massey's ability to improvise at an unbelievably young age. I would play a chord progression, and Anna would observe her surroundings or how she was feeling and just make up lyrics and a melody on the spot to complement the music. She recorded her debut EP, "I Was Lost," at age five. She sold copies in California and Europe. One memorable night at the Kalahari Resort in the Dells illustrates her abilities:

As I finished the song, I looked at my daughter to see if she was ready to come up and join me. She smiled and nodded. We hadn't rehearsed because you can't rehearse complete improvisation. I introduced her to the crowd, "Ladies and gentlemen, please welcome Anna Massey to the stage." She slowly sauntered between the tables and stepped up in front of the piano. The sparse, waterpark-fatigued audience half-heartedly applauded, not much caring about anything, let alone a kid taking the stage.

Five-year-old Anna grabbed the mic like a seasoned pro. She surveyed the audience with a casual dismissal and looked to me to start her accompaniment. I smiled and launched into a boogie piano groove and sat back and waited.

She started by swaying to the tempo, holding the mic flippantly, and looking around the room for inspiration. Then she just started singing clearly and confidently. She sang about the room. She sang about her dad playing the piano. She sang about what she had for dinner. She sang with a powerful tone and then dynamically soft when her story warranted.

The lounge where I performed was part of an open-air lobby in the resort, and you could hear the music throughout the cavernous facility, and people started streaming in. As the crowd grew larger, Anna was unaffected. She might have sung for an hour if I didn't get her attention to wrap it up.

Very quickly, it was standing room only. People lined the back of the substantial room, and all the tables were full. Families were wide-eyed with wonder at the charisma exhibited by the pint-sized powerhouse. I was loving the moment, knowing what was coming at the conclusion of Anna's performance. As I put an exclamation point on the end of the piece, there was the briefest silence, and then the room erupted in cheers and applause. It was an overwhelming response, but my daughter just smiled and shrugged, put down the mic, and walked off stage. No big deal.

She would perform with me many times in many venues through the years, until she outgrew her innocence. It's a source of great pride and happiness.

78. ATTACK OF THE DELICIOUS
(Michael Massey)

IT TOOK MORE THAN two years to write, record the tracks, and mix the album *Attack of the Delicious*. A little more than ten years into my sobriety, I was able to stretch and grow in the songwriting process, and coupled with newer technology, different flavors and song structures began to emerge. Becoming familiar with the efficiency of working with thirty- and sixty-second increments for advertising gave the songs a streamlined feel. Efficient and trim, every note counted. I wanted to work with Mike Ripp and Tony Cerniglia to flesh out the record. They were lifelong friends and were "my" guitarist and drummer. I compiled a demo CD of the songs I wanted to put on the album, and Tony took it with him on a trip to Jamaica to listen and strategize. He liked what he heard and signed on to play drums and co-produce with me.

Ripper, Tony, and I were all recording with the digital audio workstation Pro Tools, which allowed us to work individually in our home studios on tracks and then integrate them later at Tony's Spike Studios. Sometimes we'd go into Spike and work together or if I wanted someone else to turn the knobs while I was concentrating on a vocal delivery. It was like riding a bike working with these guys again. In the Chaser days, we had a flow of creativity that seemed endless. We experimented, improvised, and perfected. That process with a sober mind and healthy body took me places

MORE

I didn't know I could go. To approach inventiveness with a new lucidity was a rush that exceeded any high drugs or alcohol could provide. I was delighted with the arrangements and musical parts Mike and Tony were contributing. It was raising the music to another level.

All of this was being done between being at home with the girls, walking them to and from school, attending Emerson PTO meetings, picking up a few ad projects, and playing various gigs around southern Wisconsin, as well as every Thursday with Francie at The Ivory Room. I was living a full and rich life, something that was only facilitated by sobriety. The sheer energy required to keep my head above water with all the balls in the air would be inconceivable to my addict self.

We got Stevie Johnson involved in the engineering and mix process for the album, so the whole damn Chaser family was back together. Stevie has some of the best ears in the business and lent considerable audio expertise to the end result. Mark Whitcomb, owner and operator of DNA Studios in Madison, mastered the record and gave it the final polish to completion.

On February 10, 2006, we played an album release show for *Attack* at the High Noon Saloon in Madison. I called in every favor and contacted all the press and media I had known throughout the years, and we sold it out. I brought in Madison's best and brightest musicians to bring the album to life, and my good friend Jack LeTourneau, an accomplished Chicago record producer, videoed the show. We had a thirteen-piece band and recreated every note of the record, one of the proudest moments of my life. My parents came to the show, and we set them up with VIP seats in the balcony. They had never been fans of the rock bands I had been in and always thought I should do something "legitimate" for work and stop chasing dreams. But when they saw the show and the production and the size and reaction of the audience, it was like a light bulb came on. They couldn't believe it. My music became real to them that night, thirty years after my first club gig.

My good buddy John Urban produced the show and made it run like clockwork. Cabaret friend Gretchen Bourg (Anita Johnson) acted as production assistant, provided creature comforts, and thought of everything we might need. Thank you again.

The band consisted of my Chaser pals Tony C. on drums and Mike Ripp on guitar, with Stevie Johnson doing front-of-house sound. Cabaret alums Jay Moran (John Velvet) on guitar, James "Pie" Cowan (Bongo Gigolo) on percussion, and Jessica Lee (Klitzy Licious) and Francie (Ivana Getchakokov) on backing vocals. World-class musicians and husband and wife team Chris Wagoner on violin and Mary Gaines on bass had tracked many an ad with me. My Dells partner Mare added to the backing vocals, and Kimmie Vernon reprised her role on the duet "One More Day." The single most talented man I know, Dave Adler, added keys. Randal Harrison Hoecherl was a touring musician and a parent from Woodland and joined Chris on violin. And Bob Westfall played a mean mandolin. We had rehearsed in segments, gradually melding the different facets of the music together. The night was a rousing success, and because it was so time-intensive to bring the music up to speed and play it with a professional polish, I paid the musicians very generously, running out of money before I paid Brenda Allen-Johnson for photography.

Sadly, when you pick the best musicians to play a show, their availability is limited. It was the only full show we played after all of that rehearsal. I believe that *Attack of the Delicious* is some of the best work of my life and has yet to see adequate exposure.

The album won Best Pop Album in the 2006 Madison Area Music Awards. Tony C., Emily, and Anna accompanied me on stage to accept the award.

79. AIN'T TOO PROUD TO BEG
(Norman Whitfield and Eddie Holland)

MY MOM NEVER MISSED a school function or performance by the girls. She loved every second of it. Her children and grandchildren were her legacy and proudest achievements, and she supported us enthusiastically. That September, she came to a school music performance at Emerson and looked terrible. Her color was gray, and she was weak. I called her later that night and asked if she was okay, and she said the doctors told her she had numerous problems. Her heart and liver were struggling.

Mom also fought with alcohol. Dad was traveling for work, so she was alone much of the time, including the night I went to try to intervene.

I called my mom and asked if I could pop over for a bit. Robin asked if I'd like her to come along, and I said it would probably be better if I went alone. I was going to talk to her about the amount she was drinking. She would sometimes call me in the evening, badly slurring her words, and would have no memory of the call the next day. Her health was suffering, and I was worried.

There was one lamp on in the modest room, and my mom hid in the shadows in her customary rocking chair where she had held growing grandchildren on her lap. I sat down and asked how she was doing. The doctors had told her that her liver was working too hard, not efficiently, and congestive heart failure was beginning. She had been diabetic for years, and adding these health concerns to the mix was devastating. I asked if there was a treatment plan, and she said there wasn't much they could do. I told her that I thought her drinking was a significant contributor to her troubles. She agreed.

In that dimly lit room, we talked about drinking. Although my parents were supportive of my efforts to get clean, they had kept their distance from the treatment facility during my stay. I suspect it hit too close to home. I asked her to quit. I said she was too young to surrender. There was so much left to do, so much love yet to give. She remained unmoving and quiet. I said I would do anything to help. After no response, I tearfully got on my knees and asked her to stop drinking so she could see her grandchildren graduate from high school, so that she could create new memories. I couldn't begin to fathom the depth of her despair when a single tear ran down her cheek as she slowly shook her head and said, "No."

Although my mom was immensely proud of her family, I suspect that unfulfilled aspirations finally caught up with her. She was salutatorian of her high school class and couldn't attend college because she was six months pregnant with me when she got her diploma. She could have done or been anything she desired in life and instead spent it lovingly supporting everyone else's dreams.

In late October, I got a frantic phone call from my father at two in the morning after I returned home from a gig. He said my mom was ill and I should get over there right away. When I arrived, my mom was listless and sitting on the floor. I asked if he had called 911, and he hadn't. I immediately directed him to do so. We got her to the sofa and tried to make her comfortable until the ambulance arrived. Sitting in the car waiting for the ambulance to head to the hospital, I asked my dad for a cigarette, effectively ruining two years of abstinence. I would smoke until 2014. My mom never came home again. She went from the hospital to hospice care.

My mom was in and out of consciousness when we visited her in hospice. I was scheduled to play Giada's on Friday night, but an inner voice told me to cancel the gig. It turned out to be one of the best decisions of my life. We went as a family, and my mom was in great spirits, conscious and lucid. Emily and Anna drew pictures for her, and we talked and laughed into the night. When we left, we all had a chance to tell her we loved her, and she returned the love only a mother and grandmother can give. That night she fell into a coma and never regained the light. The evening we spent with her was a priceless final gift from the woman who had given me life.

Nancy Dodge Massey passed away on November 1, 2006, fittingly, All Saints Day.

Rest softly, mom. You've earned it.

80. DO YOU HEAR WHAT I HEAR?
(Noël Regney and Gloria Shayne)

THE DEDICATION ON my Christmas album *The Present* reads, "Dedicated to Nancy Massey. May I have inherited one-tenth of your strength."

I had hatched the plan to record an instrumental piano Christmas album during the summer of 2006 while lying in the sun poolside at the hilltop home of Joe Hildebrandt, surrounded by friends and frolicking children. Knowing the length of time it takes to conceive, record, produce, and manufacture an album, I laid down the tracks in July and August for a Christmas release. It was sometimes difficult to find the right frame of mind.

Exactly one month after my mother's death, I played a show at Café Montmartre in Madison to release it. Here is the *Isthmus* critic's choice recommendation for the evening:

> *FRIDAY DECEMBER 1*
> *MUSIC*
> *Michael Massey*
> *Café Montmartre, 7 pm*
>
> *Michael Massey has been a vital member of the Madison's music scene since the late '70s as a member of Chaser, Boys In White,*

and more recently as a solo artist and key participant in the Mad Cabaret troupe. A pair of 2005 albums demonstrate his diverse nature: Be Careful How You Say Pianist is a laid-back set of solo piano instrumentals, and Attack Of The Delicious is a lush, highly produced pop-rock album with strings, synths, guitar, and Massey's weathered, slippery voice. Even more sides should be on display here as Massey celebrates the release of an instrumental Christmas album, The Present, featuring original arrangements of traditional holiday carols.

The day dawned cold and windy, and I was having an electric grand piano delivered to the club by my old friends at Forbes-Meagher music. The roads started getting precarious, and it was no easy task to get that piano up onto the stage at the Café, but Mike Sullivan is the best piano mover in history, so he came through. As I was parked in front of the club to unload some gear, I slipped on snow, hit the curb, and took a chip out of my kneecap. I didn't even realize it until days later.

I didn't know how successful the evening would be as I left after sound check to go home and shower and prepare for the show. I was hoping the weather wouldn't stop people from attending. December in Wisconsin can be a crap shoot. The CDs hadn't been delivered from the manufacturer until the day before, causing some panicked moments, so I was hoping the feeling of dread was my imagination.

My anxiety was unfounded as there was a line around the corner to get in. The show sold out, and I sold half of the inventory of a thousand CDs that night. I played an inspired show in that warm, inviting atmosphere and kicked off the Christmas season in style for all who braved the elements. Later that week, I had the Forbes folks deliver an acoustic grand piano to the set of *Urban Theater*, John Urban's music television show at the studios of WISC-TV. We taped the first of two Christmas specials that aired for years around the holidays. My dad would find immense pride in watching those specials, and I would find validation in his eyes.

81. COME AWAY WITH ME
(Norah Jones)

I MARK THE PASSING of time in the second half of the decade with our family vacations, our daughters growing older, and by losing loved ones. My parents couldn't afford to travel extensively during my childhood, and it's something I fervently wanted to provide for the girls. Strap in for a quick travelogue of the Massey family vacations:

We started our adventures by getting a hotel in downtown Chicago for a weekend here and there, exploring the city. Anna would accompany me on my late-night walks in Chicago, and memorably one night, we found the ESPN Zone and spent hours there while Robin and Emily wondered where we were.

In 2007, we stayed in a hotel right on the shore of Lake Superior at the canal in Duluth, Minnesota, and watched the iron ore boats, some more than a thousand feet long, come in from ports unknown. I was fascinated by the enormity of the vessels. One of the trip's highlights was taking a train with a steam locomotive up the north shore of Lake Superior.

In the summer of 2008, we traversed the country in our hastily purchased used Volvo and landed in Sedona, Arizona, for a fantastic time among the vortexes, red rock formations, and azure skies. A side trip to the Grand Canyon topped it off. Mika's album *Life in Cartoon Motion* was the soundtrack of the trip. Anytime I hear one of the songs, I can feel the Arizona sun.

Summer 2009 found us in the nation's capital, and we stayed at the historic Mayflower Hotel. We toured Ford's Theatre, found the tidal basin, and circled it at sunset to visit the Jefferson Memorial. We reverently visited the Vietnam, Korea, and WWII memorials; the Tomb of the Unknown Soldier; and Arlington National Cemetery, where Robin's uncle Bill McDonald was buried with full military honors. And we marveled at the Smithsonian Air and Space Museum. When we returned, Robin started a new job managing both the east and west pediatric clinics for UW Health. It was an enormous responsibility and a personal victory that came with a substantial raise.

82. FATHER AND SON
(Yussuf/Cat Stevens)

WHAT IS IT ABOUT a certain vintage man who has an aversion to doctors? Is it misguided immortality? Early in 2008, my dad complained about a sore in his mouth that wouldn't go away. Likely it had been an issue for months or even years, and he hadn't been to a doctor in at least a quarter century. When the discomfort became too much to bear, he reluctantly had it checked out. It was advanced oral cancer caused by years of tobacco and alcohol use. He was immediately scheduled for surgery. Bill Massey was clueless. He had no idea about the gravity of the situation. During preparatory appointments to ready him for what was to come, he repeatedly looked to Robin for clarification. And she was able to put it in language that was understandable to the rest of us. This was serious.

They took half his jaw, and the surgeon felt he had done the best job possible. He was optimistic it could be successful—if my dad would change his habits. Can a leopard change his spots? Bill Massey was sixty-nine years old. He had been smoking and drinking every day of his life for the previous fifty years. We discussed making changes, and he considered it. After a long convalescence in a nursing home, he was finally cleared to be released and bought cigarettes and brandy on the way home.

He was scheduled for an aggressive round of radiation, but his surgeon was disgusted, and the assisting doctors were angry that he was squandering their efforts and his chances for a longer life.

The rest of that year, I spent a great deal of time with my father. I took him to most of his appointments and watched many a ball game on a brand-new forty-two-inch HD TV that his siblings had bought him as a gift. I would bring dinner to him, and we'd sit in companionable silence while television paraded an endless array of drama, comedy, and sports in front of our preoccupied faces. We regularly had deep conversations, mostly reminiscing about his life, triumphs, and losses. We laughed but never cried. And we never talked about death, even though its shadow loomed ever closer. As the radiation ran its course, the doctors talked about a radical chemotherapy approach, but with the terrible side effects explained, my father opted against it. I was still making it out to the Ivory Room for Thursday nights with Francie and Bruce, but life revolved around my dad, and I was becoming severely depressed.

In November, even as his health deteriorated, Dad was extremely proud to cast his ballot for Barack Obama in the presidential election. Since his surgery, the majority of his nourishment had come via a feeding tube, but on Thanksgiving, which Robin and I have hosted for more than twenty years for family and friends, he enthusiastically ate a large holiday meal, one of the few for months prior and one of his last.

Bill Massey left the physical world on January 10, 2009, twenty-four days shy of his seventieth birthday. As with my mother, substance abuse played a large part in depriving us of more time with him. Especially aggrieved was his older brother Gary. No two brothers have ever been closer, and he safeguarded many of my father's secrets, even in death.

83. REFLECTIONS
(Holland-Dozier-Holland)

I HAD LOST BOTH PARENTS and my beloved paternal grandmother, Helen, in twenty-six months. That much loss of those closest to you pushes the reaction beyond grief into anesthesia. Since my siblings lived far away, caretaking and cleaning out my parents' home fell to me. It was a monumental undertaking, and I spent months sifting through their belongings, trying to decide what to keep for sentimental purposes and what could be donated or trashed. Every room, drawer, and cupboard were full. I sometimes stared at an object for an hour, reminiscing about its use or purpose. It was impossible to be ruthless in discarding the remnants of their lives. I was numb. Looking back now, my daughters and wife agree that I was in a deep depression for more than two years while caring for Dad and taking care of the business of death.

I could put on a brave face for gigs, but I was not myself. Thankfully, I wasn't tempted to relapse even in the darkest hours of that post-death desolation. Even in my dull despondency, I knew I would ruin my own life if I let down my guard to addiction. Ironically, as the house gradually became more vacant, I would go and sit alone in the silence and smoke cigarettes.

I had removed most of the furniture except for one chair, the rocker my mom had favored for so many years. I would sit late at night by the light of a solitary lamp, rocking slowly, almost imperceptibly, and let my memory wander. I would travel back to my earliest childhood and see my parents in the most vibrant of youth. I could put myself anywhere on the timeline and see and smell and taste history. It was an emotional cleansing that I sorely needed, and I slowly emerged from the fog.

Autumn found the utility company, Madison Gas and Electric, leaving a notice of discontinuation of service. This represented a quandary to me. First, I wasn't completely finished with cleaning and staging the house for sale. It didn't make sense to make the payments for service on an empty property, but there were still things to be done that would be impossible in the dark. Second, I wasn't sure I was ready to let go. Jeff Newman was CFO and treasurer of MG&E and a regular at The Ivory Room. He knew I had lost my dad and was settling the estate. I had written a poem one late, hushed night at the house that I shared with him:

THE ONLY CHAIR

The mail stopped coming, they disconnected the phone
Now it's just a house when it used to be a home
The walls are echo empty, family pictures taken down
Weeds between the sidewalk, a for sale sign on the lawn
But I still hear the laughter, feel the love that's hiding there
When I close my eyes and listen, rocking in the only chair
Now they're coming in the morning, put a notice on the door
They're turning off the power, there'll be no light here anymore
So, this will be the last time I can daydream late at night
To drift among the shadows, to talk to you and cry
You'll always be a part of me, a presence shining there

But I'll never be as close again as rocking in the only chair
MM 10-6-09

I will forever be grateful to Jeff and Madison Gas and Electric for the kindness shown to me in granting the power to remain on at minimal cost through that winter. It allowed me to keep the cocoon and continue healing.

I spent the rest of the winter and early spring finalizing my parents' house for sale. The economy was in the tank, and prospects were dim for a profit. The property wasn't sexy enough or inexpensive enough to attract first-time buyers, and the realtor feared it would go to short sale. After my father's death, I stopped making the mortgage payments, and the bank was running out of patience. After I had everything out and cleaned up, I still spent a lot of time in the house, mostly at night, just in a reminiscing state. It was comforting to go there, and I gradually came out of the cloud of my deep depression by working things out in the stillness.

84. ON BROADWAY
(Barry Mann and Cynthia Weil
in collaboration with
Jerry Leiber, and Mike Stoller)

OUR MOST EXCITING family vacation to date was scheduled for August 2010 in New York City. The plan was to drive to my brother Keith and his wife Adriana's house in Landing, New Jersey, and stay there while they took their annual trip to visit her mother in Romania. We would take a bus into the city every day. That didn't work out so well. After giving it a try on the first day, we reevaluated the process. The last bus ran at six at night, and we would spend too much time traveling and not enough exploring. We decided to get a room at The Metropolitan Hotel, a reasonably priced, hip hotel on West Broadway in Tribeca, where Harvey and I had stayed on an earlier trip. When we figured in the bus tickets, we'd be spending a bit more, but we'd be in the thick of things. We left our van at Keith's and took the bus downtown.

Adjoining the Metropolitan was the Metropolitan Café, owned and operated by Craig Bero, a classically trained actor who had moved to New York from northern Wisconsin. After receiving a master of fine arts degree at UW-Madison, he came to the city to find acting work. He gradually realized his passion was more culinary than Broadway. Craig adopted us as his pet project and showed us places and things an average tourist could only dream about behind the scenes in Tribeca. Craig was somewhat of a neighborhood celebrity, having owned a café across the street from the World Trade Center on 9/11. He had worked around the clock to help feed emergency responders in the aftermath. As a result, everyone knew him, and all doors were open. Robert Deniro was "Bobby," and legendary baller and coach of the Brooklyn Nets, Steve Nash, was a close pal. Craig is one of a kind.

I called Tony C. from the Statue of Liberty. When Chaser came in '81, we talked about visiting the statue, and he said at the time, "We'll be back." We never were. I called him to say I had finally made it.

We hooked up with an old pal, radio icon Marc Coppola and his wife, Elizabeth, for pizza and, the next day, visited his broadcast central command on Broadway. The Masseys did a station ID that aired in San Diego an hour later.

We walked everywhere. What is it about a city that makes miles seem insignificant on foot? We walked to Battery Park, Soho, Greenwich Village, St. Mark's Place, and the Bowery. We took a cab to Times Square, and I was amazed at how family-friendly the gritty area had become. It was like a Disney mall. At Earle's suggestion, Emily took a ballet class at Steps on Broadway. All in all, it was a trip to cherish for a lifetime. Oh, and my late-night walks? I was sneaking cigarettes, so I didn't ask anyone to come with me. I decided I would find the Hudson River at about midnight one night. I headed west from our corner of Chambers and West Broadway and, after a time, found a beautiful park with a great view of midtown up the shore and a gentle breeze coming across from Jersey. Getting back wasn't so idyllic. There are diagonal streets in lower Manhattan, probably left over from Gangs of New York Five Points days, and they're dark, with warehouses and brick buildings that seemed to inhale what little light was available. I walked for quite a while, taking wrong turns, and just as my blood pressure was starting to rise, I hit upon civilization. I returned the following night but didn't make the same mistake twice.

On our last day in Manhattan, Craig gave us hastily drawn directions on a napkin on how to take the subway under the river to Brooklyn and find a park with breathtaking views of the Brooklyn Bridge and the NYC skyline.

MORE

It turns out they were shooting a movie in the park, and we watched a few takes. It was a whirlwind, memorable night.

We left the bright lights behind and went back to Keith and Adriana's to spend the night before our cross-country trek home. I went over to check on my dad's house when we arrived home. The locks had been changed. The bank had taken possession. The chapter was over. It was time I rejoined the land of the living.

85. THE ENTERTAINER
(Scott Joplin)

THROUGHOUT THE PROCESS of settling my parents' estate and cleaning out and categorizing all of their earthly possessions, I had lost enthusiasm for booking gigs and promoting myself. The shows were becoming fewer. I still mustered Thursdays at The Ivory Room but didn't have the energy for much else. In 2009 Francie had started dating Josh Dupont, a talented and entrepreneurial southern Mississippi transplant who was co-founder of a dueling pianos entertainment company called Piano Fondue. Their star was rising, and I attended some of their raucous, raunchy, fun shows with her. In fact, they had taken over a club in the Dells, and the scene we had enjoyed for so many years was shifting to their brand of music and comedy.

It was such a departure from what I had tried to cultivate in my career. Where I had attempted to be polished and rehearsed, they jumped into requested songs, often for the first time, and if it crashed and burned, it was part of the fun. But it was seldom that they crashed and burned. The talent to conjure requests for an audience is a rare talent, and they did it masterfully.

Josh started hanging out at The Ivory Room on Thursdays and sat in to play once in a while and then started playing more regularly. We became fast friends. There was talk of me trying to do their show, but honestly,

I was terrified to try it. There was so much to learn. They had it down to a science, with tried and true comedic bits interspersed with a mountain of music. Secretly, I feared it would expose my inadequate repertoire compared to their vast catalog. I felt I could probably do it, but I'd need to reverse my philosophy of being an artist first and an entertainer second.

On New Year's Eve 2011, Robin and I had another rare date with no gig. We were going to walk down State Street, have a nice dinner, and head home. As we were window shopping, my phone rang. It was Josh. He asked if I was playing that night. When I said no, he asked, "Do ya wanna?" His partner was experiencing a health crisis, and they were booked at the sold-out Brink Lounge. It was now or never. I said yes, and I had about an hour to prepare. It was probably a good thing I didn't have a lot of time to worry about it.

I arrived with my three hundred-page three-ring binder full of song charts and got a crash course in some of the ground rules of the gig. Two grand pianos were set up facing each other in the center of the room with full PA and lighting. Josh Dupont is a master of the craft, so I was in good hands just occupying the seat opposite him. It was baptism by fire, and I performed just well enough to pull it off. It helped that Francie was bringing up requests she was sure I knew. There were so many songs I didn't know or didn't know well enough to try that I ended up crumpling the request slips and throwing them across the grand pianos at Josh. On break, we went through the remaining requests on the piano, and I got a set of material I could play. After that, I settled into the gig and enjoyed the pure entertainment aspect of dueling pianos. I held it together, had fun, and started a wonderful new chapter in my professional life.

The draw, energy, and sheer excitement of dueling pianos weren't lost on proprietors Jack and Julie Sosnowski, and the days of The Ivory Room as an intimate destination piano bar were coming to an end. One of the cruel realities of the music business at any level is its extraordinarily transient nature. Even the greatest scenes have a shelf life. I've advised many of my compatriots to enjoy the good times because they won't last. The world keeps movin' on. The key in music, as in life, is to recognize those magical moments as they happen and keep them forever in memory.

Jack and Julie decided to knock out the back wall, giving them State Street exposure and tripling the space. It was a gold mine. Working with Piano Fondue, it became the go-to downtown venue for a wild time. Thursday through Saturday nights, standing-room-only, raucous crowds request everything from classic rock to rap and everything in between and sing along en masse. The proximity to the University of Wisconsin lent a ready-made student population, and there was special debauchery reserved for Badger football Saturdays. These people had been drinking for hours before kickoff and found their way downtown after the game. The result was pandemonium.

When I speak of changing my philosophy, it refers to a paradigm shift in how I approach a performance. All my life, I prided myself on preparation. As an artist in Chaser and Boys in White, we rehearsed exhaustively to perform a choreographed show to the best of our abilities, night after night. As a solo singer-songwriter, it was the same. Playing with Piano Fondue and at The Ivory Room meant preparation in learning a vast music catalog, but you never knew what you would play next. You couldn't prepare for the unknown. Song requests come at you at blistering speed, and the show is high energy with no breaks. In many instances during a show, you would be playing songs you've never done before, flying by the seat of your pants and hoping that chord chart from the internet was close to accurate. It was all about the audience, not my ego. For so many years, I hated playing "Piano Man" or "Sweet Caroline." After seeing the joy those songs and others brought to an audience primed to sing along, it changed my way of thinking.

Once I was able to reconcile myself to the term "entertainer," it was liberating to play and have fun, with the sole purpose being the engagement of the audience. My skills as an artist improved exponentially, finding new influences, playing all genres of music, and adding some of the flamboyance and humor Piano Fondue taught me. It's a demanding gig that is ever-changing and updating, and I continue to learn every day.

86. VAMPIRES WILL NEVER HURT YOU
(Matt Pelissier, Ray Toro, Gerard Way, Frank Lero, and Mikey Way)

THE BUTTERFLY EFFECT is real. It happens every day to all of us, and only in retrospect do we see how daily decisions affect our long-term future.

Since meeting over the ill-fated musical years before, Earle Smith and I had cultivated a great friendship based on mutual admiration and shared interests. Emily had been a student of the School of Madison Ballet throughout, and I was privy to stand backstage and watch the energy of the productions from the wings. I have always loved everything about ballet. In a parallel dimension, I was (am) a dancer. I loved even peripherally being a part of it. I was thrilled when Earle wanted to set one of my piano pieces. In May 2011, I edited an existing piece to eight minutes, and he choreographed a wonderful, whimsical ballet to match. It was first performed in Austin, Texas, by former New York City Ballet soloist Michele Gifford and reworked for a performance at the Overture Center in Madison as part of Madison Ballet's *An Evening of Romance*. I played the 1926 nine-foot Steinway D grand piano live, onstage, with the accomplished and exquisite Genevieve Custer Weeks dancing the part. I was ecstatic! It ranks high as a milestone in my life, inching toward legitimacy as an artist and strengthening my self-worth.

Not long after, Earle and I were having lunch, and he mentioned he was going to fulfill a dream he had of creating a rock ballet based on Bram Stoker's 1897 novel *Dracula*. One direction he was contemplating was getting the rights to use classic metal and rock songs for the soundtrack. Commissioning a composer to write an original score was another, and he had already begun a national search.

Earle was unaware of my former life as a rock and roll singer, only knowing the softer piano side of my songwriting. I asked if he would consider listening to a few things I had in my pocket and see if they were along the lines of his vision. I had recently done a score on the heavier side for a short film by my good friend John Urban, so after lunch, I sent parts of that and parts of some other ideas I had been working on and waited impatiently for a reply. I wanted this badly.

They hit home. They were exactly the kind of feel he was looking for to give the project an edge. I was hired as composer for *Dracula: A Rock Ballet*.

Every Wednesday for almost two years, Earle would come over to my project studio, and we would brainstorm and create. It was a daunting task to compose ninety minutes of music for a full-length story ballet, but we loved every minute of the process. It is the greatest experience I have had creating music so far in my life. We would talk through the story. He wanted to stay close to Bram Stoker's classic tale and not swerve into pop culture vampires. He would explain the vision of the choreography for different scenes, and I would either come up with something that fit or say I'd have that idea ready for our next session. I was immersed in creating. I still played shows with Francie and Piano Fondue, but my head was in this monumental experience of composing music and marrying it to dance. In the end, we would have twenty-four pieces of music, all written for specific characters and choreography. I only missed on one piece in the composition stage, where Earle told me to go back to the drawing board. Pretty good odds, but it speaks to the chemistry we shared during its creation.

For the performance, we would have a seven-piece band playing live on a platform fourteen feet high built into the industrial/steampunk set designed by Charles Trieloff II, known affectionately to everyone as Jen.

I set about recruiting a band for the cause.

MORE

It was a no-brainer that my old Chaser mates and lifelong friends Michael John Ripp and Tony Cerniglia would be on guitar and drums. In fact, the guitar parts I wrote were with Mike in mind, knowing he would make them his own. For the other keyboard and to conduct the band with precision and discipline, I chose my friend, and still the most talented man I know, Dave Adler. Dave and I would play orchestral sounds on some pieces and piano and organ on others. We could not have done it without him.

Dave and Stage Manager Neen Rock made the show go. Neen was everything theater, a friend, and the best I've ever seen at calling a show. She could handle a gaggle of kids for a *Nutcracker* performance, traveling Broadway casts, and self-important rock bands, and commanded the respect of even the most grizzled stage crew. For our show, she gave lighting and dancers cues and then called Dave on a direct-line telephone to cue the band so he could count us in. It was simply astounding how good she was. Sadly, we lost Neen in 2021, way too young. Her passing leaves a large hole in the Madison arts community.

On bass guitar, I wanted someone solid, creative, and, most importantly, a friend. You can see a theme developing here. One of Dave's long-term projects was a band of killer musicians and exotic characters called The Gomers. Gordon Ranney played bass, and I adored him. Gordon was not only an extremely accomplished musician, but his sense of humor and warmth also endeared him to everyone he knew. He learned twenty-four pieces of music, ninety minutes that had to be consistently perfect for the dancers, and had his cues on one index card.

The music called for electric violin, and we tapped Gomers' alum, Biff Blumfumgagnge. He fit the friend qualification, and his improv skills and sound processing gave the music an edge we hadn't known was missing.

A second guitar was all that remained. Jay Moran was the leader of The Slingbacks, a respected member of numerous successful bands, a Madison mainstay, and a friend. He teamed with his guitar buddy Michael John and rounded out the vagrant bunch. We named the band The Renfields after the inmate in an asylum in Bram Stoker's novel.

Now I had to physically score the damn thing.

87. NOSFERATU
(Helen Robbins and Joe Bouchard)

A WEAKNESS OF MINE is that I cannot sight-read music notation. I can write it as fast as I can read it. With the help of the computer program Sibelius, I knew just enough to slowly discern right from wrong. I set out to create the book from which Neen could call the show. It was painstaking work. Twenty-four pieces, a master score, and seven parts to separate for the players. I worked eighteen hours a day and slept six for a solid month to finish it by showtime. Jay Moran stopped by one day and was horrified at the gaunt, unshaven Massey who greeted him at the door. I knew the project was a monumental undertaking from the outset, but until you do it, you really have no idea how much work it is.

The band set up in the School of Madison Ballet studios, and we ran through the show twice before hitting the theater. I have never felt more alive or more accomplished. To see Earle's exquisite choreography slowly get less tentative and grow into a comprehensive whole was a thing of beauty. We felt like proud parents.

Tech week in the thousand-seat Capitol Theater at the Overture Center was an experience like none before in my life. My heart soared as I walked in the stage door, climbing the steps to the theater. There is a hush backstage in a theater. It's not quiet; it's an absence of sound like the room is swallowing it. Walking down the darkened wing and looking up to our eventual home on a platform built into the set fourteen feet off the stage was the culmination of all the hours, days, weeks, months, and years spent composing the music for this show. The hard part was over, and now we get to play!

We set about raising all of our equipment to the platform. Extensive sound checks for front-of-house, monitor mixes for us, and stage sound for the dancers went well. I had played on numerous big stages back in the day and done many television productions, but the live, in-the-theater energy with all the dancers, crew, and musicians was naturally intoxicating and erotically foreign. Earle's notes for tech rehearsal Wednesday night found us pushing the tempo because of adrenaline, so Dave was told to hold us back. For all of the musicians, keeping a rigid tempo when the music wanted to race was an unfamiliar concept. Music naturally breathes with subtle variations in speed depending on dynamics. We explained to Earle that utilizing this phenomenon would be the best possible outcome. As the week progressed and the dancers perfected their craft and warmed to our rhythm, he agreed. The dress rehearsal was a little rough, but you know what they say, you don't really want dress to go well; save it for opening night.

We were to do four shows on the first run from March 8-10, 2013. Friday night, Saturday matinee, Saturday night, and a Sunday matinee. Opening night was a near sellout. It wasn't a perfect show, but the adrenaline, energy, and unique nature of the spectacle resulted in a standing ovation and three curtain calls. I had the honor of leaving the platform and descending to the stage to join in bows. I can honestly say that standing center stage and bowing as the composer of the score was the pinnacle of my musical career thus far. It didn't seem real. All the blood, sweat, and tears expended after that fateful lunch date with Earle had been worth it.

The weekend would challenge all of us to our core. Though we'd rehearsed the music extensively, playing it with dancers and choreography top of mind was new to all of us. Live performance is never without its foibles, and we had our share, but they were disguised enough not to affect the show. Shaking it off and moving forward from them in the moment was the dicey part. In one piece that had difficult time signature changes,

I had to blow a whistle at one point while playing the piano, and it was a difficult silence break in the music, an odd count, and then the band came back in together. As the cue was approaching, I dropped my whistle. Only by the grace of God did I get the count right. If it had crashed, so too would have the dance. Crisis averted. All four shows were well attended with exuberant, responsive audiences. It is part ballet, part rock show, and everyone who attended left feeling sated in both respects.

We recorded the show for a live album with our front-of-house audio engineer and sound designer, Conrad St. Clair, on the board. Press was generally glowing about the show. One of the things I'm most proud of is that we delivered much more than anyone expected when they bought a ticket. They came to support a local production and walked away knowing that "local" in Madison means the sky's the limit. In June, The Renfields played the score in its entirety at the High Noon Saloon to celebrate the live album release. Biff brought a copy of the original *Nosferatu*, and we performed the soundtrack to *Dracula* with the black-and-white classic as a backdrop. We would reprise the entire show Halloween weekend in the Capitol Theater. We were making plans for the future and hoping to get it to touring status.

88. GOOD RIDDANCE (TIME OF YOUR LIFE)
(Billie Joe Armstrong)

WHEN I SET OUT to write a book, my fervent wish was that I could tell my story and possibly help others who might find themselves in similar straits. I hope I have sufficiently conveyed some of the horror and shame of addiction. I hope that I've made you feel despair and desperation. Now that we're on the other side, I also wanted to share my triumphs. The first half of this book is a thrill ride fueled by youth and excess. It has been a challenge to make the beautifully mundane seem interesting by comparison. I've gone into detail about day-to-day events over the past few chapters, not to pat myself on the back or boast, but to show what's possible. Far from having the capacity or endurance to manage projects and a performance schedule, I would be dead if I hadn't changed.

There would be no marriage, no Emily and Anna, no *Dracula: A Rock Ballet*. A different family would have occupied the Cape Cod on Dayton Street. The world would have kept turning, but it would be different.

In our youth, we were all convinced we would be agents of change, a necessary idealism to get us through the growing pains of being ignored by those clawing to keep their spot in the American dream. We were going to be the next Jagger or Bowie. The next Idina Menzel, the next Leonardo DiCaprio. Cure cancer, code the next software to improve lives.

The resiliency, concentration, and stamina required to carve a career in music, or any other field, is impossible if a monkey is on your back.

I proudly call myself a blue-collar musician. I've never been, nor will I ever be, a virtuoso. I play solo and in duo acts with multiple partners, I play dueling pianos, I play with some cover and tribute bands, and I perform my own original music. I compose music for advertising and video and film. I've created art. I consider myself a moderately talented musician who, on a really good night, approaches but never quite achieves greatness.

Only in sobriety, with Robin's and my daughters' love and support, do I realize that success isn't measured by fame. Prosperity shouldn't mean material wealth. Family, love, happiness, and contentment are priceless commodities. Feeling truly grateful for what you have and built through adversity is the most rewarding of confessional.

89. DON'T STOP BELIEVIN'
(Steve Perry, Jonathan Cain, and Neal Schon)

YOU CAN PUT the greatest individual musicians together in a room to play and expect the outcome to be good. But not until time has been spent together with repetition, more time, the tweaking of arrangements, and still more time do they become one entity. Reaching the point in a project when you feel the music, as opposed to playing it, is hard to describe. The nuances that ebb and flow, learning everyone's subtle rhythms and how to enhance and counter them is an ongoing process.

Tony C., Michael John Ripp, Francie, and I had entered into a cover band project we called Big Bang that was designed to make money and have fun. We enlisted Kyle Henderson on bass and his outstanding vocals. Kyle had experienced great success in the eighties with Atlanta band The Producers and had relocated to Madison. We spent time building a repertoire and perfecting the songs, and Kyle decided he'd rather sing than play bass. Auditions for a bass player proved comical at first while we endured various degrees of ineptitude until a handsome, gentle giant named Frank Queram walked in. Frank checked all the boxes as a musician, and we loved him from the first moment. Alas, life's changing priorities interrupted the process, and the band was short-lived, playing only one gig.

Tony C. and I felt that the core of the project was worth pursuing and decided to see what would come of writing some new material with this crew. Stop the Clock was born. Time was spent. Music was created, written, and recorded, and something different was there. But in the revolving door that is the music business, Mike Ripp and Francie had to bow out. Frank played in another band with prodigious blues/rock guitarist Joel Pingitore and asked if he'd come down and give it a shot. Joel played with a different edge. Right away, his familiarity with Frank created a synergistic rhythm section that breathed new life into the music. It became a sum greater than its parts, blending our various musical influences into a cohesive whole.

The night Briana Hardyman auditioned to replace Francie was dark and windy. Briana was a soulful country blues singer and seemed extremely nervous at first, tentatively singing through a prearranged song but showing flashes of brilliance. Just as we were going to try another, the power went out. Now what? Briana made lemonade out of lemons, played acoustic guitar, and sang with such passion by candlelight that she melted our hearts. A prolific songwriter, Briana's songs were prime for our developing flavor. Time was spent, music was created, written, and recorded, and the result was truly genre-defying. It had country elements but was deeply rooted in rock and blues. We made a ten-song album, *Gifted at the Hula*, named after yours truly inexplicably doing the hula between songs at a rehearsal. We had a lot of fun, easy chemistry, and the band was slowly becoming that tight musical unit to which every musician aspires.

90. THE SOUND OF MUSIC
(Rodgers and Hammerstein)

AS 2014 ROLLED IN, we settled into living. Emily had graduated from high school and was embarking on a musical journey of her own. Anna was in high school at her dad's alma mater and playing varsity volleyball. Robin was managing the daily crises that arise at pediatric clinics, and I was ever onward.

Francie and I moved our Thursday night duo show to Genna's on the Capitol Square. Owned and operated by lifelong friend Kristi Genna and her husband, Jack Williams, Genna's was a hip, stylish venue and a who's who of Madison's cool factor on a nightly basis. Jack and Kristi had also operated the Slipper Club.

I was fortunate to do two high-profile ad projects for the premiere advertising agency Stephan and Brady. Creative Director Emily Tuszynski Shea contacted me to do an instrumental for Jones Dairy Farm and a jingle for Badgerland Financial. The Jones spots would play coast-to-coast.

One night at The Ivory Room, my aunt and uncle, Sandy and Wally Staley, brought Lara Gruhn, a distant cousin traveling from Switzerland. Discovering family you didn't know existed is a marvelous feeling. To have an immediate connection with them is even better. A delightful young woman, Lara and I immediately became friends. I had never been to Europe, and when I excitedly told Robin of the meeting, we dreamed of traveling as a family to visit. A decided step up from our domestic adventures.

And in August 2014, rationalizing you only live once, we did just that. Lara and her boyfriend, Philippe Noser, picked us up at the airport in Zurich. They had arranged to stay with Lara's parents, Liz and Horst Gruhn, and graciously gave us their apartment near the city center to use as our own. Lara was a wonderful tour guide, showing us a side of the Swiss city that ordinary tourists would overlook. Our relationship as distant cousins quickly turned into a deep and abiding friendship. We became family, and I treasure Lara and Philippe without rival.

Philippe loaned us his car to travel the three-and-a-half hours to Konigsbrunn, Germany, to see Robin's lifelong friend, Chris Munger, and her family. My first time driving on the autobahn was in a four-cylinder Toyota, but we were very grateful for the gesture. It is a bit disconcerting to pull out to pass a vehicle with the gas pedal to the floor, slowly gaining ground, and have an Audi or Mercedes appear in your mirror going 150 kph. Somehow, we arrived unscathed, with Emily navigating, only getting lost once in Austria. An illegal U-turn later, and we were back on track. We stayed with Chris and her family for a couple of days, drove back to Zurich, and flew to Paris. I really wanted to take the train, but it was more expensive than the flights, so I'll save the European countryside for another trip.

Paris was everything I'd hoped it would be. We stayed in a lovely Airbnb in Marais and could walk to the Seine, Notre Dame, Centre Pompidou, the Louvre, and many more of the city's attractions. We took the metro to Champs-Elysees, Sacré Coeur and Montmartre. And yes, I took my late-night walks through the cobblestones and romance. I found French Marlboros to be delicious, but my sneaking cigarette days were numbered.

We flew back to Zurich for a birthday party on our last evening in Switzerland. They had rented a boathouse on Lake Zurich for the party, and the gentle breeze, wonderful friendship, and sunset kissing the mountains made for a breathtaking time. We grilled sausages over an open flame. Anna and Emily swam in the crystal-clear water. It was a splendid night and a perfect end to our first trip across the ocean.

In September, Chaser was asked to play a reunion! Mike Gomoll was a friend who had worked at Madison's premiere club Headliners back in the day, and he was producing a benefit for epilepsy, having tragically lost his son to the disease. Joey's Song was to take place at the 550-capacity Majestic Theater in Madison. Chaser would open for The Know-It-All Boyfriends, a band comprised of Garbage alums Butch Vig and Duke Erikson; songwriter and singer extraordinaire Freedy Johnston; and Mad Cabaret buddies Jay Moran, Pie Cowan, and Stick Bielefeld. The show was a rousing success, raising substantial money for epilepsy research, and it was an incredible feeling playing those songs again with the Chaser boys. I could close my eyes and be in any number of clubs across the country. It was muscle memory, nostalgia, and, most of all, it was reclaiming our youth, if only for a while. It occurred to me a week into rehearsals that I had likely never performed this music sober, but playing it again was a soaring natural high.

    I was asked to join a Steely Dan tribute band called Steely Dane. Madison is in Dane County. I was truly honored to be asked to be a part of a band that included Madison's elite musicians. I spent the duration of my time with them, never fully feeling like I measured up, always nervous before shows because I wanted so badly to excel and justify my involvement. We played high-profile shows, theaters, and festivals in the Upper Midwest.

    While in Switzerland, I had received an email from musician/producer Scott Lamps asking me if I would consider signing on to do a project with a theatrical bent. *Are We Delicious?*, the brainchild of impresario Tony Trout, was the idea that you write, rehearse, and perform a series of plays in one week. In this case, they were musicals. I would be a songwriter and part of the backing band for the rest of the production. The last time I said yes to something out of the ordinary, it changed my life, and having a judicious hole in my schedule, I said, what the hell. I was out of my comfort zone immediately but relished the opportunity. I was in the company of talented actors and musicians, and an inspirational camaraderie developed. We broke into three teams and were assigned stories to abridge and turn into musicals. The script-writers were given one day. We met again on Tuesday for the first dialogue rehearsal and to provide the songwriters with insight and direction. I had to have two songs ready for Wednesday's rehearsal. It was a lovely whirlwind of activity, and we were ready for opening night at the Broom Street Theater on Madison's east side. We performed fun shows on Friday and Saturday nights to receptive and appreciative audiences. It was a delight from start to finish. I have not had a break in my schedule since to do another. Maybe someday.

Notably, the assistant stage manager on the production was Suzan Kurry, an accomplished writer, actor, and director. After the last performance, I tapped her on the shoulder and asked if I could run something past her. Intrigued, she took the bait, and I sent her a rough script and the songs of the musical Billy Nahn and I were working on with Earle way back in 2003. I waited impatiently for her opinion. When I spoke to her after a couple of weeks, she said that the script would need a lot of work but that we should write one of our own! In November, Suzan started coming to my project studio on Tuesday afternoons, and we set about writing a funny, thought-provoking musical.

Also, in November, I quit cigarettes for the fourth and (I hope) final time. I quit on November 1 in honor of my mother's memory and the wish that I could draw upon her strength to make it a permanent change.

91. DO IT AGAIN
(Walter Becker and Donald Fagen)

INTO 2015, I continued playing solo shows, sometimes traveling to River North in Chicago to play the famous Redhead Piano Bar. I loved the gig. It was a classic old-school piano bar with patrons singing along and cheering until the lights came on. On one memorable night, I was finishing up "American Pie," the audience was singing the choruses with me at the top of their lungs, and the doorman was giving me the slashed throat sign to cut it off—at 4:15 a.m.! I then drove home to Madison, arriving with the sun fully up. It wasn't lost on me that I was able to do that show and numerous others like it because I was sober. Life on the other side was sweet indeed.

Two more major ad projects came my way: Summit Credit Union in Madison and Theisen's Supply, a chain of twenty-two industrial-agricultural department stores in Iowa. The confidence of having the first one most definitely got me the second. Funny how it works that way. There were times in the nineties when I would make periodic calls to agencies, looking for work, and even I could hear the desperation in my voice. Not the impression you like to make. Now, meeting with the brass at Theisen's, it wasn't a necessity that I got the project, and my measured presentation won them over. I wrote and produced both ads concurrently.

Through the summer, my schedule was full, playing with Francie, Piano Fondue, and doing high-profile festivals and outdoor gigs with Steely Dane and Stop the Clock.

In October, we were going to bring back *Dracula*. Some principal dancers returned, but new blood was also injected into the mix. We would do three nights at the Capitol Theater and three nights at the Grand Opera House in Oshkosh, Wisconsin, a beautiful, ornate, haunted theater that first opened in 1883. Sadly, Gordon's health prevented him from taking part in the run. It was a harsh reality that none of us wanted to face, but the show must go on. We got primo seats for Gordon and his wife, Jeanette, to see the show at the Capitol.

Conrad St. Clair, front-of-house sound and sound designer for the first *Dracula* run, already knew the show and was part of the team. Conrad is a world-class bass player and musician. We didn't even audition anyone else. He scored all of Gordon's parts from the recording, memorized them, and then added his personality to the role. I think he might have glanced one wrong note for the entire run! He might have.

While preparing for a St. Louis run in the spring, we received devastating news. Madison Ballet was canceling the rest of the season. The board wasn't keen on the cash outlay it took to mount *Dracula* with no guarantee of a return and lumped it in with other financial difficulties. We were shattered. All of the momentum we were building was stopped dead in its tracks. The only solace we had was the knowledge that when this unique, dazzling show was resurrected in the future, it would never be outdated. *Dracula* will live again.

Stop the Clock would play that fall's Joey's Song. The show was moved to the 800-seat Barrymore Theater where we would again open for The Know-It-All Boyfriends. As a bonus, Emily's band, Modern Mod, would start the show. Sadly, just as Stop the Clock was reaching a point that was truly solid, approaching that threshold of a great band, serious personal problems derailed the project permanently. Such is the reality of the music business.

92. TOTALLY NUDE
(David Byrne, Chris Frantz, Jerry Harrison, and Tina Weymouth)

THERE ARE MANY SONGS I've written through the years that never ended up the way I heard them. I tried different genres, tempos, and instrumentation, and it just didn't get the results I was looking for. But I felt they were good songs and wanted to get them out there for public consumption and the possibility of placement in TV and movies. The original concept was to do an album of just piano and vocals, the simplest form of the song, the way they were written. I also wanted to record them on a grand piano, not digital. I called the album *Naked* and spent most of 2016 arranging and recording the tracks.

At the end of February, I learned of Gordon Ranney's death from cancer. He was a tragically young fifty-three. Gordon was a great man, a great friend, and a musician without peer. He will be missed by so many.

Joe Johnson, friend, ex-boss, and all-around good guy had a six-foot Yamaha grand piano in his home. He was in the process of moving and wouldn't be around much. He generously offered the opportunity to come in and mic the piano and take as much time as I wanted to get the basic tracks. As with most major projects, it routinely takes twice as long as you anticipate, even with the best concentration and intentions. After getting the mics placed and acclimated to the action of the instrument, I recorded about twenty songs, twelve of which made it on the album. From February 28 through March 15, I practically lived at Joe's house after dark and often until dawn.

With piano tracks in hand, I called my old pal Doug Schoebel, who was manning the controls at Concept Productions. It would be a nice full circle to go back there and record after all these years. I worked out a deal so I could get the keys to the studio and go in after hours with a laptop and a Neumann U 87 mic borrowed from Tony C. to spend time doing the vocals. I loved going into the big room, where I spent so much time in the nineties, and singing for hours. And it became apparent to me as I got good tracks that I was not going to let this live with just piano tracks. I still wanted it to be sparse and delicate, but I needed more substance to the songs. I called on my talented friends again, and it was a labor of love to recreate parts sung years before and add new instrumentation here and there.

Kimmie Lockwood (nee Vernon) and Mare sang backgrounds on "Mary," the same parts sung on the original demo recorded at Randy Green's in '98.

Side note: When we recorded the original version of "Mary" at Randy's Recording, we had finished the background vocals on the first chorus when the pizza arrived. I worried we'd lose continuity taking a break and consuming food, but what can you do? I was right. We never quite matched the first and second choruses in tone, as much as we tried.

Emily Massey contributed a duet vocal to "Save Me a Memory." Chris Wagoner and Mary Gaines added violin and cello. Stop the Clock buddies Joel Pingitore, Frank Queram, and Tony C., this time on cajón, lent their expertise to a few songs. Michael John Ripp reprised his "Tears Disappear" acoustic guitar. Conrad St. Clair played some velvet fretless bass tracks, notably the hauntingly genius accompaniment to "More," adding to the despair and ultimate redemption of the lyric. Francie sang backing vocals and took the lead on "Not Pretending." Her texture lifts everything. Al Falaschi, saxophonist and singer extraordinaire of Steely Dane and Phat Phunktion fame, among many other things, smoked a sax solo for "Hang On." Kyle Henderson sang an impeccable harmony for "The World Keeps

Movin' On." Michelle Grabel-Komar and the Dudes in Suits, Harvey Briggs and Bruce Geiger, added harmonies on "Friends Forever," all having sung it with me in different forms for twenty years. Jeff Komar produced the record and gave it an organic polish. By the time we had finished, more than a year had passed doing a project I had thought I could easily finish in six months. It always takes twice as long.

In July, finding airfare for half of what we had paid two years prior, the Masseys returned to Switzerland for Lara and Philippe's wedding. American Airlines was half the fare and half the comfort and decorum of Swissair. My extended Massey family made the trip as well. Aunts and uncles and cousins descended upon Zurich and made our presence felt. There's an indescribable feeling of being in one's country of origin. Even five generations after my Swiss ancestors immigrated to America, it still holds a mystique and strange sense of belonging.

October found Robin promoted to clinic manager of eleven specialty clinics at the University of Wisconsin's Waisman Center. She was to oversee Genetics, Autism and Developmental Disabilities, Pediatric Brain Care, and much more. It resulted from the excellence she brought to every task and just being Robin. They were lucky to have her.

Between working on *Naked*, I was playing ten to twelve shows a month with Francie, Mare, Piano Fondue, solo shows, and Steely Dane. I was still a blue-collar working musician and damn proud of it.

On May 12, 2017, we performed a *Naked* release show at the Bartell Theater in downtown Madison. (The record, not sans clothing.) The material warranted a listening environment instead of a club atmosphere, fighting clinking glasses, conversation, and laughter. Most everyone who contributed to the album joined me on stage for the show. It was a delightful evening and a perfect way to release the record.

93. SOMEONE LIKE YOU
(Michael Ripp, Michael Massey, Tony Cerniglia, and Stevie Johnson)

AFTER COMPLETING THAT PROJECT, I did what I always do—move on, sometimes too quickly. It was a busy year, playing a dozen shows a month in different configurations to make money and not really concentrating on one specific thing artistically. It is the downside to the blue-collar musical philosophy. To make a living at that level, you need to do whatever comes your way, and if the schedule becomes heavy on the gig side, it's hard to find the time to conceive new projects.

In December, Chaser was asked to play Joey's Song again. Stevie Johnson couldn't make it happen this time, so we tapped the youngest Ripp brother and my Circle Park partner, Jim, to play the bass. Jim had watched Chaser growing up and knew most of the music backward and forward. Plus, his first instrument was actually the bass, although he plays dueling pianos and played guitar when we were on the road together back in the nineties. Those Ripps are one talented family.

While different without Stevie, getting back in the saddle on Chaser songs was once again a joy. I started talking about doing an album. We had never really recorded our catalog of songs as well as we should have. It was always rushed demos while waiting for the major label deal, and I strongly believed the music was worth spending the time with current technology to help. Mike Gomoll, executive director and founder of Joey's Song, came to a rehearsal the week before the show. He wanted to sit and listen to those songs he knew from all those years ago. Mike's presence must have provided a spark because we ran through a spirited set with energy and attitude.

We were set up to record rehearsals so we could listen back and make improvements. Those takes, run through as a set, live, just like the thousand shows we played in another lifetime, became the basic tracks for the album *Jack's Bootleg*, named for Chaser's longest and most ardent fan, patriarch of the Ripp family, Jack Ripp. Jack became like a father to me after mine was gone, and he was the first human to hear the tracks outside the band. Not long after, his health took a turn for the worse, and while he was in hospice, there was a copy of the unreleased rough tracks of the album playing around the clock. In a unanimous tribute, we named the album *Jack's Bootleg* in honor of his unwavering support through the years. A great man. I was lucky to have known and loved him.

Joey's Song was an extravaganza. We videoed the passionate set for posterity, and it felt great to play those songs again. I can't describe it better than I did earlier. It is reclaiming youth. It is drinking from the fountain and watching the years melt away. It is soul-nurturing. In addition to the Know-It-All Boyfriends, troubadour, master songwriter, and performer Dan Navarro joined us on the bill. Dan is a prolific songwriter, vocalist, guitarist, and voice actor who, with his duo partner, Eric Lowen, cut quite a swath through AAA radio and a stage near you for twenty years. Sadly, Eric passed away from ALS in 2012. One of the things Lowen and Navarro are known for is writing "We Belong" for Pat Benatar, which reached number five on Billboard's Hot 100 in 1984. Dan calls that song "the gift that keeps on giving." I could not have been more delighted to meet him and strike up a friendship. Dan is quite simply the nicest guy you'll ever meet. He brought Francie up on stage to sing "We Belong" with him at the show. It was a night for the ages. In an "it's a small world" connection, Dan knows Pam Turbov from writing songs for the Bangles.

Dan Navarro is a troubadour in the most genuine sense of the word. He continues to play a hundred shows a year, ranging from theater productions to river cruises on the Danube to intimate house concerts. He simply loves performing, meeting people, and spreading joy throughout the world. He's an ambassador of music who does it for all the right reasons.

Later in December, Conrad St. Clair recruited me to sing Frank's vocal parts in a Frank Zappa Tribute band called The Furious Bongos. It was to become an incredibly difficult and rewarding musical challenge.

So here I am looking at sixty years old, and I'm playing solo shows; performing as a duo with Francie and Mare; playing dueling pianos with Piano Fondue; singing with Steely Dane; singing with Furious Bongos and jumping around a stage like I'm twenty-one with Chaser. I think it's safe to say that sobriety is the most significant contributing factor to my longevity and continued energy. Tony Bennett was still touring into his nineties. Life goals.

94. SMALL TOWN
(John Mellencamp)

IN 2007, we got a loan and purchased five acres of land in Barneveld, Wisconsin, on the farm where I had proposed to Robin. My uncle Jim now owned the homestead where my father had grown up. Jim is my father's youngest sibling, only five years older than me. Throughout my life, he's been more of a brother than an uncle. After years of idle, passing talk about the remote possibility of building a house somewhere on the land, Jim lit a fire under our asses and made us an offer we couldn't refuse.

I am William Massey IV. My father is III. My great-grandfather William Massey I bought 160 acres in 1911 and farmed it until he passed it on to my grandfather, Allan (William II) in 1933. Allan Massey sold his estate in 1977 but kept forty acres, the 1889 farmhouse, the barn, and the outbuildings intact. The heart of the property remained a familiar place to come home. After my grandparents' deaths, Jim and his wife of forty-eight years, Anne, moved back and did a beautiful renovation of the old farmhouse.

I spent glorious summers in my adolescence and teen years visiting for weeks at a time, helping with the dairy operation and harvesting hay. Traveling in a pickup down dusty gravel roads, Jim and I listened to the diverse pop music of WLS, interspersed with reports about mystical, faraway places like the Loop, Halsted Street, and the Kennedy Expressway. I learned to drive at thirteen, in a cornfield in a Chevy pickup with three on the tree. Lunchtime ham sandwiches and cold water from the deep well were ambrosia from the gods for a tired crew after a morning on the tractor. I felt a strong kinship with the land, not only because it was a legacy but because it was ancient, driftless, and a magic current hummed just below the surface.

We enlisted an architect and started looking at designs. And then, the bottom fell out of the economy, and my father fell ill. I was designated to take him for treatment and medical visits. It soon became all-consuming. Plans were put on indefinite hiatus.

In 2018, in an effort to finally get us back on track, Jim asked if we'd like to revisit the placement of our property. The agriculture patterns had shifted since we initially surveyed for our parcel in 2007. What was once a cornfield was now open pasture and fair game for revision. We walked the land and settled on a spot on a ridge between two trees with a breathtaking view down into the valley. I could envision it. It was becoming more than a gossamer concept. We surveyed again for our new lot and finally started moving forward with the necessary permits to build our dream home in the country.

95. I WON'T BACK DOWN
(Tom Petty and Jeff Lynne)

I'M FREQUENTLY ASKED how I negotiate bars and clubs and the music business, surrounded by profuse alcohol use. It seemed daunting in the beginning, before I fully threw myself back into the fray. But after confronting the elephant in the room a few times, I found that the strength of my convictions and the mindset born in a subdued hospital room of alcohol never again being an option for me held true. Being in the moment and clear was euphoric amidst so many for whom last night's details might be a little fuzzy. I felt the energy of the people around me and turned it into fuel. I could laugh just as hard, sing just as loud as anyone, and I wasn't going to let sobriety be staid.

I will say, though, someone repeating themselves more than twice in a conversation results in me simply walking away. I don't even apologize. If you've repeated the same thing to me three times, you will not remember me walking away without a goodbye.

For the sober among us, especially the newly recovering, anxiety ramps up when the inevitable "Let me buy you a drink" is proclaimed in a club. Don't let that moment get to you. Reclaim it for your own. You have a secret power.

Early on, I dreaded it and having to explain why I wasn't drinking. I had been attending an aftercare program for a month after discharge from NewStart, and I asked my counselor how best to respond in that situation.

After the obligatory "Why are you putting yourself in those situations?" lecture, she gave me a few strategies to try, and I wasn't confident in any of them. I figured I'd get used to it, and it was part of the process.

On the last day of aftercare, it came around to me to talk about how I felt about my prospects going forward. I stood up and said, "I feel like a phoenix rising out of the ashes." I was going to reclaim my life and work to improve everything I did—every day. I'll never forget the joyful look on her face when she responded, "You're ready. You're ready to be out there!" Not until much later did I realize that success stories are in woefully short supply in her business, and my resolve on that day gave her the energy to do the important work of continuing to help others.

I hit upon the solution quite by accident. You have a secret power. I had an acquaintance saunter up that I hadn't seen in a while, and he clapped me on the back and drunkenly decreed, "Let me get you a drink. What are ya havin'?"

I looked back with steady eyes, my defense mechanism slowed down, and I simply said, "Thanks. I don't drink," and smiled. It is a secret power that fills you up inside. It is pride in that statement. It sets you apart from the others and confirms your convictions. There's no need to explain why you're not drinking. You just told them. Case closed. Besides, it's none of their fucking business anyway.

I am not judgmental, nor do I remotely condemn alcohol use, but in people's reactions, you immediately see where they are in their own lives with alcohol. If you make them nervous, they're questioning themselves about a possible problem. If unaffected and they say, "What else can I getcha?" they're probably doing okay.

Another question I've fielded many times in twenty-nine years is, "What's the definition of alcoholism?" There are countless complicated answers, but a no-nonsense counselor told me a simple one: "If drinking is affecting your life adversely and you can't stop, there's a problem." Pretty straightforward. I know from personal experience that you can wrestle with your conscience for a long time before you actually admit there's an issue, but internal conversations with yourself were happening long before.

I am not a counselor. The best I can do is tell my story. I don't consider myself an inspiration; I am an example. I believe that if I can do it, you can too.

It's a secret superpower that is justified to have while conquering demons. Four words. "Thanks. I don't drink," and a smile. Absolution, courage, and spirit. There's a lot behind that statement, and its use kills apprehension and plants you on firm ground.

"Thanks. I don't drink." Don't forget to smile.

96. BEHIND BLUE EYES
(Pete Townshend)

IN MARCH 2018, Chaser played a show at the High Noon Saloon with The Loud Soft Loud, a hard-rocking band with Mike and Jim Ripp's nephew, Jake Ripp-Dieter, on guitar. It was a nearly sold-out house. We recorded some crowd participation parts for the album.

The album.

I borrowed Tony's Neumann mic again and set up a vocal booth in my project studio. I soundproofed it so hard that Robin couldn't hear me, and I could sing into the wee hours of the morning. My schedule is whack. I've always loved the night, but when I was working on scoring *Dracula* during crunch time before opening, I was working until six in the morning, sleeping until noon, and repeating the process. I've more or less stayed there since then. Many mornings, I've just finished working, and I'm reading or watching TV to wind down when Robin gets up to go to work. At that moment, we are in two different days. Her today is my tomorrow.

"Good morning, honey."

Slits for eyes, straining against the light. "Hi." "Did you sleep well?" Shuffling into the bathroom, mumbling, "mmphrrmph..." "I'm gonna head to bed now. I love you. Have a great day."

From the shadows of the darkened bathroom, "G'night. Sleep well." She would come out of the bathroom and bestow a kiss on my forehead as I hunkered down into the covers. Sometimes I hung around until she reached actual consciousness, and we'd have a good conversation, but many days, it was like crossing the International Date Line in a time machine on Dayton Street.

It was exciting to spend time getting the best possible vocal tracks for the Chaser record. Even in New York in '81, time was short, and we settled more than I would have liked. I worked diligently to get myself into shape to sing these songs, all still outside my comfortable range like they always were. It's a different physicality to sing rock and roll, and I gave it all I had. I was also adding orchestration that we heard all those years ago, and what would have needed a soundstage in the eighties was now at my fingertips with a Mac. It struck me profoundly one late night that I was working on these songs forty years after Chaser hit the road for the first time. I still believed in the music, but even more, I cherished the enduring friendships with those guys who are my brothers. Forty years. When we're playing, I don't see the deepening lines in our faces; I see the idealism of youth, a single mind, and I am home.

In May, Robin earned her master's degree in nursing administration from Edgewood College. An incredible feat, and we couldn't have been more proud of her.

97. BLACK FRIDAY
(Donald Fagen and Walter Becker)

JULY 8, 2018, dawned on a beautiful summer day. Steely Dane was scheduled to play Summerfest in Milwaukee, the largest music festival in the world, opening for Boz Scaggs. We had done well there in the past, and the progression of stages got bigger as we proved ourselves. I was doing a couple of songs I hadn't sung before and spent many hours rehearsing, preparing, and hopefully perfecting my performance. I spent the drive from Madison to Milwaukee warming up my voice. Singing Donald Fagen well is extremely difficult. Not only is it in a deceptively high range, but the inflections, rhythms, and melodies are intricate and complicated.

After soundcheck, I wandered around backstage, continuing to warm up, wanting to stay limber and knock it outta the park for this gig and the estimated crowd of 8,000. I had been recording the Chaser songs for the album, and I felt like my voice was exercised and could be the best it's been for a long time. I was introduced and walked onto the stage and into the warm Milwaukee night.

The band started the intro for my first song, and suddenly something seemed off. I've never really been a victim of nerves, but I felt like a string stretched taut, straining to the breaking point. An odd, almost claustrophobic feeling took my breath away. All of the hours I spent on the song disappeared. I felt like I was standing there naked in front of thousands. As I hit my cue, my pitch was on the wrong melody note. My face was burning hot, and my eyes started watering. It was only a second or two before I found the right pitch and recovered, but the psychic damage was immense. I was shaken. Like every performer is supposed to do, I put on a brave, smiling face and threw myself into the rest of the song like nothing was wrong, but every note was a struggle, and every movement felt contrived.

I don't know if I warmed up too hard, I don't know if the physicality of singing the harder rock songs for the Chaser album threw off my mechanics, and I don't know why after hours spent rehearsing these cues, my brain and body malfunctioned. I walked off the stage and wanted to cry. It was my worst nightmare come true. The other songs I did that day weren't bad, but they weren't quite up to the standards I set for myself. My confidence was shattered.

Later that week, I got a call from Dave Adler asking me to meet him and Dave Stoler at a restaurant for a chat. I had an idea of what was coming, but I didn't expect the how. I ordered a coffee, and the Daves got drinks. They told me that there were disparaging comments written on the Steely Dane Facebook page about my performance at Summerfest. Then abruptly, Dave Stoler went on a rant about people walking out of the show and how they would probably never play Summerfest again because of me. I was speechless. Dave Adler disputed that account, but I was surprised by the degree of animosity leveled at me by Stoler. I was hurt and ashamed and was done as a member of Steely Dane.

Dave Adler softened the blow by talking about all of the good things I do and that singing Steely Dan songs "just isn't my thing." He was right. The anxiety I felt every show proved that. But I had done the one thing I feared most—I had let the band down. I hadn't felt lower in many years. Even though I was succeeding on many fronts and making another album, a nagging feeling of failure followed me. It continues to be a source of angst even now. Dave was right. It wasn't my thing, but it was small comfort to my bruised confidence. Steely Dane never missed a beat without me. Summerfest wasn't affected, and if someone was walking out, it was probably to get a beer. I miss them all terribly. I loved being a part of it.

98. DADDY LESSONS
(Beyoncé, Kevin Cossom, Alex Delicata, and Diana Gordon)

IN AUGUST, Chaser played the High Noon Saloon with Emily's band. Slow Pulp was on the rise, had relocated to Chicago, and with the drawing power of the two bands, we easily sold it out. Chaser opened the show. Our crowd has curiously become of a vintage that is more comfortable with an early time slot.

Many of my daughter's friends knew I was a musician but had never seen me perform. Imagine their surprise when I hit the stage in a leather jacket open to skin, a scarf, and full makeup. After getting past the fact it was Emily's dad, they wholeheartedly joined in the fun. One of the greatest compliments I've ever gotten was when Emily told me her crowd loved Chaser. I asked what about four old guys playing eighties-ish rock they loved. She said it was sincere and authentic and that there were a lot of new bands trying to do what we do but that it was forced and an imitation. Chaser's sincerity is a source of pride. Say what you will about the band, but most of the music was written together by four guys with a shared mindset. Those guys played a thousand shows and glimpsed the brass ring. And the friendships that resulted have lasted a lifetime.

Slow Pulp hit the stage and proved why their star was ascending. The band's musicianship and accessibility poured across the audience in waves, and their audience adored them, singing along to every song. That they are genuinely nice people is apparent in everything they do. It is perhaps the biggest repeated lesson I have impressed upon my daughter. I have implored her to be herself from the beginning of her musical career. To be warm and friendly, to be sincere. Though she's inherently nicer than I've ever been, I still like to believe I have succeeded in helping her avoid the arrogance and misguided entitlement of her father in his youth. It is worth my failures to be able to teach her well.

99. EVERYBODY HURTS
(Michael Stipe, Peter Buck, Bill Berry, and Mike Mills)

IN OCTOBER, Robin and I returned to Europe to lend our support to our friends and family who were suffering. Robin's friend Chris Munger had tragically lost her eighteen-year-old son to an accidental overdose laced with fentanyl two months before. Tristan was a delightful young man with a bright future and became yet another senseless statistic of the world's opioid crisis. We went to Germany just to be there and to love her and her family. To take her mind off things, Chris jumped into promoter mode and devised a plan for me to play a show with Natalie Rohrer, a wonderful pianist, singer, and songwriter who also happened to be her children's music teacher. Chris secured a venue and scheduled a rehearsal.

Natalie came over, looked at a set list I had with Francie, checked off some songs she knew, and we immediately had chemistry and a comfort level that normally takes more time to achieve. Natalie is a consummate pro. Instinctively, we felt the rhythms together and harmonized easily. She had learned my song "Tears Disappear" and took the harmony to a completely different place, which was lovely. We played a ninety-minute show in Konigsbrunn to an attentive, receptive audience. A large group came back to Chris's afterward, and we kept the neighbors awake late into the night, singing songs and sharing fellowship and laughter. It was a good distraction from the tragedy, and for just a little while, everyone was happy.

Lara and Philippe's son, Dimitri, born in May, was afflicted with esophageal atresia. He had been in the ICU since birth, and Lara and Philippe were exhausted and sad from spending so much time at the hospital and witnessing their brave little boy endure so many surgeries. We drove to Zurich, this time renting a Mercedes and doing the autobahn the way it's meant to be done. (It was only ten dollars more per day, and I hit 145 kph, just to do it.) We wanted to be there and support family who had become so much closer than the distant relatives they were. They were like first cousins, or more accurately, the best of friends. We visited Dimitri in the hospital, and Robin had brought a soft, cuddly monkey from America as a gift. He immediately took to it. We walked outside and got him a little air in the warm Swiss sun. And we loved him, them, all of them.

Jennifer Kedinger was a Wisconsin transplant to Switzerland and had become a good friend to Lara and Philippe. She was out of the country during our visit and graciously loaned us her apartment in the city center, within walking distance to Lara and Philippe's and to Europeans accustomed to walking in mountainous cities. We were huffing and puffing pretty good when we arrived for dinner at their apartment. After a lovely evening, we walked back to Jennifer's. The downhill was much easier.

I had never been on a motorcycle in my life until this trip. Philippe came to pick me up on his Vespa the next morning to go fishing. You haven't lived until you are white-knuckling it on the back of a scooter, whizzing through the busy, confusing streets of a central European city, narrowly missing pedestrians and other vehicles. It was an initiation I'll never forget. We got on Philippe's new boat and headed out on the foggy, crystal-clear lake. The morning chill gradually gave way to the sun's warmth, lifting and dispersing the fog. Fishing is seldom all about catching fish, especially if you're on a lake in Switzerland surrounded by mountains. It was utopian just being present. Lara and Robin had gone on a hike in the mountains above the lake, and we met up late morning so they could join our Lake Zurich excursion.

I really didn't want to say goodbye, but we had to catch our flight in Munich the next morning, and it was a five-hour drive on unfamiliar roads, far preferable in daylight. We promised we'd be back and bid our lovely friends adieu. We'd offered ourselves as a distraction from sadness and the distress of long days. Instead, we were the ones filled up with joy.

100. SPIRIT IN THE SKY
(Norman Greenbaum)

DURING THE COURSE OF writing this book, a friend was reaching acute stages of addiction to alcohol. As much as our intentions are honorable and good when trying to help someone, we quickly discover alcoholism is a formidable opponent. I want to include some of our dialogue and my philosophies. Though I'm not trained in offering help, I've lived it. I need to emphasize my respect for drug and alcohol counselors here. Their work is considerable, difficult, essential, and far too infrequently rewarding. The success rate is abysmal, but every victory is worth the effort.

I was surprised when he called me. The halting, slurred speech was nothing like the thoughtful, sensitive young man I had watched grow up. Knowing he was going through rough times, I had reached out before to no avail, so I was pleased he thought enough of me to call in a time of vulnerability. Recently, he had spent four days in detox in the hospital. To the dismay of doctors and family, he checked himself out prematurely and jumped right back on the downhill train with no brakes. Because it's easier. I know. I've worn those shoes. It's astonishingly easier to find comfort in a bottle you know is killing you than to face the prospect of change. To drink solely, not to shake. To stave off weakness and nausea. Unless you've been there, it's impossible to describe—and harder to understand.

He said he didn't know what to do. The small rational part of him that remained knew he was in trouble, but at that point in the throes of addiction, the other side might as well be a galaxy far, far away. We talked about how to move forward, starting with another stay in the hospital. I said I'd been in that bed. I could still feel it. He hated it and talked about the tubes and wires and judgmental nurses. I said the tubes and wires were helping him through the withdrawal that could be fatal and that the nurses were the opposite of judgmental; they were only concerned for his well-being. I said I remembered my time fondly in the hospital as a time of healing and the beginning of a new world. I didn't know if anything I was conveying was getting through or if he would even remember, but I hoped I was at least planting the seeds of comprehension.

He said he was scared. I said I knew how he felt but that the only thing he had to fear was what he had just gone through. I said he had been so close. He knew how to face that fear; he'd done it just a couple of weeks ago. Things would have gotten better if he had weathered the detox to fruition. The small victories I passionately believe in would have started to mount. I told him of the return of a voracious appetite that feels like it is accompanied by sunbeams and a choir of angels. It struck a chord when I talked about balance. He was the first person to ever understand, on the deepest level, my triumphant hands-free walk down the stairs so many years ago. He said he's forever holding on to handrails and walls to get around. I talked about clarity, explosive creativity, and building relationships with a clear heart. And I talked about death.

The immortality of a thirty-two-year-old alcoholic man is manifest. You are bulletproof until you're not. Nothing can harm you, and the world is soft around the edges until the ground gives away. Caught in the cycle of drowning reality, you don't see the truth until it buries you. I said his path was killing him, and it seemed to give him pause. Somewhere deep inside, it resonated with the kind, intelligent man he was, and he was silent.

But most importantly, I talked about how the only thing he needed to worry about right now was getting well—the only thing. Nothing else mattered. Addicts are experts at excuses. Nothing is ever our fault, and there's always a reason something happened or can't happen. He said he couldn't do rehab. He needed to work and pay rent. I told him if he continued this way, he wouldn't have a job and that if he diligently worked on getting well, there were people in his life who would help him with rent. After quelling more excuses I'd heard a thousand times, many times out of my mouth, he stopped. The truth is, without a change, there will be nothing left to make excuses for.

There is an unburdening that comes with surrender. To finally admit you don't want to live this way anymore and give yourself over to whatever it takes to be healthy again is an epiphany of meteoric proportions. To be small, helpless, and exhausted in the face of substance abuse is as hopeless as submission to the thought of change is glorious. Devoting laser focus to getting well and tuning out the distractions of a cacophonous world is a relief beyond measure. It is a chance to start over, to live, and to love.

This chapter remains unfinished. Our troubled young man has counselors, family, and friends doing all they can to help, yet he continues to struggle. He has the power to succeed, but it has to come from deep within. We can't do it for him as much as we wish we could. I'm optimistic. I believe that the enormity of his crossroads is beginning to sink in. We will all be here to do everything we can.

Update: Our friend is tenuously holding on after an intensive inpatient stay at a prominent rehab facility. While none of us are ever out of the woods, he is struggling to rebuild a life and navigate this uncertain world.

101. INCA ROADS
(Frank Zappa)

I HAD BEEN A MEMBER of the Frank Zappa Tribute band, The Furious Bongos, since December 2017. My role had been to sing Frank's baritone parts, and while it was a challenge for me musically to read the music and enter on cue in the complicated pieces, it was by far the easiest role in the band. The music is enormous. It is genius. It is incredibly difficult.

We had done some successful shows in the Madison area, and then Conrad's brilliant wife, Denise, accepted a job in Washington, D.C. It wouldn't end the project; it would just look different. After the move, Conrad had set about assembling a hybrid East Coast-Midwest version of the band and had booked a tour for May 2019.

(Conrad and I have formed a club, completely without irony, called The Luckiest Man in the World Club. We are the charter members, but to be an associate in good stead, you need only have a loving partner in life that makes you better just by association. Robin and Denise are the archetypes. The only benefit they derive from the club is having charming husbands.)

Fantastic guitarist, singer, and songwriter Lo Marie, virtuoso percussionist and vibes player Geoff Brady and me from Madison; rising young sax prodigy Vince Szynborski and Crawdaddy's guitar legend Christopher

Huntington III from Baltimore; opera star and part-time rocker Corey Crider from Lexington, Kentucky; drummer extraordinaire Lou Caldarola from New York; and for this tour, Conrad had enlisted the services of none other than Frank Zappa bass player, the original "clonemeister," Arthur Barrow. Besides working extensively with Martha Davis of the Motels, Robby Krieger of the Doors, and Giorgio Moroder, Arthur was with Frank's band for four tours. He can be heard playing bass, guitar, and keyboards on a dozen Zappa albums. Arthur and I developed a kinship as the elder statesmen of the band. For the tour, Arthur would play keys and sing lead on some of Frank's humorous, dramatic pieces. He had the inside track.

Conrad St. Clair called me and said, "We're losing our keyboard player for the May tour." I asked who he would get as a replacement, and he said, "Mike Massey." He'd been hinting at getting me to increase my role for a while. I needed to think about it. I felt I could probably do it, but it would take a significant amount of time.

On February 7, I opened with a set of original music for Dan Navarro at Café Carpe in Fort Atkinson, Wisconsin, a venerable, respected venue for touring artists. In January, I met him at the National Association of Music Merchants show in Anaheim, California, and asked if he'd consider it. After my set, Dan said to leave the piano set up and that I should join him during his set for a few. It was an honor and a fulfilling evening of heartfelt music.

Conrad finally sold me on the idea when he said that learning this music would make me a better player and performer. He said it would bolster my technique, even in delivering my piano ballads. I accepted the challenge.

I was dragging my feet a little before I jumped into the Zappa catalog, thinking I had plenty of time. Conrad would make periodic calls to check in and see how I was doing, and I said I hadn't really gotten into it yet. He gently chided me and said time was going to get away from me. The tour was coming up fast.

I started looking at the music between my Piano Fondue gigs in March. There were many moments when the task ahead seemed utterly impossible, but I kept chipping away at the stone. Learning fifteen seconds of one piece well enough to confidently play took hours. For some of the more precarious passages, I translated the notes into letters I could read to learn the brisk and complicated pieces. Twice, Conrad had to talk me off the ledge. I didn't think I could do it. Learning one song to the point of being solid was taking me days. We decided that I could make my own brand of improv fit with the groove on some songs. On others, I would play "footballs," simplified longer-held notes rather than the viciously fast musical gymnastics that others were taking care of. So, I was indoctrinated with Frank Zappa Lite, but I still had to count through changing and diverse time signatures for cues. He was right. It made me exponentially better. After immersing myself for a minimum of four to five hours a day for two months, I was a better player. I had a much better grasp of music notation than at any time in my life and felt a different sense of accomplishment than ever before.

We all converged on Conrad and Denise's new home in suburban D.C. for four days of intensive rehearsals and hit the stage in Baltimore on Mother's Day, May 12. The tour continued to Buffalo, Cleveland, Chicago, Three Oaks, and ended at the High Noon in Madison. Robin drove down and met our daughter Emily at the Chicago show. The tour was great fun, and we parted company knowing we'd be doing it again in November.

While traveling down the road from Buffalo to Cleveland, I got an email from Tag Evers, a Madison promoter who asked if Chaser could do a set at the Madison Fourth of July celebration, Shake the Lake. I wrote him back and said I would check for availability. Everyone was in, but then I realized I was booked to do the music for a wedding in Milwaukee at two that afternoon. I talked to the guys and said I could do the gig if we didn't go on until about seven.

That would give me one hour to do the ceremony, half an hour to pack up my gear, an hour and twenty-five minutes to drive home from the lakeshore, fifteen minutes to pack Chaser gear, a half hour to shower, fifteen minutes to drive to the festival, twenty minutes to get from parking to the stage, and forty-five minutes to set up my gear and transform into a rock singer. Did I mention it was a humid ninety degrees all day, and I did the wedding in direct sun? When I hit the stage at seven, my freshly changed shirt was already soaked through.

MORE

We played a good set for a wonderful audience outside on Lake Monona, not very far from where we played in the summer of 1981. It struck me again that night. I was nearly sixty-one years old and had completed an endurance test that would challenge anyone half my age due entirely to sobriety and its positive effects. Not only had my life been spared, but I honestly didn't know my age and had no intention of slowing down.

The Halloween-ish tour for The Furious Bongos started with a few changes and a week's worth of rehearsals at Chez St. Clair. Arthur didn't make the trip and was replaced by Berklee professor and Grammy-award-winning mastering engineer Jay Frigoletto for the first half of the tour and composer and Madison Opera accompanist Scott Gendel for the second half. Geoff Brady couldn't join us because his wife, accomplished musician Kia Karlen, was struggling with acute health issues. Geoff's shoes were rented by fabulous vibes player Matt Peters. Corey didn't make this trip either because he was doing the Dallas Opera. Damn divas. Seriously kidding. To add a different brand of musicianship and mayhem, we called on Madison violinist and singer Randal Harrison. Randal is an acclaimed composer, singer, and instrumentalist and had played with me way back in the *Attack of the Delicious* release show.

With those changes in place and well-rehearsed, we traveled to Poughkeepsie, New York; Manchester, New Hampshire; Burlington and Brattleboro, Vermont; Albany and Buffalo, New York; Baltimore, Maryland; Lexington, Kentucky; Columbus, Ohio; Three Oaks, Michigan; Fremont, Ohio; and Chicago. We had a great time playing the music and enjoyed each other immensely. There was always laughter happening somewhere.

As much as I pride myself on my resilience, I was dragging ass when I got home. The road hadn't changed since I was twenty-one, but I begrudgingly admitted I had.

102. BAD MOON RISING
(John Fogerty)

MARCH 1, 2020

Sitting at a stop light, lost in thought about house dimensions, I heard Robin's quick, astonished intake of a breath. As I turned to look at her, the world exploded.

It wasn't in slow motion like the movies. It was instant, violent, and brutal. I felt myself blow backward and then slam forward, spidering the windshield with my head. I landed back in the broken seat, and it was silent, dust slowly descending through the sunbeams. I lay stunned and disoriented.

We were hit from behind at a high rate of speed and pushed into the car in front of us. I calmly called Robin's name. Before I could check on her, I slowly moved my extremities one by one until I felt pretty sure nothing was broken and I wasn't paralyzed. The only pain I felt was in my ankle. It wasn't broken, but something hurt. I called to Robin and got no answer. She was leaning forward, slumped into the steering wheel. I touched her back and softly started rubbing it while continuing to call her name. I knew I shouldn't move her, but I also couldn't bear to see her in that position. Something just felt terribly wrong.

I decided to lean her back in the seat. It would allow me to assess her injuries and support her head. Afterward, she would say that she felt like she was floating in a sensory deprivation tank and couldn't breathe until I moved her. When I moved her back, she couldn't support her head, and I caught it before it moved too far and held it up. At the same time, I heard voices coming from outside. They asked if we were okay. I said, "No."

Nurses are angels. I know because I'm married to one. But Stacy McAtee is a special brand of angel. She opened the door, kneeled next to Robin, and started talking to her in soothing tones. I told her I had moved her back in the seat and saw the trepidation in her eyes, but she kept talking to us, keeping us calm. Stacy got behind Robin to support her head, and finally, Robin spoke. Until that moment, I wasn't sure if she was alive or dead. She couldn't swallow and was choking on saliva. It was an eternity before the first responders arrived. It didn't just seem like it; it was a woefully inadequate response time. Throughout this nightmare, Stacy McAtee called on all of her abilities to help us reach the ambulance ride.

When EMS arrived, we directed them to Robin first, and they put a neck brace on her and got her out of the car and onto a gurney. It felt like they were very rough with her, but I'm sure they were just doing their job. When she was safely in the back of the ambulance, they came to my side of the car and asked if I could walk. I wasn't sure I could, but they just walked away and left me to negotiate a steep embankment to walk around to the back of the car to find my own gurney. I'm still a little surprised by that. But it gave me an opportunity to tell Stacy's daughter her mother was an angel as I gingerly found my way to the stretcher and readied myself for the ride.

Lying in the back of the rattling ambulance on the way to UW Hospital, the thoughts that ran through my mind were calm and methodical. I mostly prayed my wife was going to live. I hoped against hope she was going to be okay. I didn't know the extent of her injuries, although I knew it was bad. She hadn't had any feeling in her extremities as they were taking her away. Whatever happened next, whatever condition we were in going forward, we would make it together. I hadn't for a second even thought about my injuries. They seemed inconsequential compared to Robin's.

My ambulance arrived first at the hospital and was whisked into the emergency department. It seemed odd that I would arrive first when Robin's ambulance had departed before I was out of the car. They cut off my clothes and examined me for cuts, bruises, and breaks. I kept asking about my wife. They said she had arrived and had a team of doctors working on her, and they would let me know her condition as soon as they could. I had X-rays, an MRI, and a CT scan. I had lost my phone in the accident. I was holding it when we were hit, and it was nowhere to be found. But I picked up Robin's phone and started making phone calls.

I called Anna, who was coming back from Milwaukee. I told her we were in an accident, and when she had an immediate, highly emotional response, I decided to tone down my description and say we would be okay but that she should come to the hospital when she got home. I called Emily in Chicago and was a little more descriptive. I told her more about the situation, and we decided she would come home the next day. When they came in and told me Robin was going into emergency surgery, I called Em back and said she should come now. She and Teddy Matthews might have exceeded the speed limit on the interstate.

When the doctors examined Robin, her injuries were so severe they put a halo around her head to stabilize her. As the screws were going in, the anesthetic wasn't working, and she said, "Just do it!" And as her neck was straightened, she said to the doctor, "I can feel my hands." It was music to their ears. It meant she had an injured spinal cord but that it wasn't severely damaged.

Anna called again, and I got a little more in-depth with her. I said her mom was going into surgery and she should try and see her beforehand. She stopped at home and was going to come right up. I called her again, bringing her along slowly, then told her we were pretty severely injured and not to be surprised.

They wheeled me in to see Robin, and I took her hand and said, "We'll get through this," the soothing mantra she has used all these years. Anna made it in to see her before she went for surgery, and I had prepared her well. She was strong for her mom.

Someone from the fire department came into my room with my red iPhone XR and asked if it was mine. They found it on the road under the car! I said yes, and while the case was a little worse for wear, it worked fine. I called Mike Ripp and left a message. I called Jim Ripp, and he came to the hospital. I called Jennifer Brazelton, Robin's friend and former boss, because I knew she could be the person to call Robin's contacts at the hospital. I made these calls, lying on a board in the emergency department of UW Hospital, floating on a cloud of fentanyl to dull the pain that was starting to envelop my body. An ophthalmologist came in to give me an exam because I had a blank spot in my left eye. My vision was a little blurry, but there was a disconcerting patch in the center of my vision that was blank. Not black, just a clear circle devoid of image.

They moved me to a room, and family members started arriving. Emily and Teddy had broken land speed records and breathlessly arrived. Emily took over and called all of Robin's siblings, and they were all there when the doctor came in around ten that night and told us Robin's surgery was extensive but successful. She'd had four cervical vertebrae fused with metal from C1 to C4. She also had a concussion. She had a long road to recovery, but the prognosis was that she would have full movement in her arms and legs. Family was allowed to go and see her, and although she wasn't totally conscious, it comforted the family that she was going to live.

My injuries? A broken C7 vertebrae, three broken ribs, a lung contusion, a laceration on my forehead, and a concussion. I also had a mysterious laceration on my ankle that hurt worse than all the rest, and nobody seemed to care about it. I had to ask to have it treated. I guess that was the least of their worries. When he delivered the news about Robin, I asked the doctor if I could still make the two gigs I had scheduled for that week. He failed to see the humor and didn't dignify it with a response.

I'm still puzzled as to the logistics of the accident. We were plowed into by a Dodge pickup truck going at least fifty. The driver walked away from it and was never tested for any substances. He claims he was daydreaming. I call fucking bullshit on that. If he hadn't hit us, he would have run the red light we were waiting for and perhaps caused a worse accident! And, of course, he was underinsured.

Even with all my anger, Robin and I decided we wouldn't ruin his life. He was a seventy-eight-year-old man, and we could have taken him for all he was worth. That's not who we are.

Relieved that my incredible wife was in good hands and out of immediate danger, our family went home and left me to the shadows and muted sounds of a late-night hospital. I slept very little, reliving the sound and sensations of the impact and its aftermath. As I cultivated the myriad thoughts of the day, including self-pity and "Why did this have to happen to us?" I came to another conclusion that life is so incredibly fragile. The clichés had already been spoken about how lucky we were, it could have been so much worse, etc. But they weren't clichés. Robin and I were alive in a world-class hospital. The surgeons at UW Hospital had the expertise, ability, and facilities to perform emergency surgery that literally pieced Robin's shattered neck back together and gave her a chance at living a normal life. The outcome likely wouldn't have been as positive if we had been anywhere else. We weren't lucky; it was miraculous. When my wife was taken away in an ambulance, she had no sensation below her chin. She couldn't even swallow. I lay in my speeding ambulance, looking at the ceiling wondering how we were going to negotiate a changed life. The slightest variable in the speed or angle of the collision could have resulted in irreparable injuries or death. Even as I write this, I realize I should never again wonder why it happened. There is no answer.

103. IT'S THE END OF THE WORLD AS WE KNOW IT (AND I FEEL FINE)
(Bill Berry, Peter Buck, Mike Mills, and Michael Stipe)

AS I FINALLY DOZED OFF into a tentative sleep, the door opened, and a phlebotomist came in to draw blood. I was exhausted, my body was beat to shit, and I had a headache that wouldn't quit. I said, "You've got to be fucking kidding me." She justifiably wasn't too pleased with my reaction, and there was an immediate tension. Realizing I had said my thoughts out loud, I apologized for my rudeness and complimented her on what was the smoothest stick I'd ever gotten. So much for sleep. A cavalcade of doctors were in and out of my room. Many I saw once and never again. I asked each how Robin was doing, and they had no idea. My nurses, bless them all, gave me information whenever they got it and sometimes inquired for me.

One particular nurse decided she would take me over to see Robin if I was up to it. I jumped at the chance. She wheeled me through the circuitous, bustling hallways to the intensive care unit. I didn't see the tubes and electronics aiding Robin's recovery; I saw the most beautiful woman in the world. As I held her hand, she floated in a semi-conscious state. Just then, I was overwhelmed by immense fatigue caused by the medication I had taken before our trek, little to no sleep the night before, and trying to do too much too soon. I asked if my nurse could take me back, and I fell into a shallow, often interrupted sleep.

The next day, I felt better. I decided I would do as much as possible to convince my healthcare team I was ready for discharge. My cousin, Denise Gronli-Terrian, a nurse at the hospital, wheeled me for another visit to ICU, and we found the staff walking Robin down the hall. She was walking! I wept tears of joy. It would be a long, painful recovery, but she was walking. It was the first significant step. Neil Armstrong got nothin' on Robin.

I went back to my room and underwent a battery of physical and cognitive tests to see my status. I forced my way through some of the physical challenges and likely should have stayed another night in the hospital, but I wanted to be a visitor in Robin's room, not another patient. I got a somewhat reluctant green light to go home from the docs, showered, and changed into street clothes from the worst attire known to humankind. What is up with hospital gowns? Can't someone do something about that? It's the twenty-first century.

Yet another nurse wheeled me for the last time through the sixth-floor cacophony to Robin's room. I was a visitor.

Robin had walked again for a few steps, unassisted. I saw in action what I already knew about her. The strength and resolve in her face told me she would attack her recovery and rehabilitation with a vengeance. My wife is a bona fide rock star.

I went home with Emily and Anna. I was more than a little anxious riding in the car, but I couldn't wait to get a decent night's sleep, even though I had to sleep flat on my back in my cervical collar, with no pillow because of my injuries. At least I wouldn't be awakened every hour for tests.

Our daughters grew up quickly on that fateful day. They were thrust into the role of caretaker for their parents and performed magnificently. Part of their challenge was a cantankerous father who challenged and flirted with the limitations placed upon him by medical staff. In retrospect, I never took my injuries seriously. I never once complained because, in my mind, I was injured far less severely than Robin. It was she who I concentrated on and worried about. I should have brought myself along more slowly and Emily and Anna, difficult as I was, did a great job putting their foot down on some things and looking the other way on others.

Robin improved slowly during the week, and we spent as much time visiting as we were allowed. Her pain level was acute, and I wished more than anything that it was me instead of her. If anyone on earth didn't deserve this twisted karma, it is my saintly wife. The most compassionate and caring person I knew didn't merit this set of circumstances. The universe fucked up. It got it wrong.

It seemed abrupt to me, but the doctors planned on discharging Robin to the UW Rehabilitation Hospital on Friday, March 6, just five days after the accident. I found it impossible to comprehend that someone with her injuries would be moved from ICU so quickly. Part of me was happy, and the other part thought she was being discharged prematurely. But what do I know?

And we were going to transport her. Another surprise! After an expert ambulatory drive by Emily to the far east Madison facility, Robin was installed in a private room at the rehab hospital and set about diligently working to heal.

104. VIRUS
(Björk and Sjón)

ON MONDAY, MARCH 9, UW Hospital unofficially acknowledged that COVID-19 was a serious threat. The rehab hospital started limiting and changing the number of visitors. They were trying to get a handle on what was the appropriate response. On March 10, UW–Milwaukee announced it was moving classes online. UW–Green Bay followed suit the next day. On March 13, the governor ordered all schools in the state to shut down by March 18 with no possibility of re-opening until April 6 at the earliest—if only. We were at the beginning of a global pandemic. This was uncharted territory, and my wife was in a rehab hospital, in a cervical collar, with severe injuries from an auto accident, recovering from major surgery, with a feeding tube for nourishment because the injury to her neck still made swallowing too painful to eat.

Through it all, she stayed positive.

And through it all, Emily and Anna selflessly cared for us with compassion and wisdom learned by observing their mother all these years.

On one of our early visits to the rehab hospital, my daughters and I decided it was a Culver's night. As we headed south on Stoughton Road, I realized we were going to pass the accident site, and I brought it up. Emily said we could go a different route if I was uncomfortable, and I said, "No, I'm fine," not sure if I actually was. We were coming up to the location of the crash, and my heart started racing. I had been in a severe auto accident as a six-year-old, and every time throughout my life I've come close to that site, I've felt heightened anxiety. It's never gone away. But this day, I felt every muscle in my body relax, passing the place on the road where I had a brush with death just days before. It was the oddest sensation. I hadn't realized until that moment how clenched and tense every muscle fiber had been for over a week! I slept like a baby that night.

Robin had been losing weight because of her inability to take nourishment. She tried hard to eat soft foods and soups, but the pain in her throat wasn't abating. If she lost any more weight, it would jeopardize when she could come home. A target had been set for a March 21 discharge, but if things didn't improve, she would have to stay longer. Then mid-week, they abruptly canceled all visitors. Robin had been complaining of a sore throat and cold symptoms even before the accident, and they continued all through her stay in the ICU and rehab, and now she had spiked a fever. The overriding fear was that she had COVID and had infected the hospital. We breathlessly awaited test results and were relieved with a negative result. But she had some undiagnosed viral infection that was still concerning.

We had been taking turns visiting. We could only send one person every twenty-four hours, and now we couldn't visit at all. We got our status reports from phone calls to Robin and her nurses. She gained a couple of pounds after forcing some supplemental real food in addition to the feeding tube. We resigned ourselves to caring for the feeding tube for a while at home. Then they changed their minds. Robin would be coming home on Friday, March 20, if she didn't lose more weight. We were thrilled! I couldn't wait to get her home to make her as comfortable as possible. But then came the word they feared a false negative on her COVID test, and she would have to quarantine at home for a week. Are you kidding me? What could possibly be next?

We did get some good news that they removed her feeding tube before discharge, but she would have to have it re-inserted if she lost weight again. Initial insertion was incredibly difficult. Speculation was that her throat was damaged from intubation at the accident scene. We would work hard to avoid that and celebrate every pound gained.

Everything was being canceled. Schools closed their doors, and restaurants, bars, and shops shut down. The government was categorizing businesses as essential or non-essential and ordering non-essentials closed. Governor Tony Evers quelled pandemonium by declaring liquor stores in Wisconsin essential. If he hadn't, there would have been pitchforks and torches in the street.

And Robin was home! After all she had been through, we needed to keep her quarantined from us under the fear that she had COVID, even after a negative test. She was sleeping quite a lot, so it wasn't terrible when we set her up in the basement on the futon and waited on her hand and foot. It didn't last long, though. We finally came to the conclusion that it didn't make any difference where she was, we were coming into contact anyway, and we threw out the rule book and brought her upstairs.

We watched as the world fell deeper into chaos and shutdown. We would have had a long, secluded recovery, but now everyone was right there with us in their own bubbles, wondering how bad it was going to get.

On March 30, we awoke to the catastrophic news that friends had been abducted from their home and brutally murdered. We were numb. It couldn't be real. Was the world truly going completely crazy? We had been casual friends for years, socialized occasionally, and our children attended the same preschool. They were beloved by all who knew them and many who didn't. They lived their lives helping people and making the world a better place. It was a senseless and violent act in an already turbulent year. One more surreal event to be processed by fragile, wounded brains.

And we were in for yet another shock. Our thirtieth wedding anniversary dawned tragic with the news of the passing of one of Robin's dearest friends, Helen Chung. Helen had been valiantly battling lung cancer, and her death was sudden and unexpected. We had known Helen and her husband, Brent Smith, since Emily attended kindergarten with their daughter Caitlin. Robin and Helen's friendship was deep, abiding, meaningful, and a source of joy for many years. Although Robin's grief was profound, she kept a brave face to be strong for Caitlin and her younger sister Mairin. And amid a pandemic, wearing a cervical collar and recovering from massive injuries, Robin Valley-Massey took on the role of executor of Helen's estate. It is one way she has chosen to honor her.

105. I WANT TO THANK YOU
(Otis Redding)

APRIL 9, 2020, a day of giving. Masterminded by Madison CBS affiliate WISC-TV Anchor Charlotte Deleste; Robin's sister, Karen Broitzman; and Robin's coworker Ryan Brown, Valley-Massey Strong combined a fundraiser with the internet to provide us with funds to take care of medical bills not covered by insurance and living expenses while we were convalescing. The outpouring of love from the community was beyond comprehension. Once again, our ever-present lifelong friend John Urban stepped up and produced the event in association with Big Dreamers United, a company he founded with Lea Culver to provide promotional materials for nonprofit organizations. As usual, John went above and beyond the call of duty to help people in need. This time it was us.

I have included an unedited thank you post from Facebook on April 13, 2020:

> We alternate between tears of disbelief and joy, and a numbness. We spent the day feeling like we were underwater. How could any of this be real?
>
> When Charlotte Deleste and Robin's sister, Karen Broitzman, first floated the idea of a benefit right after our accident, we were both in a terribly fragile state and were grateful and humbled by the thought.

Now after the longest six weeks of our lives, that vision has turned into a reality beyond our wildest imagination!

There are no words to express our gratitude for the people involved in bringing the event to fruition and to all of you for your generosity and wonderful, kind words. It sparks a renewal to feel all the good in this world that all too often these days seems severely lacking in compassion and warmth.

It's hard to accept help. Truer words were never spoken than, "Tis better to give than to receive." We struggled all day with not feeling worthy of this enormous outpouring of love and support. Every time John Urban posted a new, unbelievable total, it triggered another round of surreal tears. But in speaking with some close friends during the course of the day, they assured us that it feels good to help. It feeds the soul to be generous. So in that spirit, we are honored and humbled by all of your uplifting words, songs, good humor and love as well as your amazing, selfless donations during a time when so many are experiencing hardship. Our hearts go out to everyone suffering in the midst of this pandemic.

Although "thank you" isn't remotely enough, we'd like to try; Charlotte Deleste, Karen Broitzman and Ryan Brown for the vision. John Urban and Lea Culver of Big Dreamers United for the fabulous promo video and John's tireless producing and monitoring of the event. Leanne Marso, Ryan Brown, Dr. Maria Stanley, Beth Kille, Erik Kjelland, Rick Tvedt and Tony Cerniglia for lending their cinematic talents to said video.

James (Jim, Jimbo, Jambo, Jam, Slam) Ripp for posting a treasure trove of music from a dusty vault, taking some of us back quite a few years and testing the memories of even those who wrote and played them! Tony Cerniglia for being media consultant and Jonathan Suttin and Kitty Dunn of 105.5 Triple M and Charlotte and Mark Koehn of WISC-TV 3 for having him on their shows.

Jay Moran, Clay Konnor, Emily Wicker, Josh Dupont/Francie Phelps, and Erik Kjelland for recording videos of performances that brightened everyone's day.

MORE

Siobhan Killeen-Toomey for above-and-beyond meal preparations and collecting a generous neighborhood donation out of the blue.

Mark Geistlinger, Kristin Meyer and Zoe Meyer (you're it) for maintenance, yard work and being the very best of neighbors and friends.

And to all of you. Everyone who sent flowers and cards and letters or brought meals to us. Everyone who's called with inspirational words. Everyone who has posted an uplifting message. And to everyone who donated during a difficult time for all. Personal email thank-you notes will be forthcoming. We can never thank you enough.

Never.

Robin Valley-Massey and Michael Massey ... Valley-Massey Strong

Not expected and incredibly appreciated, the event buoyed us beyond measure. I'll say it again. We can never thank everyone enough.

Only two people reached out to me in the middle of the aftermath of the accident and the pandemic, asking about my alcohol recovery, both recovering themselves and knowing the disease of addiction doesn't pander to logic. My dear friend and Stop the Clock bassist Frank Queram called and asked if I was doing okay. We had a lovely conversation, and I assured him that I was in a good place regarding relapsing. My cousin Doug Gronli also asked through his daughter Denise who had wheeled me through the hospital. It touched me that they thought to ask, and it surprised the hell out of me that I hadn't even thought about it until they brought it up. It gave me an odd feeling that drinking wasn't even on my radar in the midst of some of the worst stress and trauma of my life.

106. BIRTHDAY
(John Lennon and Paul McCartney)

A TWENTY-FIRST BIRTHDAY is a big deal. For everyone. You spend years of your life pining for the moment when you're "legal for everything." When you're an adult. When your fake ID can be passed on to the next crop of younger revelers.

Anna's twenty-first was going to be spent in isolation. She had made huge plans pre-pandemic, and those vaporized amidst the virus—a grave disappointment.

Emily is a good big sister, and Anna will agree half the time. This is one of those times. Emily enlisted her friends Desi and Carina to help devise a special birthday, and they worked on a plan to create "Club Q(uarantine)." It was kept a tightly guarded secret until the moment of reveal. They transformed our former master bedroom into a dance club.

I set up my PA, mic, stand, and lights. They constructed a bar generously stocked with tequila and strung garland, glitter, Christmas lights, and streamers on the wall. They made a sign for the door. There was going to be a bouncer. We found karaoke tracks to sing with online and sound checked. Everything went like clockwork.

In an endearing act of levity in the middle of hardship, Emily and her friends (they were Anna's friends, too) had given us a respite. It was an escape from the gravity of healing, and it gave us the ability to forget, if even for a little while, the insane status of the world.

We danced, we sang, they drank. We partied into the night. Though not the celebration Anna had envisioned for herself, it was much more memorable in many ways.

107. UNWRITTEN
(Natasha Bedingfield, Danielle Brisebois, and Wayne Rodrigues)

WHEN EMILY ABRUPTLY dropped everything and came to our rescue, she took a hiatus from the band in the middle of working hard on writing and recording its first full-length album for Winspear Records. Even with a pandemic, the label was on schedule, and the pressure was mounting to deliver a finished product. The problem was that Emily was sheltered in place in Madison, a caretaker for recovering parents.

Slow Pulp was positioned well in the Indie Rock scene. Their earlier releases were in the millions of streams and climbing on Spotify, and all other platforms and YouTube were monetized. They had some very good industry traction after successful supporting slots on extensive U.S. tours. This album and subsequent headlining tour could take them to the next level.

One major limitation the medical staff had laid on us was that we should avoid stairs whenever possible. This caused a major shuffling of rooms, bringing our upstairs master bedroom down into the project studio I had loved for two decades, moving my studio into the dining room, and setting Emily up with a workspace to write and record ideas in our former master. She would sequester herself for hours, and we'd hear traces of melodies wafting through the ceiling. The album wasn't even entirely written yet, the deadline was looming, and Em was getting more stressed by the day.

Henry Stoehr, Slow Pulp's lead guitarist and producer, suggested we do Emily's vocal tracks at the house. We could record the tracks and send the files to Henry in Chicago, where he would place them in the mix. In theory, it could work. She wasn't too excited about the idea at first, but there was really no other choice. She couldn't go back to Chicago. Everyone was in quarantine, and Em wasn't in the band's pod because of the accident. I called on my buddy, Tony C., yet again. I procured his Neumann U 87 microphone once more. Then we set about creating an environment conducive to creativity as best we could. We draped quilts and blankets over my PA and lighting poles to build a makeshift vocal booth. Emily referred to it as the "blanket fort." I configured a metal coat hanger into a makeshift circle, stretched an old pair of nylon tights over it, and placed it in front of the microphone for a pop filter. It would have to do. It really is all about the performances.

Emily felt completely overwhelmed as we dipped our toes into moving forward on the project. Not only did her parents cheat death, and she was caring for them during recovery, but the parents of friends were murdered, her mom's best friend passed away, and she was under pressure to finish writing the melodies and lyrics for unfinished songs and record the vocals for five of them. I said to calm down, chip away at the stone, and we'd get there. And we worked.

We must have made quite a sight, me still in my cervical collar manning the controls of Pro Tools and Em, in headphones surrounded by bedding in a converted dining room. Unfortunately, there is only one photograph documenting the operation. All we thought about was getting the work done.

It's worth noting how immensely the music industry has changed since Chaser went to New York in the early eighties. In that era, you needed to go into a studio or rent the gear to make a recording. Now, you have the equivalent of $100,000 worth of gear on a laptop and can record an album just about anywhere. The downside is that if you listen very carefully to the isolated tracks, you can hear traces of the television in the other room where Robin and Anna were trying valiantly to co-exist with an album being created mere feet away. Or the sump pump in the basement kicking in periodically. Oh well, it gives it texture.

After the head injury, my reaction times were slower than normal. I felt a strange sense of detachment for the first couple of months after the accident. It was like I was watching my life instead of living it. I would forget what I was talking about in the middle of a sentence. Working on this music with Emily slowly brought me closer to reality and cleared the cobwebs. There was one very dramatic episode where after a particularly good vocal take, I thought I had inadvertently deleted it. Pro Tools has safeguards against such disasters, but my brain wasn't working at its peak, and I felt complete panic as Emily melted down over my ineptitude. I figured it out, and the track was saved, but it was a moment that was a breakthrough of sorts for me. It jolted me into being wholly present and putting any remnant of self-pity to bed. At this point, I was her engineer, not her father.

Both Emily and I had trepidation about working together. We are very similar in many respects, and I hoped it wouldn't be abrasive. Instead, we developed a good sense of bouncing ideas off each other, and I gently nudged her in directions of diction and emotion. The potential adversarial vibe never materialized, and we surprised ourselves by becoming a potent, creative, and efficient team. I was immensely proud of my daughter. Her natural sense of melody is formidable, and her work ethic and drive to finish the project amid chaos were admirable. As we worked on recording the vocals for the completed songs that the boys in the band had approved, she was also writing the remaining lyrics and melody to finish the album. It was a brutal schedule, but it gave us both a purpose and distraction from the accident and the evening news.

Before we knew it, the load had lightened. We worked slowly and methodically, taking time and care with each song. What had seemed insurmountable amidst tragedy and turmoil became accomplishment. Henry was extremely happy with the tracks we sent, and the rough mixes sounded lovely. He even enlisted me to arrange a piece he had written for the piano. After learning it comprehensively, I gave it my personality and am honored that it landed on the album. We finished the last vocal track

MORE

and sent it to Chicago one day before the deadline. Henry expertly mixed, produced, and sent it to mastering. The record landed with Winspear Records on time.

So, in the middle of the worst year of my life, I had an opportunity that would have never happened in a normal world. I cherish the time working with Emily toward a common goal, and I credit it with helping me to recover from the nightmarish beginning of the year.

Update: as of this writing, Slow Pulp's streams are more than sixty million, and the band's catalog averages more than 1.2 million streams per month. Slow Pulp was cheated out of the normal progression of things by COVID-19, scheduling, canceling, rescheduling, and canceling again two U.S. tours and a European tour. Their first headlining U.S. tour narrowly missed completely selling out in November and December of 2021, playing twenty-four of twenty-eight scheduled dates before a positive COVID test shut it down.

Currently, Emily and I just finished recording the vocal tracks for Slow Pulp's second full-length album in my studio in our new home, a world away from the dining room blanket fort. A new deal with a larger record label is only awaiting signatures. They are about to embark upon a thirty-city U.S. tour supporting the Canadian band, Alvvays, and are scheduled to support Death Cab for Cutie in Europe in March 2023. The new album will be released in spring 2023, with headlining U.S. and European tours to follow. Slow Pulp: coming soon to a city near you.

108. START ME UP
(Mick Jagger and Keith Richards)

IN MAY 2020, Josh and Francie were brainstorming ways to keep Piano Fondue in front of an audience and to keep our roster of entertainers engaged and fresh. We didn't know how long COVID-19 was going to fuck up the world, and they rightly weren't going to wait around to find out. Piano Fondue instituted the Showcase Countdown, where our online fan base would choose songs for each of us to record each week. I wasn't sure I was ready to perform, but I jumped in with both feet. Some of the earlier recordings were a little rough, shaking off the rust of an accident and not playing for a couple of months, but we all got into the swing of things and created a fun weekly diversion for ourselves and the audience. Besides, we had a little more control over the finished product than a one-off live performance.

I credit the Showcase Countdown and Piano Fondue for bringing me fully into recovery mode. It was a purpose and a mental and physical workout every week. It made me realize my brain was a little lethargic from injury, but we would work through it.

In June, we started live-streaming weekly shows. Ninety minutes on Facebook, YouTube, and Twitch. Michelle Grabel-Komar commented in the chat window after the first show, "Thanks for the hang," and it became "Mike Massey's Monday Evening Hang" from that moment forward. It was a great way to sharpen our live performance chops after months of dormancy. With the Digital Setlist app, developed by Josh and Francie, viewers could request the songs being played and comment in the chat window, so there was instant dialogue across the internet. We all chose an evening. I took Mondays; Dr. Josh Dupont continued his famous Tuesdays; Jim Ripp commandeered the "Hump Day Happy Hour" every Wednesday; Josh and Francie did a duet night on Thursdays; Taras Nahirniak landed the "TGI Taras" on Fridays; and Josh and Francie reprised their duets on Sundays with a weekly theme night. Piano Fondue had an ongoing presence of live music six and sometimes seven nights a week. A good time was had by all.

A couple of months into the rotation, I added about thirty-five of my songs to the setlist and did an all-original night. Subsequent weeks became a mix of classic hits and Massey songs, and I found myself playing some of them better than ever. There's something about playing in the cocoon of your own studio while knowing people are listening that lends itself to experimentation and reaching for the best performance you can give. There isn't the conversation, laughter, or distractions of a club, just pure concentration and performance. The best kind of meditation and escape.

Robin continued attacking her rehab with a vengeance. She faithfully attended physical and occupational therapy sessions and implemented all treatments, aided by her medical knowledge. And we walked. Robin sometimes walked miles a day with her Exerstriders, poles similar to cross-country skiing designed for walking. She and I would walk together all around Madison's east side, often ending up at the breakwater of Lake Mendota at Tenney Park for the sunset and a rest on the bench lakeside. I didn't think it was possible to love and respect her more than I already did, but she proved me wrong. The woman is superhuman. In June, she was given the green light to wear her neck brace half of the time and was able to lose it permanently on July 1.

She went back to work in early July at the Waisman Center, supposedly four hours per day, but it was always six. I felt it was too soon, but they needed her, and I think she wanted to feel more normal as well. It resulted in evenings where she was wiped out and bone tired, and I hoped it wouldn't be a detriment to her recovery, a recovery that doctors said would take at least two years. It was still a very long road ahead.

In October, Robin's brother Brian built us a driveway to the new house site. The house was staked out, and excavation was going to start soon. When I saw the location of the stakes, I asked our builder, Derek Carpenter, to move the stakes eight feet west from their location. It still didn't feel exactly right when I saw his handiwork at the deserted site on an off day. I called and asked if I could move them again and assured him that I would accurately keep all of the dimensions secured. He was justifiably hesitant, but I convinced him I knew what I was doing. My uncle Jim Massey and I, armed with the GPS compass on my iPhone and a tape measure, moved those stakes another eight feet due west, and the house clicked into its rightful place in the world. I will forever tell that story to anyone who is forced to listen.

In November, they broke ground, poured concrete footings, and then the foundation proper. This house was real. It was a culmination of years of preparation, a dream coming true.

109. ANGEL OF THE MORNING
(Chip Taylor)

MIDDLETON—*Joni Sue Massey, age 52, of Middleton, passed away on Thursday, Dec. 10, 2020. She was born on July 28, 1968, in Madison, the daughter of William and Nancy (Dodge) Massey. Joni graduated from Madison East High School and attended MATC.*

Joni previously worked for UW Health as a Med Flight dispatcher. She relished the fast-paced environment and excelled in her role helping the emergency helicopter find people in their direst hour of need. She loved gardening, reading, and playing the piano. Joni also enjoyed using her creativity to re-purpose vintage finds, adding touches of paint to worn flowerpots and making them works of art. Or rescuing antique pieces of furniture and giving them new life.

Family was most important to Joni; she was enormously proud of her children and grandson, celebrating accomplishments large and small. She held a special place in the hearts of her family as the "Angel of the Morning," so named for a song that was on the charts the day she was born. A lone sister beloved by her four brothers and parents.

Joni is survived by her daughters, Justina (Ben) Kimmel and Caitlyn Olrick (Ian Seaman-Gilberts); sons, Andy Olrick and Hayden Olrick (Mariana Rubio); brothers, Michael (Robin Valley-Massey)

Massey, Scott (Elizabeth) Massey, Keith (Adriana) Massey and Kevin (Shari) Massey; grandson, Milo Olrick-Gilberts; former husband, Kevin Olrick; and many other relatives and friends. She was preceded in death by her parents.

Virtual services will be held at a date and time to be determined. Please feel free to reach out to a family member if you would like to participate.

In lieu of flowers, memorials to the Monona Serenity Group or the Lupus Foundation of America, Wisconsin Chapter, would be appreciated by the family. Online condolences may be made at www.gundersonfh.com.

MY SISTER WAS BORN in the summer of 1968. Merrilee Rush and the Turnabouts had a top ten worldwide hit with the song "Angel of the Morning," and my father immediately deemed it Joni's theme song. She was indeed our angel.

Joni was dealt a bad hand in life. She was diagnosed with lupus and rheumatoid arthritis in her thirties. After surgeries, pain management became an ongoing struggle for the rest of her life. Like so many unfortunates in this pharmaceutical-dominated landscape, she flirted with and succumbed to opioid addiction.

Joni was young to become a mother. She was seventeen when Justina was born on November 28, 1985, and Andy, Caity, and Hayden came along in succession. Her marriage to Kevin Olrick was blessed by these beautiful children but struggled under the weight of being kids themselves who never had a chance to grow up. Thrust into the role of adults, much like our own parents, Joni and Kevin worked hard to provide a good life for their family and succeeded for a time. But misfortune, Kevin successfully battling throat cancer, and Joni's illnesses took their toll.

After the divorce, Joni fell into a pattern so familiar to the millions of Americans battling opioids. She took her pain meds too early and could not get the prescription refilled, so she resorted to black-market drugs.

She was a woman of extremes. She loved her children passionately and would do anything for them, but addiction robbed her of clarity and resolve. In November 2004, after three grand mal seizures caused by her lupus and opioids, Joni slipped into a coma for a week with acute respiratory distress syndrome and was placed on a ventilator. We all thought we would lose her and steeled ourselves against it.

Miraculously, she pulled through, but she had lost some cognitive ability and seemed unable to comprehend responsibility for her actions.

A shift was taking place. There was less use of pain meds but an alarming increase in alcohol consumption. There were more frequent episodes of acute intoxication, and we all tried to help. She began repeating the mantra, "At least I'm not as bad as Mike was." Truth be told, she was quickly approaching my level of degradation, and I knew it, but she wouldn't listen to me. Like so many of us in the throes of substance abuse, Joni never took any ownership of her disease. She struggled with reality as opposed to her sense of self. This was exacerbated by the damage done while in a coma. She no longer possessed the will or the awareness to successfully institute change for the better. We constantly heard her say she didn't drink that much or that she could quit anytime. It was a flashback for me, and I feared for her well-being, for her life.

After a particularly bad episode where she was taken by ambulance to the hospital for detox, the staff suggested a hard-core residential treatment facility in Georgia that was covered by Medicare. Joni was excited by the prospect and said all the right things about wanting to get clean and turn her life around. We were thrilled! After a couple of nights spent with us, we put her on a plane bound for Atlanta, and for the first time in many years, her family and friends found cause for optimism.

But alas, after a month at the facility, she said she needed to come home to attend to business and relapsed on her way home from the airport.

This started a pattern of relapsing, hiding it for as long as she could (she couldn't), ending up in dire straits and detoxing again in the hospital, and going back to Georgia, each time promising it would work. There were four stints at the treatment facility, staying a bit longer on subsequent trips. The last time, she lived in Georgia for six months and sounded great when we had phone conversations. We all implored her to stay permanently, knowing it was her best chance for success. But she wanted to come home. She missed her family and wanted to see her grandson Milo grow up. She returned to Madison and got set up in a nice one-bedroom apartment, and things seemed better for a little while. I talked to her on the phone and knew she had relapsed again. She denied it, got defensive, and cut off communication, which wasn't uncommon, but after a week or so of not talking to her, we tried again and got no answer. Her daughters tried as well, and when there was no response, with a feeling of dread, they called the Middleton Police Department for a wellness check.

On December 10, 2020, Joni had drifted softly away, free of her earthly struggles at last.

There is much more to her story and life than I have depicted here. It could be a book of its own, filled with tragedy and comedy, love and loss. I deeply mourn for her, as do her family and friends, but we also feel a reluctant relief. She is no longer fighting a dragon with every breath. In watching Joni's slow, painful demise, I saw what could have been my own, twenty-nine years prior. I watched the disease of addiction tear apart the ones she loved and methodically kill her. I struggle with feelings of guilt because I'm recovering, and she could not. Daily, I wish I would have done more, a residual, perpetual side effect of the disease that devastates the loved ones of the afflicted

110. LOOKIN' OUT MY BACK DOOR
(John Fogerty)

THE YEAR 2021 saw fleeting hope on the horizon for an end to the COVID-19 pandemic. Vaccines were being administered to people in stages, and Robin was among the first due to her position in healthcare. Emily was next, being a ballet teacher in Illinois. Anna returned from her newly adopted Phoenix, Arizona, home to get a shot because of her association with the Madison Metropolitan School District as a virtual junior varsity volleyball coach for East High. I got my Pfizer vaccine in April. There was light at the end of the tunnel. The world was awakening. COVID infections declined exponentially, and plans for a return to normalcy were being made.

Live performances were being scheduled. Francie and I played our first show together since December 2019 on May 8 outside at the beautiful Botham Vineyards in Barneveld. We were a little rough around the edges after the layoff, but it was glorious to sing together, harmonize, and have actual live humans applaud.

But wishful thinking and overconfidence gave way to another surge. While logical, empathetic members of society took it seriously, misinformation and misguided politics led to half of the population eschewing science for a false, selfish, perceived liberty. Restrictions came roaring back.

On a hopeful front, construction had begun on the new house. Supply chain issues, our builder getting COVID, and numerous other setbacks severely delayed the process. Still, Robin and I watched the slow transformation of a virgin prairie, ancestral land, assimilate the home of our dreams. The walls and the floors gave us our first glimpse at the reality of our vision. What had been entirely conceptual was taking shape with wood, iron, and cement. We sold our home at 1950 East Dayton Street to a lovely couple with two daughters about the same ages as Emily and Anna were when we moved in. A serendipitous, enchanting circle. In seventy-one years, the home had never been listed with a realtor. It has always been sold with pride by word of mouth. And here's hoping its new occupants share our enduring love affair with the property.

I'm going to miss living in Madison, eight minutes from downtown, within walking distance of shops, theaters, and the lakes. I've lived all but a couple of years of my life on the east side and will always have that sense of pride. But as I embraced a radical change in my life when I got sober, so do I look forward to this new phase of discovery and serenity, stability, and a continued drive to create art. A prospect that is only possible due to my sobriety.

111. LIFE'S BEEN GOOD
(Joe Walsh)

I'M STRUCK BY HOW my definition of success has changed over the years.

The younger me wanted fame and fortune, limousines, and tens of thousands in the audience. Now I'm touched and consider it the highest compliment when someone reaches out and says my music comforted them in their time of need.

The younger me lived a promiscuous and lascivious lifestyle, resigned to the thought I'd probably die alone but would have a blast getting there. The current me looks at how incredibly fortunate I am to be in love with the woman I married thirty-two years ago and who saved me.

The younger, stupider me drank alcohol nearly every day of my life for twenty years. I made a change twenty-nine years ago and celebrate every moment that has happened since.

I've lived two different lives.

I am grateful every day and sometimes feel guilty about my abundance of riches. I'm not financially wealthy, but I'm alive and love deeply. Our daughters are intelligent, compassionate, delightful, socially and politically active contributing members of society, which should be the goal of every parent.

The changing definition of success. Though I haven't sold a million records yet, I have people that appreciate and love the music I create. I have dear friends who I would do anything for, and them for me. I share my life with a woman who I love far more than on our wedding day. If that's not success, change your dictionary.

Throughout the course of this project, I have been alternately depressed from reliving some of my darkest moments and elated by the joys and victories that have come with sobriety.

To finally put all of the stories I have told through the years in one comprehensive place is soul-cleansing. In my pursuit of producing something that I hope will be a comfort and help people who are struggling, I have helped myself. I told my good friend, Michael John Ripp, as he contemplated asking Courtney LeClair to marry him, "Life is a series of chapters, and it's up to us to write them."

The steam from my coffee rises, illuminated by the morning sun on the screen porch of our beautiful new home. I survey this lush green valley, legacy land, in the family for 111 years, with Frank the cat on my lap and Cora our three-legged rescue Terrier sleeping on a chair across the room. Every day I find it difficult to believe this exquisite reality. It is beyond anything I ever imagined.

It is here, in this dream come true home that Robin and I will live, love and create new stories to be told another day. It is here I feel the magic of the earth and the influence of generations of sweat, back-breaking work, laughter, tears and integrity. And it is here, in these pages, that I make peace with all that has gone before, what has landed me in this moment.

I feel a sense of a life well lived with hard-earned contentment. For no apparent reason, providence has made me a fortunate one. I am recovering. I can anticipate. I can reminisce. Too many of our compatriots didn't get that opportunity. The books of their lives ended tragically early and unfinished.

It is in their memory I dedicate this endeavor.

And it is in their honor I have so much yet to do.

More.

MORE

MORE

My life in tatters, bleeding
Pouring on the floor
Drowning what control I have left
Cracks that line the ceiling
Mock me to the core
Darkness steals my soul

I'll never laugh again or sing as loud
I'll never play that song to adoring crowds
I'll never dream as big or breathe as deep
I'll never feel your love raining down on me
There's got to be more

I live between the shadows
Don't know what is real
Or if I can believe what I see
Help me find an answer
Show me how to heal
Teach me how to grieve

I'll never laugh again or sing as loud
I'll never play that song to adoring crowds
I have no love to give or the will to weep
For what I've lost, guilt is killing me
There's got to be more

Searching deep inside through twisting passageways
To find the man I was before
I throw away the bottle and the mask it made
To find my calm before the storm
To find the key, unlock the door
I found the key unlocking more

I know it won't be easy

MICHAEL MASSEY

Changing what is past
Finding who I am again
If happiness is fleeting
I'll take it when I can
Give it second chances

I'll laugh just as hard, sing just as loud
I'll play my songs to a mindful crowd
I'll dream just as big, breathe just as deep
I'll feel your love raining down on me

I'll laugh just as hard, sing just as loud
I'll lie down in the grass to see faces in the clouds
I've got love to give, pride is my reward
I'll open up my eyes, see what was here, all along

More

CAST OF CHARACTERS IN ORDER OF APPEARANCE

MY ESTEEMED EDITOR tells me I have too many names in this book. He's right, of course, and I have deleted many at his behest. But here is a primer to the main cast of characters. There won't be a quiz.

Robin Valley-Massey—My wife of thirty-two years, and so much more.
Jim Ripp—Lifelong friend, musician
Scott Massey—Brother
Kevin Massey—Brother
Keith Massey—Brother
Joni Massey—Sister
Bill Massey—Father
Nancy Massey—Mother
Mark Davini—Lifelong friend, musician
Michael John Ripp—Best friend
Ron Hoffman—Musician, Lucifer drummer
Rick Paulson—Musician, Lucifer guitarist
Charlie Ferguson—Neighborhood friend
Mick Whitman—Friend, musician
Harvey Briggs—Friend, musician, mentor, Dude in Suit
Bruce Geiger—Friend, musician, also Dude in Suit
Laura—First love
Linda—Also first love
Rob Fish (West)—Friend, musician
Fred Carr—Teacher, musician, mentor
Tony Cerniglia—Lifelong friend, Chaser drummer, musician
Pat Hynes—Friend, early Chaser bass player
Scott Duckwitz—Friend, roommate
Chris Kammer—Friend, promoter, dentist
Billy Erickson—Lifelong friend, musician, hallucination
Joe Cerniglia—Tri-State Security, Tony's dad
Rick Ambrose—Friend, manager, mentor

Stevie Johnson—Lifelong friend, Chaser bass player
Cameron Crowe—American author, writer, director
Pamela Turbov—Friend, impresario, queen of cool
Tim (Cheesie) Ringgenberg—Lifelong friend, Chaser crew
Mike Murray—Lifelong friend, Chaser crew
Paul Ripp—Friend, musician, Chaser assistant manager
Tony Toon—Rod Stewart's publicist, lech
Bernie Taupin—Lyrical genius
John Waite—British songwriter, singer, musician
Ian Anderson—British songwriter, singer, flautist, musician (Jethro Tull)
Sharon Osbourne—Ozzy's wife, TV personality
Bebe Buell—American model, singer
Orly Kroh—Friend
Bill Murray—American treasure
Kay Cerniglia—Tony's mom
Roger Probert and Genghis—Atlantic Records A&R, staff producer
Andy Warhol—Twentieth-century icon
Ron Goodrich—Lifelong friend
Brian Kroening—Friend, Boys in White guitarist
Rod Ellenbecker—Friend, Boys in White bass player
Hal Spear—Writer, comedian, Star Search contestant
Ed McMahon—Johnny Carson's sidekick, Star Search host
Duane Vee—Coworker, matchmaker
Lara Cody—Colleague, National Academy of Songwriting
Michael Goldstone—Music industry giant
Ted Wingfield—Friend, musician
Joel Rogers—Friend, musician
Joe Johnson—Lifelong friend, boss, musician, purveyor of pianos
Stephanie Virchow—Friend, musician
Joe Ferraro—Agent
Jerry Goeden—Friend, boss
Jeff Kincaid—Friend, statistic
Dr. Ken Felz—Doc
Nick Shabani—Sleazebucket

Rick Murphy—Murphy Music
Michelle Grabel-Komar—Friend, musician
Jimmie Nahas—Friend, musician
Dan Geocaris—Friend, Concept Productions
Rod Barelmann—Friend, Concept Productions
Doug Schoebel—Friend, Concept Productions
Joel Jackson—Friend, manager of the Wigwam Lodge
Robert J. Conaway (Bobber)—Friend, fishin' musician
Sharon Olson—Friend, inspiration
Mare—Friend, musician
Randy Green—Friend, musician, producer, mentor
Sheila Berg—Friend, muse
Kimmie Vernon (Lockwood)—Friend, musician
Emily Massey—Daughter
Nancy Mayek—Colleague
Amy Kruger—Friend
Jim and Ann Stanger—Lifelong friends
Anna Massey—Daughter
Kelly Maki (Gorton)—Friend
Dale Maki—Mortgage banker, lifesaver
Kay Drew—Robin's lifelong friend, now mine, too
Brad Bensman—Friend, marketing genius
Todd Nelson—Friend, entrepreneur
Billy Nahn—Friend, writer, director
W. Earle Smith—Friend, choreographer, artistic director Madison Ballet
Joy Dragland—Friend, musician
Francie Phelps—Amazing friend, musical partner
John Urban—Friend, confidante, star of television and radio, photographer, videographer, producer
Gretchen Bourg—Friend, Cabaret dancer, Madison Ballet
Jay Moran (John Velvet)—Friend, musician
Craig Bero—Actor, restaurateur, friend
Josh Dupont—Friend, musician, Piano Fondue founder
Dave Adler—Friend, musician, conductor

Neen Rock—Friend, stage manager Overture Center, miracle worker
Gordon Ranney—Friend, musician, Dracula bass player
Biff Blumfumgagnge—Friend, musician
Conrad St. Clair—Friend, musician, sound designer, audio engineer
Kristi Genna—Lifelong friend, owner Slipper Club and Genna's
Joel Pingitore—Friend, Stop the Clock guitarist
Frank Queram—Friend, Stop the Clock bass player
Briana Hardyman—Friend, Stop the Clock singer
Lara Gruhn—Friend, distant cousin from Zurich, Switzerland
Philippe Noser—Friend, Lara's husband
Suzan Kurry—Friend, actor, director, playwright
Mike Gomoll—Friend, Joey's Song
Dan Navarro—Friend, songwriter, musician, troubadour
Chris Munger - Robin's lifelong friend, my friend, singer
Natalie Rohrer—Friend, singer-songwriter, Germany
Stacy McAtee—Guardian angel
Desi Fisher—Lifelong friend
Carina Vargas-Nunez—Lifelong friend
Henry Stoehr—Slow Pulp guitarist, songwriter, producer

ABOUT THE AUTHOR

MICHAEL MASSEY is a composer, singer, songwriter, pianist, performer, and producer with a story to tell. He has written or collaborated on over 350 rock, pop, country, and instrumental songs, as well as the full-length Dracula: Rock Ballet score. He has eight critically acclaimed albums, including Pop Album of 2006 and Unique Albums of 2014 and 2018, at the Madison Area Music Awards. Michael also won Instrumentalist: Piano at the same awards in 2009, 2019, and 2020 as well as numerous ADDY, TELLY, and WAVE awards for excellence in original music for advertising. He lives on the driftless prairie in southwestern Wisconsin with his wife, Robin.

Photo by John Urban

ACKNOWLEDGMENTS

THANK YOU TO Matt Guenette, world-renowned poet and Madison College professor, who took this initial mess of mine and shaped it into something readable; Jim Massey, for his considerable expertise in editing punctuation and grammar; Sabra Stiemke, for another round of edits; Scott Massey for inspiring me to jump in feet first and attempt this endeavor; and accomplished author Keith Massey for valuable insight along the way. Thank you to my readers who saw through the rough state of the manuscript to give me feedback and constructive criticism to make it better, and Kristin Mitchell and Shannon Booth of Little Creek Press for molding it into an actual book.

On the recovery side of things, the doctors and nurses in Intermediate Care on the eighth floor of Meriter Hospital are a special brand of humans to lend support and compassion to those of us who land in their auspices. I want to thank David H. Back, my AODA counselor at Newstart, who admitted he didn't give me much chance of success at the outset of my treatment but later applauded his misjudgment; and Misty Morey, a lifelong friend who helped me navigate my very early sobriety and led some comfortably gentle AA meetings. Thank you to my family and friends who never gave up on me, even after all of my failures and deception. You all gave me repeated chances to right the ship when I gave you no reason.

My daughters, Emily and Anna, you gave and continue to give me purpose, grounding, and joy. As we progress into adult/parent relationships, I hope you can overlook my missteps along the way as a guy just trying to do his best by you.

And most of all, thank you to my partner, wife, and rock, Robin. There are no words to portray what you mean to me. Without your selfless support and unwavering faith, my life, our beautiful life together, would not exist.

MORE

CPSIA information can be obtained
at www.ICGtesting.com
Printed in the USA
JSHW010010281122
33946JS00002B/8